The Horse Riding Tourist

Near and Far

Rachel Lofthouse

Cover designed by Simon Avery

This book is a work of non-fiction. Though the names of hosts who feature in this book, and their staff are accurate, the author has replaced some of the names of the tourists where it has not been possible to gain the permission to use their real name.

Rachel Lofthouse
Visit my website at www.thehorseridingtourist.com

First Published in: Jan 2019
By Lofthouse Books

ISBN-978-1-9995802-1-6

To all my friends, who have endured my absence while I worked on this book.

Table of Contents

Part One

The Land of the Tölt

Transfer to Kjóastaõir Farm

A crisp 9°C (42°F) on a late afternoon in early October isn't exactly bikini weather. But a bikini is all that I have on as I step outside away from the comfort of a heated building. A building where other tourists and post-work weary locals are either browsing the gift-shop, chatting over coffee, or exchanging ski jackets for swimwear. My only protection from the chill is a complimentary spa towel wrapped tightly around me. The floor is cold. The transition brisk. After four or so strides, the towel is whipped off and deposited on a towel rail. A few more strides then down the slippery steps into the steamy milky-blue water... bliss. The water is 37°C (98°F), like a freshly ran bath, but instead of the sweet smell of the bubble bath, the steam carries the pungent-aroma of sulphur. That is because this is no bath, it is the Blue Lagoon one of Iceland's most popular tourist spots.

I'm in southwest Iceland on a four-day horse-riding tour packaged as a short break. The schedule includes visits to several of Iceland's famous tourist sights, the experience of riding tölt, the silky-smooth gait of the five-gaited Icelandic horse, and if I'm lucky a glimpse of the elusive Northern Lights (aurora borealis).

The Blue Lagoon is 29 miles (46.6 km) outside of the capital, Reykjavik in a cracked-lava field close to the coastal town of Grindavik on Iceland's southern peninsula. The lagoon is not a natural phenomenon. It is an artificial lagoon with water supplied by Svartsengi, geothermal power plant situated 1.5 miles (2.4 km) to the east.

The main building is two-storey, L-shape and primarily glass featuring lots of 45-degree angles, rectangles and topped by a flat roof. It is a contemporary building designed to complement the surroundings. Separating the building from the lagoon is a patio where spa-towels dangle in bunches to resemble collapsed garden umbrellas amongst metal chair and table sets forsaken by spectators who have opted for the warmth of indoors. Arched aluminium-rail bridges join plank walkways that span away from the building out to this end of the lagoon and the banks of lava rock on the far side. The lagoon is busy with a crowd that resembles a busy day at my local leisure centre pool. Heads bob on the waterline like a colony of seals watching a boat chug by from the safety of the water. The atmosphere is infectious: relaxed tinged with excitement. Drifting in the steam over the lagoon's surface is the resound of voices.

Edda, my group tour guide, reminds me and the present newly-acquainted-trip companions of the advice she gave us on the coach:

'Don't put your head in the water because the sulphurous element will suck out the moisture from your hair and leave it as dry as straw baked in the sun for a week.'

Edda is a vivacious medical student beautified by natural long-blonde hair and a massive smile, who is fluent in English, Norwegian and German. She lives and studies in Reykjavik. Her family home and where she grew up is a farm close to Kjóastaðir Farm where the horses are and where my group will be staying for a couple of nights. Kjóastaðir Farm is located in the Haukadalur Valley, a valley roughly 90 miles (144 km) northeast of the Blue Lagoon.

We are close to the waterside bar, a rectangle box not dissimilar to a modest-sized garden shed. Partly submerged underwater the frontage is open to display an array of bottles and optics along the length of the back wall. The barman stands below the level of the lagoon's surface so he is on a par with the bathers who swim up to purchase drinks. He is having a busy afternoon: there is a crowd of two-people deep waiting for their turn to be served.

Engulfed in steam within the crowd, you don't get a sense of the scale of the lagoon. What I do discern in this busy lagoon is I need to become familiar with the 14 faces of my newly acquainted travelling companions. All of whom I met 30 minutes ago in the arrivals hall at Keflavik International Airport. My travel-fatigued brain is finding it difficult to remember names and faces significantly enough to pick any one of them out in an overcrowded lagoon of bobbing heads, so I have to ensure at least one person in my group is in my line of sight. It wouldn't aid the schedule if I got separated and lost in the first hour of the tour.

To keep connected, I chat with Christina and Véronique who like me have travelled to Iceland on their own. They are both slim women in their late-twenties. Christina possesses a youthful face framed by strawberry-blond hair cropped in a neat bob. She is from Germany and akin to many Germans speaks fluent English. Valerie is from Belgium. She has pixie-like facial features accentuated by her cropped-brown hair. She understands some English though speaks little. Mutually, we decide to swim away from the visitor centre and bar to the less-crowded outer end.

Further, into the lagoon the water begins to clear of people and the jagged rocks of the lava mounds in the foreground and moss-covered hillocks behind are uncloaked. It is a set of contrasts: dark rock, pale water, rising steam and a lowering sun in a cloudless blue sky.

At the mid-way point, we swim to join another trio in our party, two brunette English women and their Swedish friend. They're in a fit of giggles with a beer in hand and faces covered in grey-lagoon mud. Us, new arrivals follow their lead and scoop the mud from the supply provided. The consistency is the same as the watery rifle-green liquid that runs through my fingers and down my forearm when I forget to shake the bottle of the face mask I have at home. The difference is the colour and the sulphurous smell. I take care to avoid my hairline and eyes as I rub the clay on my chin, nose and cheeks. An action made tricky by the laughter of me and my companions. Christina, in her holiday enthusiasm, covers her face and gets a splatter of wet mud in her hairline.

The English ladies are from the home counties of England. They are more or less my height (5 ft. 5 in/1.67 m), in their thirties and tipsy having consumed a couple of beverages on the plane. The look of one of the ladies suggests Asian parentage, which is emphasised by her dark skin and long straight hair. She's visited Iceland on a riding tour twice before. It was on one of these previous visits when she'd met the Swedish lady, a slim woman also in her thirties with short blonde hair. The Swede is fluent in English. She lives in the world of horses having at least two of her own at home. The other English lady is spindly with straight hair cut to below her ears. She is quintessential home counties in character and clipped accent.

Cocooned in warm water and steam, I relax in the company of my new-found friends. This tourist hotspot may be overcrowded and over-publicised; nonetheless, it's still awesome. Granted the locals will know of a quieter hangout away from the tourists. For me, after a long day of trains, planes and automobiles this is a perfect spot to start a mini Icelandic adventure.

Refreshed and back on the coach, Edda does her best to make the two-hour transfer comfortable. For the first hour, she assesses the mood on the coach just right by letting the people who want to talk amongst themselves and leaves the rest to sit quietly and take in the scenery of the lava fields and dark rocky hills. The classification of the coach is a midibus. A midibus is larger than a minibus yet smaller than a single decker. It is an older style vehicle comparable to the coaches in service in Great Britain throughout the late 1980s and early 1990s. The interior has upholstered seats with a garish swirly-pattern. As a result of a non-existent suspension, the coach judders when it goes over bumps or rough ground. Inside, 14 travel companions are spread out either sat together or on their own. I'm in the row behind the English ladies. The lady with the clipped accent takes an interest in my daily life in Cornwall; where I live and what I do for work. She had visited Cornwall roughly 10-years ago when a friend had invited her to stay at their family home. I know the village where she had stayed as it is 10 miles (16 km) from the town where I live. At the end of this conversation, I settle down in my seat to admire the countryside. The coach heaters ensure the crispness of the dwindling day remains outside.

Southbound, the journey skims the outskirts of Grindavik then curves to the west using the Suðurstrandarvegur Road (427). Mile after mile the road snakes through low-lying lava fields where purple and green mosses carpet the grey-brown rock-strewn land, and white telegraph poles forge long chains. Here and there, the broad horizon yields to shallow hills of bare rock and grass. There are frequent glimpses or long stretches of the North Atlantic Ocean and its uninviting steel-grey water. Apart from a scant number of cars driving by, the ocean seems to be all that stirs in this isolated landscape.

Dusk is upon us as the road traverses a spit of land shielding Hliðarvatn lagoon from the ocean. In the rapidly fading light, reflections from the dwellings on the off-lying banks twinkle and dance on the lagoon's ink-black surface. On the east side of the inlet at the lagoon's most southerly point the coach stays on Suðurstrandarvegur for a short time then takes a right and switches back to roll to a standstill in an ample, well-maintained and empty carpark. In the shelter of a dry-stone wall, everyone but the driver disembarks.

Wrapped up in ski jackets, hats and gloves the warmth of the coach is exchanged for a serene atmosphere: crisp air and the mellow crash of unseen waves. Away from the wall on the northeast side of the carpark, in a landscape of rolling meadows, is a raised grass bank supported by a dry-stone wall. On the vertex is a small-scale box-shape church made from wood painted pale-grey. It is a simple design with the most elaborate feature an orb and a cross sited at the peak of a wooden steeple that protrudes up from the slate-grey pitched roof. Everything is neat and in good repair. This place of worship is Strandarkirkja Church, a landmark famous for a legend bound to it since the 12th century. The legend concerns sailors caught out of sight of land in stormy weather. The sailors prayed to God. If they made it back to dry land, they vowed to build a church in the spot where they landed. Thereupon a light appeared to guide them. This light got brighter and brighter, and then a shining figure was seen on the shore. The current incarnation of the sailors' church has the year 1888 painted above the entrance door to confirm its construction was during the late 1880s. Wall-lights illuminate the interior. The glow from the bulbs emits light through the four windows on the south-facing long side. In the fast diminishing daylight, the church beckons you to enter its warmth and light.

Our stop here is not in the schedule. It had been planned earlier due to the delayed arrival of the Swedish flight. To demonstrate Icelandic hospitality, the local tour operator had acknowledged most of us would not have eaten since lunch and because of the flight delay would not be eating again until late this evening at Kjóastaðir Farm. To ease any hunger, Edda had been instructed to lay on a light picnic. In the dusky light, we huddle at a picnic table. On the lee side of a walled bank and steps going up to the church. Edda hands a brown paper bag to each of us. Inside is a sandwich, a slice of cake, a piece of fruit and a drink.

As we eat the vast sky covering the lowland and sea transitions to its darkest blue-grey. The sun drops below the western horizon to leave an orange hue above the land and sea-line. A headland up the coast becomes a black silhouette. Sparse rows of gravestones, rocks and walls in the foreground mere outlines. On a high mound to the west is a statue stood on a plinth; from our picnic spot, it appears as a featureless figure. Faint lights transmit from nearby dwellings projecting the promise of shelter from the dark and cold. Be that as it may, the obvious choice for further investigation is the close-at-hand church.

When I reach the top of the stone steps going up to the church something catches my eye, and I hesitate. Down an unevenly-paved path going away from the church is something quirky and unexpected. Sucked in by the distraction, I go to get a closer look.

Stood on pieces of level stone is a row of six tiny houses the size of a child's doll house. Left to right there is triplicate unattached houses and triplicate lower attached house. There are no sides or backs just fire-red painted facades displaying white pitched roofs and frames. The houses are at the base of a dune mound covered in green and yellow grasses. I know what the houses represent as I read about the Huldufólk in advance of the trip. The Huldufólk is the Icelandic version of elves. These houses are álfhól (elf houses) and apparently can be found throughout Iceland. Article statistics claim a high percentage of Icelandic people believe in this unseen folk. This may be true, nevertheless for someone like me who grew up in a locality where the culture includes an element of folklore, legend and small supernatural beings (the closest to home being the infamous Cornish Piskies) I can't help surmise the Huldufólk are kept alive to primarily delight the children and amuse the tourists.

Back on track, a peak around the church door reveals an equally neat interior. In fact, so neat it looks practically unused. There is enough room for a modest congregation to gather on the six rows of wooden pews set out on both sides of the central aisle. A low-hung rope in front of the alter suggests visitors should not step across to a modest alter set up with a tall chest draped in a crochet cloth and adorned by candlesticks holding unlit candles. A painting of a figure wearing a white robe hangs above the chest. The figure has a halo of light encircling their head and a long staff held in an outstretched arm. I'm not close enough to see if the figure is male or female. Maybe this is a portrait of the figure seen on the shore by the sailors on the fabled stormy night. An upright piano is in the corner to the left of the altar and a pulpit on the right.

Ellisa, a petite woman wrapped up in a woolly black-and-white bobble hat and purple jacket stands at the back of the rows of pews in quiet contemplation. This place of worship must be incommensurable to the synagogue she attends at home in San Francisco. Our words are hushed. Ellisa signs the visitor book before we shut the door behind us and go back to the coach.

Back on the main road, the coach hugs the coast for a few miles then turns inland onto a north-easterly orientation. Even though dusk had passed the sunlight is not quite finished in this part of the world. The land of Iceland may be out of reach. The moon is not. A transit of a full moon had recently happened and tonight's waning gibbous moon remains magnificent. Momentarily the moon's saucer shape gleams an orange-red. Edda tells us the transformation is a frequent phenomenon that transpires just as the sunlight disappears. After the moon returns to its usual shade of pale the rest of the transfer is in relative darkness.

Most of the settlements passed are sleepy hamlets or small-scale towns faintly illuminated in the engulfing dark by a scattering of streetlights and glows from houses. A couple of cars whoosh by on the outskirts of the larger towns. At intervals, Edda stands and makes a brief announcement using the intercom. She discloses the name of the town or village and jokes: 'If you look out of the right side you will see such and such. Well, you would if it wasn't dark.'

Laughter fills the interior as the delayed journey advances into the dark.

In the final leg, the coach joins the Biskupstungnabraut Road (35) and aims for the Geyser hot spring area and nearby neighbour, Kjóastaðir Farm. On arrival at the hot spring area, imaginations are used to visualise this most visited tourist sight. Somewhere in the darkness are the famous geysers gurgling and bubbling. There is a reassuring reminder from Edda: 'You will visit the geyser field tomorrow afternoon.'

The course changes to continue eastwards for nearing 2 miles (3.2 km) and then takes a left off Biskupstungnabraut onto a track. Grit crunches beneath the tyres as the coach trundles on for 200 m (656 ft.) and then takes a right onto a property with dim lights fixed to scattered buildings seen as outlines in the night. We've arrived at Kjóastaðir Farm.

In the latter stage of the transfer, Edda had briefed dinner will be served immediately on arrival as the meal was prepared a few hours back by our hosts and is ready to eat. We were asked to collect our suitcases from the back of the coach and leave them in the undercover area outside the door of the riding centre building. The final instruction is to abide by the Icelandic custom of removing shoes and boots on entering a house and leave the footwear inside the doorway.

Chatting and unorderly we're ushered into a substantial open-front barn with a thick layer of woodchips carpeting the floor. Light spills from four facing glass windows set into an interior wall. In the corner to the left of the windows, a wall-mounted light guides us to an open doorway. Luggage is abandoned outside as we filter out of the cold and into the warmth of a tidy and functional hallway. In the middle of the hallway pushed up against the back wall is a narrow wood table bookended by chairs. The table and chairs fit snuggly in between closed interior doors displaying toilet signs. At the far end of the hall is another interior door. We remove our boots and hang our coats on a rack fixed behind the entrance door. In an unorderly line of women, I filter through the end doorway into an open-plan farmhouse kitchen-diner emitting wafts of homemade lasagne. The light seen through the windows from outside emanates from this room and has drawn us in like moths.

Centremost and taking up a considerable amount of the floor space is a wood table with pew-style seats rapidly being filled by babbling guests. Smiles as warm as the room greet us. They radiate out from our hosts, Hjalti G and Asa who are the owners of Kjóastaðir Farm. They stand beside a kitchen island stacked with plates and cutlery next to two steaming lasagnes. Hjalti G must be over six-feet tall, dark with a receding hairline and a neat beard. His appearance matches his profession: a farmer who manages animals and land. Conversely, Asa is a slight curly-haired blonde standing at the height of Hjalti G's shoulder. They are both middle-aged and have healthy complexions.

I sit close to the end of the table with my back to the entrance hall in the company of Christina, Véronique, Elissa and her travel companion, Terri. Terri is an experienced rider of many years, who owns a farm close to Boston in Massachusetts. Elissa and Terri have been friends for many years. Terri was Elissa's riding instructor up until Elissa relocated to San Francisco. Possibly the oldest of the guests, Terri retains a healthy complexion and an aura of calm and responsibility. On their arrival in Iceland five days ago, they had embarked on a road trip around the island. Their tour will conclude in four days after two days' horse trekking and two nights in Reykjavik. While Terri and Elissa entertain us by summarising their recent glacier walk and other Icelandic experiences, I take in the rest of the room.

An atmosphere of excitement and anticipation accompanies the many conversations. Fuelled in part by the wine and beer partaken by the English-Swedish contingent at the other end of the table. During the transfer, I'd found out there are two more ladies who travelled from Sweden in the company of the Swede I met at the Blue Lagoon. It looks like it's going to be a long night of drinking for this merry band. In the centre of the table is a group from Finland: a middle-aged mother, her two teenage daughters, and her friend. The eldest daughter is university age, the younger still at school. The girls are pretty, svelte, blonde and healthy. I have ascertained they own Icelandic horses themselves back in Finland and only the eldest daughter speaks English.

Candles and t-lights held in a variety of containers and candleholders light the dining area and add to the cosy feel of the room. The main source of illumination though is an electric light that hangs down from the ceiling above the kitchen island. Beyond the light, someplace outside in the dark are grazing horses. I'm reminded of their presence by the skin and fir of a once tri-colour horse hung beside a thick-framed mirror on the facing wall, behind the table.

In between courses, Elissa nips outside to survey for the elusive Northern Lights that have so far evaded her. I too have an aspiration to witness this phenomenon and have to remind myself of the limited time I am at the farm. A couple of nights is an improbable window to catch an array.

Well-fed and back out in the cold, we pull or carry cases the short distance back up the track, taking a right before we reach the road. Edda brings us to a halt in a jumbled arc around her. We've stopped at the entrance to a circle of four varied-sized cabins. The dim exterior lights are assisted by stronger interior lighting pouring through the cabin windows. Edda explains how many people the cabins sleep and little accommodation factions peel off in search of their beds. The Finnish first, who take the westside cabin. Followed by the English-Swedish contingent who retire to the cabin on the east side. Terri and Elissa suggest I share the furthest away, north-end cabin, with them. We leave the still to be housed Christina and Véronique with Edda.

Our boots are removed and left in the entrance porch before going through the front door into a snug room. Encompassed within a wooden interior are a sofa and coffee table, to the left of the door, and a dining table and three high-back wooden chairs placed against the wall, on the right. Across the room is a vertical-wood ladder going up to an open-front loft. I step up the lower rungs to take a look. The loft accommodates four single beds. There is a small window in the north gable. The ceiling is so low it is more of a bunk than a room, and I will have to move around on my knees. Back at ground level, adjoining the dining-table end of the room is a kitchenette containing a sink, work unit and fridge. Adjoining the back wall of the kitchenette is a compact bathroom fitted with a shower cubicle, vanity sink, and toilet.

Terri discovers a ground-floor bedroom through a doorway aside the sofa. She makes a plea to Elissa and me as she's not confident in her ability to climb up and down the ladder. Assured in our agility, Elissa and I gracefully agree to share the loft. Elissa moves the portable heater closer to the foot of the ladder and increases the thermostat. With a clear sky, the temperature will drop below freezing overnight.

It's about 10:30 pm when I snuggle-up under the duvet on the bed beneath the window in the loft. My final thoughts reflect on the events of the day. From the moment, my flight took off from London Heathrow Airport, an

American man in his mid-thirties, who I was sat next to on the plane had handed me some unused headphones. He was on his way home to the USA via Iceland with his 10-year-old son. His son had accumulated free headphones as they had travelled around Europe by plane. As I'd stood in the cramped arrivals hall at Kalfavick International Airport waiting for my mobile to connect to a local network, an attractive Icelandic taxi driver with piercing blue eyes and a mop of brown hair kindly lent me his mobile phone so I could call the tour operator to find out the whereabouts of my absent guide. Just after, Edda arrived and bunched everyone together at the meeting point. In the activity, there was the surprise of recognising the English ladies. They had been in the seats in front of me on the plane. Their presence was hard to miss for they'd animatedly chatted while quaffing alcoholic drinks. My first words to them were, 'I recognise you two.'

They too recognised me from the plane. It was a random coincidence to find myself seated behind complete strangers, who not known at the time, I will be with for the next couple of days. It was a good icebreaker.

Haukadalur Valley

I wake at first light. A glance at my mobile phone reveals it is 7:45 am. Revitalised by a deep and restful sleep. I don't dally. So not to wake Elissa or Terri, I step softly through the cabin as I shower and dress. A thermal top, ski top, ski socks and ski jacket are hastily thrown on; though, I brave no more than jeans for my hardier legs. As I move through the porch, I pull on my long boots and ski gloves and brace myself for the dawn chill.

The air is clean. I smell nothing. Clean, fresh and silent, I hear nothing either. The sun is below the horizon. The sky, cloudless and the palest of blue. There isn't a hint of a breeze.

I pause to peruse the surroundings. Underfoot is a dusty volcanic-grey mixture of dry dirt and grit. My cabin is a rectangular box constructed using reddish-wood planks and featuring small windows and a rust-red pitch roof. There is an aerial fitted to the porch roof. Behind the cabin are grass banks that edge fields that rise and fan out to distant crests. On a crest, out to the northeast and barely insight is a populous herd of horses. The herd is too far away to pick out any describable features.

Turing away from the fields and accompanied by a soft crunch underfoot, I set off southwards and pass by the other cabins. The cabins of the Finnish quartet and the English/Swedish contingent are identical in material, yet are marginally different in size and design to my own. The most southern accommodation is a bungalow with a façade dominated by windows surrounded by dark-brown-wood planks. I assume this is where Christina, Véronique and Edda sleep.

Opposite the bungalow is the long side of a farmhouse; its façade sited on the corner of the track we'd used last night to enter the farm. The track curves east and then south around a spacious outdoor arena fenced by white metal posts connected by taught thick-white canvas strips. The track finishes outside the main riding centre building where I dined in the company of the other guests last night. I don't walk down to the building; instead, I turn right towards the road.

Facing west, you look out over the breadth of a shallow valley and its far-reaching fields of greens, yellows and browns, dotted here and there with whitewashed farmhouses. On the far side against a backdrop of a long and high earthy ridge is the rising steam of the Geyser hot spring area. In this perfect weather, the darker shade of the ridge makes the water vapour easy to spot and from my distance of 2 miles (3.2 km) away. I can pick out the funnel of water being periodically propelled skywards by, Strokkur the hot spring area's active geyser.

I double back to look down the track to the main riding centre building: A whitewashed long barn structure with a rust-red pitch roof. There is an exterior light at the point of the roof. It glows orange in the early-morning light. The building's narrower open-front faces westwards. Joined to the longer south side is a lower structure set further back. This section contains windows giving it a bungalow look. The building stands quiet and empty; there is no sign of life. Considering breakfast is scheduled at 8:30 am, I end my brief wander and go back to the cabin to sort my riding clothes and equipment in preparation for the day's trek.

There are no lit candles when I enter the dining room as daylight now filters in through the windows. The English lady with the clipped accent and one of the Swedes are seated at the table in the same places they'd sat in last night. I help myself to home-made porridge from the kitchen island and join them. In the wake of last night's high spirits, their heads are delicate and their demeanour subdued. I discover subsequently to putting their cases in the cabin the contingent came back to the dining room to resume drinking. The oriental-looking English lady and her Swedish friend were the last to retire having talked and drunk throughout most of the night. In her Clipped-English accent, I get an amusing account of a restless cabin where fuddled individuals had stumbled over suitcases or furniture in the unfamiliar lodgings during the night. On top of this was a succession of phone alarms set at a British or Swedish time going off. Her phone rang at an early hour to remind her to take her son to his beavers' club.

It's not long until the rest of the guests filter into breakfast. Last to arrive is the second half of the contingent. They look remarkably awake considering they've had hardly any sleep. As barely a couple of hours had passed since their last alcoholic drink, we conclude they're probably still a bit drunk.

Edda also experienced an eventful night. Some of her horses had escaped from a field on her family's farm. After dinner, she had joined family members in a round-up of the horses to restore them back to where they should be.

Excitement and anticipation build through the whole of breakfast. Spread alongside the toast, cereals, porridge and croissants on the kitchen island are a choice of sliced cheeses and meats, vegetables, bread and sweet biscuits. Guests have been provided with Tupperware boxes to make up a packed lunch for today's trek. Asa directs us to fill brown water bottles using the sink underneath the back window adjacent to a stove. All through breakfast and picnic lunch preparations, Edda sits with us in turn and jots down our riding experience and capability on a piece of paper along with everyone's response to the question: 'What type of horse do you want to ride?'

I report, I have a weekly private lesson on a quiet, well-behaved and responsive mare and I can walk, trot and canter in open countryside.

We're allotted 30 minutes to return to the cabins and prepare for the day. Terri, Elissa and I are back at the riding centre building within 10 minutes. We'd already prepared and are keen to meet the horses. To pass the time we explore part of the indoor area. Pew seats line the side walls of the covered woodchip area. Fixed above the pews on the nearside are a map of Iceland and other informative posters. Using the map Terri and Elissa guide me along the circuit they'd taken on their road trip. Consuming most of the dimensions on the offside wall is a display board. It has the name of the farm, 'Kjóastaðir' printed on an enlarged photo of many horses and riders fording a river in the foreground amid a backdrop of Icelandic hills and ridges. To the right of the board is the entrance to an indoor space housing animal pens not dissimilar to an indoor cattle market or the indoor pen area at a British agricultural show. The carpet of wood chips finishes at a concrete belt laid beneath the hall and dining room windows. A set of red-framed garden chairs and a table are on the concrete. Sat in front of a chair close to the hallway door is a white and tan collie with a thick winter coat. It is the farm's working dog, who is not forthcoming when strangers stand looking down at him. He curls his lip without intent. We leave him to his wait outside the closed door and go to look at the indoor pens.

The pens are in the lower half of the riding centre building viewed from the track on my brief wander this morning. A doorway on the right takes us into a generous tack room. On the wall between the threshold where we stand and an inverse outside door are approximately 20 loose-ring-snaffle bridles hung on bridle pegs. On the far wall are two tiers of saddle racks holding the same amount of saddles. In the centre of the room, 20 leather saddle bags are piled up on a wooden table. The long interior wall incorporates a large window framing a view of the indoor pens. Underneath the window are pegs holding high-visibility orange and yellow waterproof jackets and trousers. Further down is a thin two-tier table with a stockpile of about 20 riding helmets.

When we return to the wood-chip area most of the guests have come back from their cabins. In reaction to the influx of people the farm dog decides he does want attention and comes up to us for a pat and a stroke after we sit down. Everyone is present when Edda and Hjalti G arrives. Edda, in her relaxed and easy-going style, explains Hjalti G assisted by the farm dog, will go and round-up the herd of Icelandic horses currently grazing in the north-facing field at the back of the riding centre. The horses will be brought down to the pen outside. We will then collect a bridle, saddle, saddlebag and riding hat from the tack room and take them to the outdoor arena where we will brush our horse and tack-up.

Anticipating his task, the dog springs into action running at the side of Hjalti G in a state of excitement. Hjalti G and the dog get into a white multi-terrain minibus parked outside the riding centre building. The rest of us go outside to the back of the building where there is a lookout point up and across the farm's north and north-east facing fields. The terrain of moorland grass, wire fences, and sporadic rocks incline upwards towards the horizon. It is an array of green and brown colours beneath a far-reaching blue sky. There isn't a hint of a cloud nor a breath of wind, just a perfect crisp autumnal morning. Close to the brow of the north field and virtually out of sight are roughly 40 grazing horses.

Hjalti G's vehicle comes around the south back corner of the riding centre building and makes a beeline northward passing our lookout. He pulls up to open a couple of gates to gain entrance to the field and then drives up the hill to reach the horses. I'm too far away to watch the dog in action. He must have done his job well as the herd is soon moving downhill at a trot or canter. The rumble of many hooves beating the earth increases in volume as the herd approaches. On the riding-centre side of the opened gateways, they drop down to lower ground and filter in elongated order in front of a high bank. As they file by, I get the impression the majority of the horses are either dark bay or chestnuts displaying a variety of flaxen-mane and tail shades. I count three greys and two skewbalds.

On the return to the front of the riding centre building, we find the herd corralled in a white-metal-tube fenced pen. There is no grazing as the surface is a mix of volcanic soil and tiny stones. In these close quarters, some of the horses' jostle, others huddle together. Ranging from 13 hh (1.32 m) to 14 hh (1.42 m), winter-coat fluffy and incredibly cute, they are hardy and compact horses with thick-long manes. In the UK, their height would classify them as ponies and not horses. Here the breed is classified as horses. The Icelandic people can be offended if you refer to the horses as ponies. Since I heard this, I'd corrected myself a few times in conversation when I'd referred to them as ponies. Although October is in its infancy, the average temperature in Iceland is 9°C (48°F) during the day and 4°C (39°F) at night. Hence why these permanently-kept outdoor horses are in full winter coat. A small grey, easy to pick out amongst the chestnuts and dark bays, stands resting its head on the quarters of an iron grey. From what I can make out this is the lone iron grey in the herd. As I single out individuals, I wonder which horse I'll be given to ride.

We all collect a saddle, bridle, hat, and saddlebags from the tack room. Unlike an English tack room, the bridle and saddle racks are not labelled using the horse's name. The reason is the majority of Icelandic horses are a similar size and shape and can share tack. Carrying our selected equipment, we enter the arena; an area guessed to be 20 x 50 m (65 x 164 ft.) storing two tiers of cylinder-shape bales wrapped in white polythene at the far end. Edda instructs us to select a patch of ground at intervals where the horses can be brushed and tacked-up. From a black-plastic box full of brushes and combs placed at the base of the arena gate post, I select a mini plastic curry comb and a hoof pick. The spot I choose is in the front left corner of the arena where I set the saddle down against the fence.

While the riders collected tack, Hjalti G had put a bridle on a chestnut gelding possessing a flaxen mane and tail and removed it from the pen. Edda takes the reins of the chestnut. She leads him into the centre of the arena and halts him close to the entrance. A Norwegian called Audrey has come to assist Edda. Audrey is a polite young woman of university age. Blessed with Scandinavian good looks and long blonde hair, she speaks perfect English.

Audrey will join us on the ride out today. She is happy to observe Edda's lead, and when asked takes the reins of the chestnut while the rest of us gather round and watch Edda cheerfully demonstrate how to brush our horses. In the act, Edda explains because the coats of the horses are thick a plastic curry comb is used to brush dirt from their saddle and bridle areas. The demonstration moves on to introducing us to the saddle and two-part bridle. The bridle comes with a detached noseband. The part put on the chestnut by Hjalti G, combines the headpiece and cheek pieces into a strip of leather that is attached to the bit-rings. Outward-facing metal clips attach the leather to the bit and buckles allow for adjustments. There is no browband or throatlash. Reins come in plain leather or webbing and clip onto the rings of the snaffle bit. Edda takes the reins from Audrey and demonstrates how to fit the noseband. It looks similar to a drop noseband and is fitted by going over the leather of the headpiece.

Audrey retakes the reins. Edda picks up the saddle she had collected from the tack room. The Icelandic saddle is designed specifically for the contour of the Icelandic horse and is a variant to alternative designs. The closest match is a dressage saddle. Made of leather they either have a quilted or plain levelled seat. The saddle is positioned further forward on the horse than a transitional English saddle.

To conclude the demonstration Edda shows us where to position and attach the leather saddlebags. The broad piece of leather that joins the saddlebags goes across the withers. Clips at the ends of the leather are clipped to D-rings on the saddle's skirts. Lastly, the single-buckle fastening on the bags is pulled taut so the flaps are secure and any contents cannot fall out.

With the chestnut ready to ride, Edda takes the reins and demonstrates how to mount from the ground. Once mounted, she explains how to hold the reins and introduces the Icelandic riding style of using long stirrups. If stirrup leathers are too short or too long, we are to dismount, adjust them from the floor and remount repeating this action until the length is correct.

The next part of the demonstration covers the five gaits of the Icelandic horse. Edda explains an Icelandic horse will have either four or five gaits. The gaits all Icelandic horses have are walk, trot, canter/gallop, and the tölt. A lesser number of the collective national and international herd will have a fifth gait, the flying pace. Edda rides the chestnut at walk out of the arena taking the left rein and a 90-degree angle to be alongside the arena's fence on the track going back to the chalets. Edda, in sequence, walks, trots, and tölts up and down while explaining the particular gait and how to ask the horse for it. A bubble of excitement swells up inside me to replace my normal laid-back holiday mode. One of the main reasons I came on this trip is to experience the tölt. The chestnut is handed back to Audrey. The rest of us are instructed to collect our bridles and accompany Edda back to the pen where the herd waits.

Hjalti G is waiting at the gate of a confined pen that links the riding centre building and the occupied horse pen. Edda goes inside to join Hjalti G, securing the gate behind her. On consulting a piece of paper pulled from Edda's pocket, Hjalti G reaches over the fence and takes a bridle. He then goes through a gate on the right into the horse pen. He selects a horse, puts the bridle on, leads it back through the gate and hands the reins to Edda. They consult the list again and select another name. Hjalti G takes another bridle from the closest rider and re-enters the horses' pen. Edda then calls out the name of the person who will ride the horse she has. This horse is led out through the confined pen gateway and entrusted to the named rider who leads it back to the arena and begins their preparations for riding using the methods demonstrated.

With 13 riders and horses to pair the wait resembles a horse and rider version of a blind date. I watch this process over and over again before my name is called out. Then, I swap the bridle I hold for the reins attached to Gjáska (pronounced, 'Gstar'). She is cute and a surprise grullo dun with a dark-brown mane, tail, and socks. Her velvety nose has an outline of white hairs along her mouth and above her nostrils. There is a thinner band of white hairs around her eyes making it look as if she is wearing eyeliner. She is taller than the horses selected before her. As I lead her back to the arena, I say hello and tell her how gorgeous she is while giving her lots of pats and strokes. Her coat is soft and silky, and her neck is toasty underneath her long-thick mane.

Gjáska stands quietly and relishes the attention as I brush her and tack up. Conversations are scant, and talk is quiet throughout the pre-ride preparations. Most of the time riders are speaking to their newly acquainted horse. Ellisa is nearest to me. She is preparing the small grey I'd singled out in the horse pen. Close by is Terri and her horse partner, a pretty chestnut mare distinguished by a white blaze and flaxen mane and tail. Terri has put her rain clothes behind the cantle of her horse's saddle and is repeatedly checking to ensure the bundle is neat and secure.

When Edda has completed her tack inspection, she asks everyone to mount for the ride. Our troop is made up of six dark bays, five chestnuts, a pale palomino, a grey, and a dun. Escorted by, Edda leading and Audrey on another chestnut at the rear, the procession of riders dressed in ski or riding jackets ride out of the arena and onwards to the road, first, turning left out of Kjóastaôir Farm and then right to join a track laid alongside the Biskupstungnabraut. Our direction is westwards, down the valley, in the distance is the Geyser hot springs area. The weather remains unsullied without a cloud in the sky. Visibility is crystal clear, and the green of the expansive fields and dark shades of the volcanic ridges are intense. The track we're on is horse friendly and of a width where we can ride side-by-side. Its surface is formed from bedrock: light-to-dark-grey volcanic stone, earth, and dust. Periodically the horses' hooves ring out a chink as they strike a stone.

On both sides of the road herds of horses' graze in fields comparable to the size of UK arable land. A long trot takes us to where the road meets the River Hvitá. The river's rapid-flow cuts southwards through the valley and to cross our procession temporally leaves the track to use a single-lane bridge. On the other side, the Biskupstungnabraut is left behind by a change of direction: northwards onto a bridleway.

The landscape is breathtaking. There is a clear sightline as the bridleway extends in a straight line through level heathland to reach a birch forest in the distance. The dark-green trees are another rich contrast against the blue sky. On the right is the River Hvitá, its glacier-fed water in full flow. Bursts of yellow flowers compliment the heathland's mass vegetation of light-browns and purples. On the gentle lower slopes are established farm settlements then the terrain steepens in the form of high volcanic hills and ridges that contour the valley.

There are multiple bursts of trot and canter on the way to the birch forest. I'm at the back of the ride preceding just Audrey. Terri and Elissa are in front of me respectively. The horses at the back fall behind in walk and frequently trot in the walk periods to close the gaps opened by the faster-walking horses at the front. Gjáska is lazy and not responsive to light aids. I can get her to do what I want, but it takes a lot of effort. Thankfully, it's not long before, Audrey hands over the white schooling whip she's been carrying: 'You won't need to use the whip. You just need to carry it.'

Gjáska immediately ceases dragging her hooves and responds to my aids. I keep hold of the whip but never use it.

The exact spot of where the heathland ends and the birch forest begins is difficult to ascertain because unlike the woods and forests in the UK the trees in Iceland do not grow to a significant height. This circumstance of nature was affirmed at breakfast by Edda when she quoted an Icelandic joke: 'If you get lost in an Icelandic forest, stand up.'

The path reduces to hard-packed mud, narrows to the width of a horse and is hemmed in by spindly birches shaped like Christmas spruces. The trunks are visible as branches cling on to the green and golden-yellow leaves. Inversely is the overgrown foliage of the taller conifers that softly brush riders' legs as we transverse the thickets populated by these evergreens.

For the majority of the ride, there is plenty of leg room and many vistas out to the faraway hills and ridges. A brief break commences on the crown of a hillock where everyone dismounts. The hillock serves as a vantage point to look out over part of the Haukadalur Valley. It is marked by a square wooden post, approximately 2 m (6.6 ft.) high. The word 'Selhóll' is carved vertically into the post and painted white. I'll presume 'Selhóll' translates to 'hill' in English. The horses display their familiarity with the spot by either grazing or standing at rest. In the unseasonably warm late-morning sunshine, Gjáska is content to stand and receive a bit of fuss.

Far away to the north is the southern edge of the Glacier Langjökull. I had never seen a glacier. Though, it is no more than a glimpse of its true magnificence it is a wonder to behold. The glacier's brilliant-white peaks rise out from the earth on the skyline. By its nature, a stationary illusion creeping ever forward. Mountains and ridges of volcanic rock frame the rest of the valley, where green, gold, purple, and brown autumnal shades glisten in the sunlight. There isn't a lot of conversation. I presume everyone is savouring the company of their horse and the impressive view. Some of us, namely the English/Swedish contingent, may be suffering from a lack of sleep and a hangover.

The remainder of the morning and early part of the afternoon is spent riding in and around the birch forest. There is another break in a golden-rolling-hill meadow where the horses graze under an expansive sky touched only by the highest of the distant mountain peaks. A few riders sit down close to their grazing horse's head. Having trained in the traditional English style of equitation, I cannot bring myself to mirror this action.

Remounted, the ride sets of southwards on a direct course for the picnic lunch site. The path remains bound by vertically-challenged trees forming a roofless tunnel effect. Terri, Elissa and I remain at the back of the ride. Our conversation topic is the tölt. Terri, the most experienced rider reports her chestnut mare has been in tölt during the faster pace stints. Elissa and I are not as sure. I think Gjáska gives me a couple of strides in the transition from canter to trot because it feels different. On the stints when Terri is behind Elissa and me, she says she sees Gjáska and Elissa's grey tölt albeit for a mere couple of strides.

Mid-afternoon had arrived when the ride comes to a halt in a clearing at the side of a single-vehicle track. A pen where the horses can be turned loose to graze on a thick carpet of lush-green grass takes up roughly half the space. The pen is square and of sufficient size to accommodate 16 horses for an hour or so. Low-grassy banks meet in the northwest corner and reinforce the rustic post-and-rail fence as well as serving as a windbreak. Dual ropes hang horizontally from rotund gateposts, and when pulled taut become the gate. Copying the actions of the riders in front of me, I dismount and remove Gjáska's saddlebags, saddle, and noseband and put each item out of hoof reach on the ground. Having quickly deposited their own horses into the pen, Audrey is in control of the rope-gate leaving Edda free to take the horses one after the other and lead them through the gateway. Edda removes the remaining part of the bridle, and the freed horse finds a spot to have a roll. The horses' usually welcome thick-winter coats are sweaty beneath their saddles. After her roll, Gjáska stands and rests. Her coat shines in the afternoon sun, and the wet patches where her tack was starts to dry off.

Further on and bounded by conifers is a dwelling. It stands silent, and there is no sign of life. The clearing is sheltered and warm. Horses graze. Riders settle on the bank that extends away from the west side of the pen. Hats and jackets are taken off, packed lunches are retrieved from saddlebags, and eaten. Then there is silence and rest. The only sound is of the unseen placid-flow of a stream behind us. A patch of low-lying land abundant in wild grasses and trees needs to be navigated to reach the stream. Edda had told us at breakfast that because the rivers in the valley are sourced by the glacier the water is safe to drink. A consequence of yesterday's alcohol intake is the English/Swedish contingent is dehydrated and their water bottles already emptied. When they go down to the stream to refill their bottles the lady with the Clipped-English accent loses her balance and stumbles into the water.

An hour later Edda directs us to queue at the gate of the pen ready to take our horse from her as she leads them out one-by-one. A trio of dark bay horses causes a moment of confusion for the reason that to the unfamiliar eye, they are identical to look at and their riders cannot tell them apart. I don't have this problem as Gjáska is the only dun. I soon have her tacked-up and ready for the ride back to Kjóastaðir Farm. As a result of hours of riding and a consequential long rest, my legs protest at mounting from the floor for the fourth time today. Terri uses a patch of higher ground where there is a dip on one side sizeable enough for her chestnut mare to stand in, thus reducing the mare's height and making it easier to mount. When Terri moves on, I lead Gjáska into the dip so I too can appease tired muscles and gracefully mount.

Southbound and back on mud-packed trails, twisting and turning through thickets of trees, the ride progresses at a swift pace due to there being lots of opportunities for trot and canter. Though the terrain is flat, there are some challenging bends. My balance and ability to move with Gjáska's movement is put to the test when cantering around hairpin bends. My heart beats quicken at the point of negotiating a particularly tight one. For a small horse, Gjáska possesses a smooth and comfortable canter, and I soon get used to riding at this gait if the terrain allows. In the transitions, I feel Gjáska giving strides of tölt, yet I can't retain the gait as I can trot and canter. Warm from her exertion, Gjáska appreciates the wade through a couple of shallow and slow-flowing streams. As we ford, the horses stop for a drink.

The sun is low in the west as the ride emerges from the network of bridleways and turns eastwards onto the track running alongside Biskupstungnabraut. We return using the route we had used this morning. Over the bridge straddling the fast-flowing River Hvitá, and onwards up the hill to Kjóastaðir Farm. Horses in wire-fenced fields raise their heads and watch us go by.

Hjalti G and Asa are waiting for us outside the riding centre building close to the pen holding Gjáska's herd. I dismount and remove all of Gjáska's tack apart from the main part of the bridle. She gets a final pat before I hand her reins to Hjalti G, who stands inside the gate of the pen in the same spot Gjáska had been passed to me this morning. Amid the flurry of removing tack, Asa invites us to go into the dining room where there are coffee and cake for all. Shortly afterward, she will take us to visit the Geyser hot spring area before it gets dark. Riding equipment is put back in the tack room, and 14 tired yet exhilarated riders trickle into the warmth of the dining room and devour a slice of delicious homemade chocolate cake. There are big smiles and merriment at the table. Riders share anecdotes on how their horse performed. The main subject in the various conversations is the tölt and the frequency and duration of the gait. Edda reports the distance covered today was approximately 12 miles (19 km).

After coffee and cake, there is a quick change out of riding clothes back in the cabins superseded by a return to the front of the riding centre building where the white minibus used by Hjalti G to round-up the horses this morning is parked. Asa is in the driver's seat. I jump into the front passenger seat beside her and wait for everybody else to fill up the seats behind. For me this is the best seat on the minibus as I get a wide field of vision. I don't want to miss a single opportunity to admire this part of the Haukadalur Valley. The minibus trundles out of Kjóastaðir Farm and initially retraces the same route used on the outbound ride this morning: westbound, down Biskupstungnabraut. With the Geyser hot spring area getting ever closer the minibus coasts over the hump of the bridge crossing the River Hvitá and continues in a relatively straight line to use two more bridges traversing rivulets. Asa and I comment on the incredible weather today. She says the weather is unusual for October and the usual forecast would be rain. After the third bridge, the road curves to the southwest and deposits us at the Geyser hot springs.

Asa brings the minibus to a standstill close to the single petrol pump on the forecourt of the Geyser visitor centre: a one-storey red-timber building with multiple red-pitch roofs and a glass façade. There is ample parking available; nevertheless, most of the bays are empty. A well-maintained grass bank partitions the parking bays out front from the road. Red flags on white poles and a row of trees share the bank's crest. Before we alight the minibus, Asa lets us know she will be back in an hour to pick us up. She drives away leaving us to join a few other hardy souls fighting the cold in the closing hour of daylight – mostly young couples in anoraks and woolly-bobble hats. Through the glass doors and windows of the visitor centre orb wall and ceiling lights invite you to come out of the cold and into the warmth. Tempting though it is to go inside, we turn away.

Like moths to light, we're drawn, towards the rising vapour streams on the other side of the road. The group splinters to reach its goal. In the company of Christina, Véronique, Terri, and Elissa, I cross the tarmac and go through an unclosed gateway installed in a grey-painted concrete wall to funnel visitors into the hot spring area. Elsewhere in the valley, the weakening sunrays shine onto the land and tint everything (pasture, stone, wood, and rock) a reddish-gold. Here the hot spring area is cast in the long shadow of a high ridge.

A grey-brick walkway provides the scattering of visitors a safe passage through a gurgling field. Natural vents release divergent-densities of sulphurous vapour in an area of bubbling-mud, moorland flora, pooled-surface water, and shallow streamlets. Litli-Geysir is the first on the geyser circuit. Brought to our attention by a piece of rock with a flat surface engraved with, LITLI - GEYSIR. It is beside a hole in the earth the width of a boulder with steam rising from it in an unspectacular way. On a flatbed of mud and sand, Litli-Geysir is set apart from the walkway by a puddle-depth trickle of surface water. We don't linger. Enticing us onwards is the denser rise of vapour trails coming from Strokkur. This active geyser erupts throwing water and steam up to exceed the silhouette of the ridge.

At Strokkur the walkway devolves into sand that circles the circumference of a three-metre wide crater. Strokkur too has its name engraved on the flat-face of a rock; though, this rock is much bigger and placed on the path. Despite the rock's size, it's still dwarfed into miniature by the hole it sits beside. On the far side of Strokkur is a trio of benches placed just outside the splash zone. A clear seam divides the wet and dry sand. Pairs of unfamiliar visitors walk by or sit on the benches. On our approach, the seated visitors get up and make their way to the bottom of the hills that form the backdrop. Christina, Véronique, Terri, Elissa and I sit on the benches and expectantly look at the huge cloud of vapour floating up from the hole. We're ready and waiting for the next burst of water and steam. Strokkur does not disappoint. Within moments there is an almighty eruption. Vast quantities of water and steam shoot up to a height of approximately 9 m (29.6 ft.) and then drops back to earth splashing a considerable amount of water onto the ground a short distance from the strategically placed benches. The steam lingers for longer gradually evaporating into the dusky air. Strokkur is a watch in awe phenomenon. In the interval, Christina suggests, we should time the period between back-to-back eruptions to ascertain how long it takes; the result is eight minutes. In the intervals, I try to pick out the edges of the crater but without success due to a veil of dense steam.

Back on the brick walkway, we meander to the Great Geysir. Initially, the immense plume of steam coming from the Great Geysir is all you see as it floats skywards in the motionless air. It has the appearance of smoke rising out of the flames of a substantial bonfire. We pass a standing stone engraved with GEYSIR, positioned at a split in the path. A roped-off section guides you upwards in a rocky lunar setting to a squat summit where you can view the length and breadth of the 18 m (59 ft.) wide crater. Great Geysir is not active. Decades have passed since the last eruption. All a visitor can do is stare at the hole and imagine the magnitude of water and steam the Great Geysir would shoot into the air. The Great Geysir's eruptions are said to be at least another 9 m (29.6 ft.) higher than Strokkur.

In the twilight, we retrace our steps back to the Geyser-Centre. There are 10 minutes left of the allocated hour that we can spend in the warmth and light of the souvenir shop. The shop is well-lit and set out like a smart boutique (wooden floor, shelves, racks, and tables). There is Icelandic trademark woollen clothing (pullovers, hats, and gloves), neat stacks of reindeer skin and sheepskin, rows of boots, and shelves of maps, books, jewellery, candles, postcards and those funny little plastic toy trolls fashioned with a bright tuft of hair. In a corner is a stuffed polar bear without a price tag. I expect the polar bear is for display only. Elissa wants a pullover for a souvenir. She selects and tries on a few with the purpose of ascertaining the best size. She is going to buy a pullover from the limited selection she's discovered in the hallway at Kjóastaðir Farm.

Back at Kjóastaðir Farm, Terri, Elissa and I enjoy a swift bottle of beer in the cabin ahead of joining everyone else for dinner. The ambiance of the dining room is much the same as it was last night and again an array of candles produce light for the table. Hjalti G and Asa announce the main course for non-vegetarians is lamb, born and raised on the farm. I'm famished from the day's long ride and the trip to the Geyser hot spring area and make light work of my starter and main course. Dessert is served late into the evening. I've just picked up my spoon from the table and dipped it into a bowl of chocolate pudding when an ecstatic voice calls from the entrance hall. The voice, I'm not sure whose, says two words powerful enough to make me together with the rest of the room drop everything and rush to the exit. The words are 'Northern Lights.'

Precious seconds rush by while I retrieve my boots and coat from the hallway. My pull-on boots seem to take an age to put on, and although I'm one of the first into the hall, there is soon people overtaking me. I put on my coat, hat, and gloves as I dash through the outside covered area and out into the clear night. We gather at the side of the arena where the horses were brushed and tacked up this morning. Everyone's eyes look to the south-west horizon. Where the dark earth meets the night sky, there is a long green-glowing strip of light spanning the valley from hill to hill. I can't believe I'm looking at the

Northern Lights. To witness this wonder was an ambition of mine and in the few days, I'd arranged to be in Iceland they materialize.

I'm not sure how much time passes. I am sure without the Northern Lights I would not have stood outside as long for it is bitterly cold. I go back inside to finish dessert after the green glow disappears. I make light work of the chocolate pudding in a room full of elate conversation. Another 15 minutes goes by, many more since I'd heard those two magic words. Then they come again from a voice in the hallway.

The room responds at an equal pace to the previous announcement.

'Wow!'

I take up a similar spot to where I stood previously to behold the new and expanded green glow. The Northern Lights spread upward and outward to fill what was the dark sky. What an array. The light grows so tall and broad it appears to reach the pinnacle point overhead. I hear Edda's voice behind me and turn around to find her alongside Hjalti G, Asa, and Audrey. They too are awestruck. Edda explains seeing this spectacle is a rarity in Iceland. I can compare their reaction to mine when I see a full-arc or double-full-arc rainbow back home. If the conditions are perfect, I see the arc meet the land and discover there is no pot of gold at the end of this particular rainbow. Again, I'm not sure how much time elapses as I stand and watch the solar extravaganza, but I stay outside until the Northern Lights fade. Then after a brief spell back in the dining room, I retire to the cabin ahead of Terri and Elissa.

I'd changed into my pyjamas when Elissa bursts through the doorway into the main room: 'Rachel, the Northern Lights are back.'

Jeans, socks, pullover, coat, hat, boots and gloves are quickly pulled on. Out of the warmth of the porch, I join Elissa, who looks to the northwest. The green glowing light dances across the horizon in a zigzag movement west to north. Although it doesn't climb to the same heights as before, there is enough to create a wall of light. It is the movement that is striking, rapid and visible unlike the creeping climb of the second display. About 10 minutes go by before I'm beaten by the cold and return to the warmth of the cabin. My body is exhausted, and I can no longer retain enough heat. In the darkness of the loft room, I lay in bed. Close to my head is the small window. I pull the curtain back. The last thing I see before I shut my eyes is the dance of the Northern Lights.

Canyon Brúarhlöõ and Waterfall Gullfoss

I wake from a deep and refreshing sleep with an hour until breakfast. As we prepare for the day ahead, Elissa, Terri and I revisit last night's Northern Lights spectacular. I feel guilty because I fell asleep when the lights were on full display, and I do not know if I will get the opportunity to behold the splendour again. Elissa dispenses reassurance by reporting the Northern Lights had vanished shortly after my retreat into the cabin. Although she kept a vigil for an hour or so after, the lights did not reappear.

Breakfast plays out much the same as yesterday. The alteration is the English/Swedish contingent is looking somewhat perkier having consumed less alcohol at dinner and retired to bed at an earlier hour. As I polish off two servings of Asa's homemade porridge, the conversations at the breakfast table are primarily on the shared luck of witnessing such a magnificent display of the Northern Lights. It was the perfect ending to a perfect day. Before we leave the dining room, Edda informs us of the riding itinerary for today. After watching the horse round-up and tacking up, we'll ride out to the Canyon Brúarhlöõ, accompanying the gorge all the way up to Waterfall Gullfoss. We will stop for lunch at Gullfoss and view the waterfall then ride back to Kjóastaðir Farm.

In the same spot as yesterday, I stand beside Elissa at the back of the riding centre building looking up the field to where the herd of horses' graze or watch the approach of the white minibus driven by Hjalti G. The brilliant blue sky from yesterday is no more and in its place is a blanket of low-grey cloud. As a result of the dimmer light, the golden autumnal colours are drastically reduced leaving the fields a darker green and the volcanic mountains in the distance essentially black. There's a feeling of imminent rain in the air. Elissa and I concur it should be easy to spot our horses as the herd goes by. Most of the horses are either dark bay or chestnut so spotting Gjáska's dun coat and Elissa's small-grey gelding should be an easy task. However, it is Terri's chestnut mare and her distinctive flaxen mane and white blaze, who we pick out in the herd first. The mare leads the herd from the field, through the gate, down the grassy bank and for part of the levelled track behind the riding centre. I comment that the chestnut mare must be fairly dominant in the herd considering her place. To demonstrate her standing the mare pushes a dark bay in front of her and coaxes it forward from behind. Gjáska is picked out at the point when she arrives at the unclosed gateway and descends the slope. Her position in the herd is near to midway. It's a pleasure to watch Gjáska trot by in her natural environment. Her head is up and ears pricked forward, she is relaxed and free in her movement. Elissa's grey gelding comes soon after. We'd already picked out a small grey covered in mud coming down the field. Because of the mud, we can identify him only when he comes through the gateway and down the bank. I tease Elissa about having quite a lot of brushing to do.

Riding a different chestnut horse today, Edda leads the procession of Icelandic horses out of Kjóastaðir Farm. Audrey is not accompanying us on our ride, so to start I take up the rear. Elissa and her grey gelding are in front of me. Earlier, amid the ride preparations, Edda corroborated on Terri's chestnut being a dominant mare in the herd hierarchy. On receipt of this piece of information and hearing about mine and Elissa's observations, Terri allows her mare to take up a position close to the front of the ride. We are a colourful sight in the late-morning gloom. Everyone is either fully covered or half covered in high-visibility orange and yellow waterproof jackets and trousers borrowed from the tack room. Me, Elissa, Terri, Véronique, and the lady with the Clipped-English accent are the only exceptions as we've all brought waterproof gear. Edda is kitted out in a fluorescent orange set. Christina wears full yellows enhanced by reflector strips. If the headlights of a vehicle point at her, she will light up like an over-decorated Christmas tree. Conversely, the lady with the Clipped-English accent looks the quintessential traditional English rider: black-velvet hat, long-leather black boots, and a full-length navy waterproof riding coat.

At the junction with Biskupstungnabraut, Edda leads our troop straight across and bears eastwards away from the Geyser hot spring area. Initially, the terrain is akin to where we'd ridden at the beginning of yesterday's ride. On the farm side, there's the same track running parallel to Biskupstungnabraut.

On this side, the track runs alongside the boundaries of fields. Though the width of the track allows for horses to walk side-by-side, we remain in single file. The track brings lots of opportunities to trot or tölt.

Gjáska is helping me out this morning. My body is a little tired from yesterday's long ride, and there is a non-verbal agreement between us that when we're not in a walk, the tölt is going to be the gait to use. I can feel how smooth the gait is to ride now Gjáska is giving me her wonderful tölt whenever the ride moves faster than a walk and can understand why this is the chosen gait for long journeys. The tölt requires the rider to take up a stance alike to standing with legs stretched but with 'soft' knees. The rider's posture needs to have the essential straight back. The movement of the tölt feels as if the horse's forelegs are being 'flung' out from side-to-side. The movement is silky smooth and incredibly comfortable. During yesterday's demonstration, Edda explained it is more strenuous for a horse to tölt than to trot; though, Gjáska seems to welcome the change of gait from yesterday's ride. Because I can experience canter on any horse, I will be riding in walk and tölt only today.

The low-lying terrain of the farmed valley is left behind when our course bends to the northeast and begins to climb. Still close to Biskupstungnabraut the expanse of green fields surrenders to high outcrops and even higher rock formations. As the route alters northwards, we transition into rocky mountainous terrain. The surface of the trail changes to volcanic soil strewn with sizeable stones forcing the horses to pick their path carefully. In this new landscape, the Biskupstungnabraut is out of sight. This topography is how I imagined Iceland. Footpaths ascend and descend, threading between crags of rock. There are no trees. Green moss and the purples, oranges, and yellows of heathland plants are scattered amongst the sparse wild yellow and green grasses yielding pockets of colour against the dark grey of the rock and lighter grey of the overcast sky. Here and there dry-stone walls mark this wilderness as managed land.

Elissa and I interchange places sharing stints at the rear of the ride. During the climb, Elissa's grey gelding starts to trip on the rougher terrain. I suggest she rides him with a longer rein so he can pick his route. All she needs to do is look forward and keep in balance with his movement. Exactly what I'm doing on Gjáska. Terri comes back to join us. She reports the horses at the front are fizzy, they jostle and get in each other's way. Terri holds a catalogue of past experiences with fizzy horses. Now she is getting older she prefers a quiet, well-behaved horse. This type of horse is what she asked for and why she is riding the chestnut mare. The ride is calm at the back as Gjáska and the grey gelding, who like the chestnut mare, are well-behaved.

Eventually, the Canyon Brúarhlöð comes into sight on the right. It is a deep ravine with the River Hvítá flowing southwards at the bottom. The river is the colour of watered-down milk, and its paleness highlights the width of the canyon. This pigmentation is a trait of a river sourced by the Glazier Langjökull. There are various places of high ground presenting a view of the dark-grey hills on the far side of the canyon where the grey cloud hides the furthest-away crests. On our course, north-eastwards vistas of the Canyon Brúarhlöð come and go as the trail winds through the rocky countryside. In the places where the canyon is at its narrowest, the River Hvítá is hard to spot. Where the canyon widens, mudflats span the flatland from the river to the cliffs. In this terrain, the ride stays in a walk. Though, there are bursts of tölt where the trail dips to level ground between high points. With the weather closing in pauses for photos are brief as soon as the shot is taken we ride on.

Having completed the steepest parts of the climb, we leave Canyon Brúarhlöð behind and re-cross Biskupstungnabraut. The altitude is roughly 200 m (656 ft.). The surface of the track is less stony than back in the lower valley. Here the track is laid close to the road in an extensive plain of autumnal moorland and wire fences hemmed in by distant hills and ridges. In the foreground on the east side of the road is the Waterfall Gullfoss visitor complex. Parked up in a tarmac carpark are four coaches and in the region of 15 cars; though space permits the capacity for many more vehicles. The expected rain begins lightly, carried on the wind.

Edda leads us to another pen situated apart from the carpark on the north side of the complex. We come to a halt and dismount on a piece of rough ground joining the tarmac to the long side of the rectangular pen. Saddlebags, saddles, and nosebands are removed and placed carefully on the tufty yellow grass. We lead the horses to the metal gate on the roadside of the pen, Edda takes them through in turn and sets them loose. The pen was built using horizontal planks and vertical wood poles. There is no grazing for the horses. Any previous vegetation is long gone. In its place is a surface of tiny grey stones and earth. By cause of the rain-carrying wind increasing in velocity, the horses huddle together in the west facing corner. Edda will stay by the horses and tack. Everyone else aims for the visitor centre where the toilets are.

Trudging unorderly back to where the tack is set down, we make our way to the visitor centre via a path laid between five information boards on the carpark side and a red one-storey building with a green-pitch roof pen side. Beside the red building is a pair of long picnic tables placed on the pathing slabs to the left of the door. The building looks locked and out of use. 20 m (65.7 ft.) further on is the visitor centre. Its design is higher at one end, thus making its roof slant. The façade is symmetrical and fashioned from hefty charcoal-grey blocks. Five full-length windows display shop dummies draped in warm-woollen clothing. The automatic doors slide open, and we walk through a wall of warmth into the shop.

The souvenir shop bustles with tourists dressed in practical outdoor clothing who have come inside to shelter. Our footfall adds droplets to an expanding wet patch tinting the pale-floor tiles a charcoal-grey. The retail space is smaller and more cramped than the souvenir shop at the Geyser hot spring area. Numerous counters full of jewellery and knick-knacks go all the way down the length of the room. There are limited gaps between the couples and families as they try to decide whether to purchase a pullover, hat or reindeer skin. It is also lunchtime, and the shop is the thoroughfare to the café as well as the toilets. The café is larger than the shop with long tables set out in rows. Orb lights dangle from a timber-pitched roof, and natural light spills in from wall-to-ceiling windows. The setup is a self-service tray affair designed to cater to a high number of people.

We hardy horse riders don't stay indoors; we go back outside and disperse. I try to find shelter from the wind so I can eat my packed lunch without adding mouthfuls of hair. Christina and I use the picnic tables at the front of the locked building that shelters us from the worst of the rain-carrying wind. Dressed in high-visibility yellows, Christina is not going to get wet. Likewise, for now, my untested down ski jacket and light-waterproof trousers are proving their worth.

With lunch eaten, we find Elissa and Terri sat on a bench in a shallow recess on the opposite side of the locked building. Terri and Christina remain when Elissa and I set off for the wood-plank walkway on the north side of the visitor centre. Jacket hoods are pulled up in response to the rain changing from droplets blowing in the wind to consistent drops. Snaking downwards through a carpet of brown, yellow and green wild grasses and heather the walkway delivers a sweeping view: rolling hills, autumn colours and a section of the River Hvítá's white water flowing down from the northwest. Overhead an expansive sky is weighted with rain-bearing clouds. From up here the lay of the land gives the perception of being on a relatively level footing. Though there is a clue to notify the visitor of an imminent drop: Like smoke from a great fire, a continual-cloud of water vapour comes from someplace below.

We go by a posse of visitors in soggy anoraks when they stop to look at four information boards set out in a square shape at a four-way intersection. Elissa and I go straight on down a steep set of wooden steps equipped with sturdy handrails to aid a safe passage down a rocky descent covered in pink, purple and yellow heather. At the top of the steps, I get my first look at the Waterfall Gullfoss. The expanse of milky water is channelled down over a step bounded by jutting outcrops. It gives the idea of a stair for a mythical giant to step down into a pool of water stirred up by the power of tons of water pouring into the ravine.

The wooden steps end in a small empty carpark where two more information boards stand free of tourists. Elissa and I pause to read the content translated in Icelandic, English, German and French. The first board informs us, Gullfoss and its surrounding area became a nature reserve in 1979 and the management of the reserve is the responsibility of The Environment Agency of Iceland. Above the text is an aerial photograph with the footpaths marked by a yellow-dash line. The second board begins with an introduction:

Trail of Sigríður and Gullfoss
Welcome to the trail of Sigríður. By the trail you will find signs with information about Gullfoss, as well as the area's geology and history. The trail of Sigríður is dedicated to the memory of Sigríður Tómasdóur in Bratthoif, and her heroic struggle for the conservation of Gullfoss.

I'd read about the chronicle of Sigríður Tómasdóur ahead of my trip. In the first half of the 19th century, the daughter of the then owner of the waterfall single-handily secured the conservation of Gullfoss. Due to the proximity of the family farm, Sigríður Tómasdóur frequently visited and loved the waterfall with a passion. Conversely, plans were put forward by foreign investors to use the power of Gullfoss to produce electricity by building a hydroelectric power-plant. A consequence of this project would be the destruction of the falls geology. Sigríður Tómasdóur was so enraged by the plans she threatened to kill herself by throwing herself into Gullfoss. In protest, she walked barefoot from Gullfoss to Reykjavik; a distance of 76 miles (122 km) on today's road network. She arrived desolate with bleeding feet. Her efforts were not in vain. Her pleas and reasoning listened to and no power-plant built.

In addition to the chronicle of Sigríður Tómasdóur, I'd discovered the translation of Gullfoss to be Golden Falls. The information board speculates on how the waterfall gained its name:

Where Does the Name Gullfoss Come From?
It is likely that Gullfoss was given the name because of the golden evening hue which often colours the glacial water. Another theory is that the name was inspired by the rainbow which often appears when sunshine hits the water-spray thrown up by the waterfall.

Another theory about the name can be found in the Sveinn Páisson's travel journal. Once upon a time, a farmer named Gýgur lived at Gýgjarhóll. He had plenty of gold and could not bear the thought of someone else possessing it after his lifetime. To prevent this, he placed the gold in a coffer and threw it into the waterfall – which ever since has been named Gullfoss.

There will be no rainbows today; instead, visitors will have to be content with looking at the upper part of the board where a photograph is on display demonstrating this marvel of nature. The print has captured the arc of a rainbow cascading from the left side to the centre of the stepped waterfall with the bottom of the rainbow dropping down over the lower step and out of sight. Enough of photos and information it is time to take in the real thing.

Gravel crunches beneath our feet as we cross a level piece of ground to reach the edge of a platform, which provides a view of the deep gorge. There is another wood-plank walkway close to the edge. This walkway is fenced off from the sheer drop by a post and rope barrier for visitors' safety. Our amble is disrupted by frequent pauses to stop and gaze at the waterfall below. Succeeding the descent of the shallower first step the water gushes across the pool at a 90-degree angle and tumbles down the second step disappearing into the depths. The wooden planks of the walkway cease just before the descent of the continuing grey-earthen pathway. It looks like this is the place where the rainbow photo was taken.

The descending pathway snakes through moorland plants in full autumn display to end at an extensive outcrop on the near side of the waterfall's upper step. Despite the volume of spray and dense rain, I can make out tiny figures in yellow and orange high-visibility gear on the flattish upper layer of the outcrop. Part of my group is down below at the crest of the waterfall. We continue onwards to go and join them.

Spray billows up as water is forced across the length and breadth of the pool and down the lower step into the deep ravine. Immediately afterward the water is forced into a sharp change of trajectory from west to south where it resumes its course as the River Hvítá. The river's flow is bounded by the ravine's sheer-sided cliffs which reduce the width to at least a sixth of the breadth above the upper step where the waterfall begins. Here the might of Gullfoss and its appeal to hydroelectric power investors is revealed and heard. The gush and thrust of the channelled and rapidly falling water is a continual deafening roar. Terri catches us up at the base of the rock formation. I pick my footing carefully as the three of us scramble up the slippery rock and move across the top to watch the water crashing down the first step. The experience is incredible. Nevertheless, on a day like today, it isn't a place to linger. The noise is fierce, and the spray comes at us from every angle. We're soon retracing our steps back to where the horses wait.

Inside the pen, the horses are huddled together in the corner. Their hindquarters pointed to take the brunt of the wind and heavy rain. Gjáska's smartly positioned herself in the middle of the herd and uses a dark bay horse as a windbreak. Everyone gathers roadside by the pen's metal gate ready to take our horse from Edda after she has caught and bridled them in turn. There is a brief moment of confusion again with who is riding which dark bay. The dark bays look identical to the unfamiliar eye. Gjáska is selected next. In the act of going to the front of the queue and taking Gjáska's reins, Edda and I chuckle. Gjáska's dun coat makes her easy to identify. A flurry of enterprise passes as 15 people tack up their horses. After I mount I discover the reins on the bridle put on Gjáska aren't long enough. So, I swap reins with the Finnish mother.

With the weather continuing to close in, Edda takes a direct course back to Kjóastaðir Farm: Southbound alongside Biskupstungnabraut. The ride remains on the road-side track for most of the way as it leaves the higher hilly terrain and curves to the southwest on the lower slopes in the valley. The surface of the track is ideal for riding a hasty return journey, mostly ridden in tölt. The outside of my ski jacket is saturated. As the pit-a-pat of raindrops increase, I'm sure the water will come through to the inside any second. Thankfully, thoughts of this impending soaking are magically blown away because right now I have the sensation of gliding above the ground. Bringing up the rear of a lengthened procession of horses, Gjáska is bowling down the hill in tölt. The tölt is a smooth easy to sit gait, and I relish every stride. Because the rain obscures everything apart from the road and track, I use this period to delight in my Icelandic horse and the gait she is giving me to experience on this ultimate ride.

We've covered more or less 4 miles (6 km) when a couple of the fizzy horses at the front of the ride leap forward; startled by something I suppose. Was a rider unseated? I'm too far back to discern what happened. The sudden burst of excitement is explained by a waterproof covered Hjalti G holding a gate open to provide direct access into Kjóastaðir Farm from the Biskupstungnabraut. The gateway is on the south boundary of the property and up till now had not been used. Last through the gateway, I emulate the actions of the other riders by dismounting, and leading Gjáska, uphill to the pen occupied by the waiting herd. After removing most of Gjáska's tack, I say a sad goodbye accompanied by lots of pats then hand her reins to Hjalti G. As I take my equipment to the tack room, I notice the inside of my ski jacket is still dry.

Another serving of coffee and cake in the dining room, succeeded by a quick shower and a change of clothes. Towing a packed suitcase, I leave the cabin for the last time. The coach that transferred us to Kjóastaðir Farm two nights ago is back and parked by the cabins. However, preceding the departure for Reykjavik there is a final gathering in the outside under-cover area of the riding centre building. We are given a souvenir certificate each amid smiles and goodbyes from Hjalti G, Asa, Audrey and our knowledgeable guide, Edda.

Reykjavik

It's gone 9:00 pm when Terri, Elissa, Christina, Véronique and I wander down Laugavegur, one of Reykjavik's main shopping streets. Saturday night in central Reykjavik is in full swing, and Laugavegur and its side streets are buzzing as people make their way to or from packed restaurants and bars. Lights from shop displays and taverns illuminate the street where a party atmosphere has spilled out from the drinking establishments. People are laughing together or call to each other in the cold night air. Cars full of older teens, and twenty-somethings cruise down the one-way street. The procession down Laugavegur is long and slow as deep pavements squeeze traffic into a single one-way lane. The cars advance no quicker than a brisk walk when not at a standstill. The drivers don't seem to mind. They are here to soak up the atmosphere of a Saturday night in town. I recall nights of aimless cruising around Central London late at night when I was their age.

Our journey to this juncture began as we boarded the coach back at Kjóastaðir Farm and it was precisely at that time when the rain stopped. The drive time to Reykjavik was roughly two hours and as opposed to the outbound journey most of the transfer was in daylight. Using Biskupstungnabraut, the coach rolled down to the Geysir hot spring area. Then on through the Haukadalur Valley where lofty hills defined by a clearing-grey sky edge the pastureland. Periodically rivers were followed, and glimpses of lakes snatched as the coach travelled through part of southwest Iceland. Isolated settlements popped up close to the Biskupstungnabraut. I'd noted the names of two: Reykholt and Klausturholar. At someplace near the 40-mile mark, we'd come off the Biskupstungnabraut and took a right, westbound onto Suðurlandsvegur. The coach then remained on Suðurlandsvegur as it skirted the town of Hveragerdi as the day began to fade and traversed old lava fields to reach the outer suburbs of Reykjavik at dusk.

We were dropped off outside the Fosshotel Lind, a modern four-storey hotel close to the city's main shopping, restaurant, and bar district. The hotel's façade conforms to the architecture of the neighbouring hotels and office buildings: populous windows and decorative terracotta wood panels and frames.

Tonight's room allocation was pre-planned. I'm to share with a member of the English/Swedish contingent, a young Swedish woman in her early thirties with cropped mousy hair. She is the quietest of the contingent, and until now, I had not noticed her presence. Probably due to the fact she is part of a group containing louder personalities. Our room is neat with twin-beds, a veneer floor, pale-painted walls and a wall-width window on the external wall. While we relaxed and prepared for dinner, our conversation was mainly an exchange of summaries based on our lives at home. She invited me to join her and the rest of the English/Swedish contingent for dinner. An invitation, I'd declined because I had already made plans. When I take my leave of our shared room to join Terri, Elissa, Christina and Véronique for dinner, my impression of her is of a calm, clear-headed and sensible young woman.

Famously labelled the most northern capital in the world, Reykjavik has a modest population of 120,000. Terri, Elissa, Christina, Véronique and I now join part of that 120,000 looking for a place to eat. Our pace is slow as we cross from one side of the street to the other and stop briefly to read the English translation of the menus displayed outside the doors of restaurants. Many display an agreeable menu. But when we make an enquiry, we're told the restaurant is busy, and there is a long wait for a table. Subsequently, we move on ready to try our luck at the next place.

Laugavegur Street ends, and Bankastrati Street begins; though, the path remains linear. None of us had eaten since devouring a generous-sized piece of homemade cake back at Kjóastaðir Farm many hours ago. Precisely at the point when hunger starts to make us consider dropping our standards on where to eat, a restaurant adjoined by a conservatory-type structure protruding from a three-storey building behind comes forth on the other side of the street. The architecture is Mediterranean old-style: sloping roof, mustard-painted walls, green-wood framed windows prettified by shutters and flower boxes. The conservatory is full of diners. The ambiance of animated yet cosy and relaxed drifts out to five hungry tourists standing on the street peering in.

Painted above the entrance door is the date 1892. The name of the restaurant is, Caruso; the menu lists Mediterranean dishes. It takes seconds to agree this is the restaurant where we will have dinner.

Inside is a modest reception with a staircase to the first floor ahead and a doorway on the left opening into the ground floor bar and dining area. The atmosphere fulfils its promise from outside. There are people seated at the bar, and at every table. Efficient waiters and waitresses' flit from the kitchen to the tables. Candles are placed on every table to enhance the dim lighting. Amid the bustle and many conversations going on at once, the restaurant radiates merriment and relaxation. A friendly waitress greets us and explains there is a 30-minute-wait time for a table. If we're happy to wait there is a lounge bar on the first floor where we can partake of an aperitif. None of us want to leave. The warm and animated ambiance invites us to stay. Our hunger enticed by wafts of baked dough and herbs. Again, we are unanimous: a pre-dinner drink will provide plenty of time to select from the menu.

The lounge bar incorporates a high ceiling, tall-bay windows dressed with full-length green-velvet drapes, wooden tables, and various upholstered occasional chairs. The waitress directs us to the table closest to the staircase, hands out menus and takes the drinks order. The drinks are swiftly served. As we take our first sips, the waitress comes back and announces our table is ready. On the way, back down the stairs, we comment positively on the considerably reduced waiting time as 30 minutes had not slipped away since arrival. Back on the ground floor, we enter a dining area split into two sections. An L-shape bar furnished with sets of wooden tables and high-backed chairs is sectioned off from the conservatory by a white-washed-stone interior wall. The waitress shows us to a table in the back corner, close to the bar.

A couple of hours are spent in Caruso, drinking white wine and eating the dish of choice – mine is a delicious pizza. Our waiter, a handsome young local man who speaks perfect English, times his attendance perfectly and always pops up at the exact moment when we need something. The restaurant remains busy throughout the meal, which is good for us when our conversation and laughter get more raucous as the bottles of wine are drunk.

With the meal over and as we drink the last of the wine, discussion falls on what to do next. On the penultimate night of their week-long adventure, Elissa wants to enjoy Reykjavik's nightlife and party into the early hours. Because her flight isn't until tomorrow evening, Christina decides she will go on to a few more bars. Véronique agrees too even though her flight leaves at first light in the morning. Véronique's plan must be to stay up all night and sleep on the plane back to Belgium. I decide to retire to the hotel. I'm not a morning person and struggle to get up following a late night. Preparatory to arriving in Iceland I planned to visit Hallgrímskirkja Church to experience its panoramic views of the city. There is enough time in the morning for this excursion before I have to take the shuttle service to Keflavik International Airport and catch my flight back to London.

We leave Caruso not long past 11:30 pm and go back down Laugavegur Street. The street is still alive with throngs of merry people and cars cruising. Music blares out from busy bars, and restaurants are full of late diners. It is not long until Elissa spots a vibrant bar throwing out loud music down a side street. I say goodnight to Terri, Elissa and Christina, and goodbye to Véronique. My walk continues down Laugavegur Street in the company of the sights and sounds of the city on my ultimate night.

Christina is accompanying me on my morning excursion to Hallgrímskirkja Church. She is hungover and feeling the aftereffect of having just two hours of sleep. Earlier, back at the hotel as we feasted on a cooked breakfast and lots of black coffee, Christina gave an account of the bars visited and the drinks consumed after leaving Caruso. Despite it sounding great fun, I know if I'd carried on into the night I wouldn't be visiting Hallgrímskirkja Church this morning. Today's weather is classic Iceland: a blanket of grey rain-bearing clouds high in the sky and a brisk icy wind blowing off the North Atlantic Ocean. I expect the icy wind is helping Christian to stay awake.

Hallgrímskirkja Church is on the summit of a hill. My first glimpse of the church was just after breakfast when I pulled back the curtains in my hotel room. Outlined against the wintery sky the church's high setting made it easy to spot beyond the red and white pitched roofs of the neighbouring streets. It is a backdrop to the leafy square laid out with modest lawns and children's play zone directly behind the hotel. An adjoining street reminds me of the Amsterdam street where a friend had lived: Tree-lined pavements with cars parked at an angle to the kerbside, and lines of three-story apartments.

After a couple of wrong turns, we arrive at Hallgrímskirkja Church via the ascent of Frakkastigur Street. At the culmination of Frakkastigur street, the façade of the church's pale-stone tower rises into the grey sky. It has the outline of a space shuttle about to launch, featuring a pointed nose and symmetrical stepped wings. The entrance is at the bottom beneath a huge-arched window. Stacked above the window are six arrow-slit windows that end underneath the church clock. Atop the clock and forming the base of the 'rocket's nose' is the observation room, the objective of this morning's quest. Behind the tower at a third of its height is the rest of the church building extended out beneath a steel-grey-pitched roof. The church has a contemporary design, an arrangement of clean lines and angles.

Sentinel on the church's concourse close to the roadway is a statue of a man on an elaborate plinth. The man's stance is proud and reconnoitring as he looks ever northwards. The engravings on the back of the plinth inform us the statue is of Leifur Eirkisson (970 – 1020) son of Iceland. It says Eriksson was the first European to discover the landmass that is now the United States of America – 500 years earlier than Christopher Columbus.

While there are a few tourists on the concourse, the majority of people entering the church are here for the Sunday morning service. Christina is keen to see the pipe organ. Her guidebook says that a German organ builder from Bonn had built the pipe organ. Bonn is Christina's home city. My intention was not to get tangled up in the Sunday-service crowd and make a beeline to the observation room. However, as Christina is desperate to see the pipe organ, I concede to take a sneaky look at the service under the condition we're quiet and do not stay long.

On entering, the lift and stairs to the observation room and the gift shop are passed to reach the grandiose doorway into the main chamber. I'm thankful for the curiosity of tourists as we merge in with the handful who are standing inside looking to where the service is taking place at the far, alter end. The main chamber is the traditional church configuration yet has the contemporary architecture of the exterior: symmetrical pale-stone walls curving into a high dome ceiling. Grand clear-glass windows curve to a 'rocket nose' at the top and let an abundance of light filter in from outside to fill the chamber. Stone pillars carved with squared-off groves span the length of the church to support the ceiling. On both sides of the central aisle are rows of upholstered-wooden pews decorated by carved stepped ends. To increase the seating capacity rows of high-back chairs have been positioned behind and in front of the pews.

At the back of the chamber, the entrance doorway is a simple design conveying the abstract image of a giant fireplace and mantelpiece with the doors in the place of the grill. Above the mantelpiece are the organ pipes. Nine sets of pipes supported by sturdy diamond-shape-wooden shelves form an overall configuration of vertical lines that culminate in a 'rocket nose' at the apex. The pipes are silver tubes crafted at various heights. The longest sets out on the flanks. The smaller sets carry on the theme by resembling mini rockets ready for take-off. Looking down the main chamber the organ is on a low-set platform to the left of the central aisle close to where we stand. Shaped by the use of rectangles and lines the organ is carved out of the same pale wood found throughout the church. Owing to the Sunday service taking place, Christina is frilled to hear the notes coming out of the pipes and drifting through the chamber. On the hasty retreat, back towards the gift shop, I comment on hearing the pipe organ being compensation for not being able to linger and study its detail.

After purchasing entrance tickets from the gift shop, we decide to take the lift to the observation room. I have a lazy take-it-easy Sunday morning feeling and Christina, in her current hung-over state, doesn't think she would make it up the steps. I don't know how many steps there are. I do know the height of the tower measures over 74 m (236 ft.) and the observation room is not too far beneath the tip. When the lift doors open at the top, we step out cool, relaxed and breathing normally.

The observation room is square with triplicate exposed-to-the-elements arched windows carved out of the concrete on all four walls; every window is the width of a person. There are six other tourists in the room; young couples in their thirties wrapped up in woolly hats and quilted jackets. Christina and I start at the nearest and vacant southwest wall. From here, we will move clockwise visiting every window. The observation room does not disappoint and is well worth getting up and out for on a Sunday morning. This vantage point looks out over and above the residential streets, hotels and six-storey buildings and the assortment of grey, white and brick-red pitched roofs. Although this is a capital city, there is a sense of space aided by abounding outdoor zones and gardens. Many of the streets are lined by trees in blazes of autumnal colours. There is a clear view of the runway at Reykjavik Airport where a small jet lands and taxies to the terminal building. Behind the airport is the cold-grey water of the bay. In the south, far away from the outskirts of the city sunrays penetrate the blanket of cloud and beam down onto the silhouettes of table-top hills.

The northeast-facing windows funnel an icy blast strong enough to give the effect of being in a wind tunnel. Christina and I laugh in the fresh-icy air. The surge is exhilarating and certainly blows away the cobwebs from last night.

Away from the northeast wall's icy blasts, you can dally looking out towards the skyline. There are a scattering of church spires and high-rise buildings all dwarfed by the heights of the hills and ridges beyond the bounds of the city. The highest ridges have a sprinkle of snow resembling dusted icing sugar.

On the ocean side in the distance is the dockyard. It may be too late in the year for pleasure craft since the only vessels moored in the harbour are a pair of steel-grey Navy frigates and four medium-sized boats, feasibly ferries or craft used for whale-spotting tours. The dockside and decks are deserted, presumably because it is Sunday and early October. The tourist season had passed, and this far north winter rapidly approaches.

It's about 11:15 am when Christina and I take the lift back down to ground level. There is time to spare ahead of the shuttle bus departure to Kalfavick International Airport. Enough to make a brief visit to the Sun Voyager Sólfar sculpture. Christina vaguely recalls at some point the merry band of her, Terri, Elissa, and Véronique had stumbled to the sculpture in their wanderings last night. As it was dark and the memory blurred, she is happy to visit again. Progressing northwards up Frakkastigur Street, I ask Christina how she came to speak fluent English considering she has always lived in Germany. She explains several years back, her social circle was made up of many nationalities and the common language they share is English, so this is the language they use when they are together.

The city holds the morning after the night before look and feel. Traffic is bordering on non-existent, and there are scarcely any people meandering from place to place. Going to Hallgrímskirkja Church, I was so engrossed in finding our way using Christina's tourist map. I hadn't noticed the cleanliness of the streets. Buildings are in good repair and freshly painted. Wet from recent rainfall, the roadways and pavements have a glistening sheen. Detritus is exclusively recently shed leaves scattered at the base of stunted trees. Reykjavik is a lovely city.

At the crossroads adjoining Laugavegur Street, I recognise a number of the establishments we'd passed yesterday evening. Christina espies a bar the merry band visited. The bar triggers the recall of memory on how they found their way to the Sun Voyager Sólfar on her first visit.

The Sun Voyager Sólfa is on the water side of Saebraut Street and is a landmark on the Sculpture and Shore walk, a designated esplanade at the edge of the bay. As we step out from the shelter of the streets to cross the Saebraut, the icy gusts of wind coming off the ocean batter us. The wind cajoles us into not staying at the sculpture for long by biting through the down of our ski jackets. The sculpture has the appearance of a Viking longboat with five oars on both sides. These 'oars' are the sculpture's supporting legs. Attached to each of these legs is a five forked welding with curved prongs pointed skywards. In my mind, the forks represent the heads and bodies of the Vikings manning the oars. The main frame skirting the 'oars and Vikings' is a parody of a boat's hull displaying a tall mast close to the stern and bow. It isn't a Viking longboat. There is a sign identifying the sculpture as a dream boat, an ode to the sun. Made from steel it was designed by, Jon Gunnar Arnason. The wind strengthens further. Christina and I go back to the shelter of the enclosed streets.

An hour later I'm outside the Fosshotel Lind in the company of the English half of the English/Swedish contingent. We're waiting for the hotel shuttle bus bound for Reykjavik Bus Terminal. There we will board another bus that will take us to Keflavik International Airport. Like the outbound journey, we're booked on the same flight back to London. The sun is out, and the buildings are sheltering us from the icy wind. They've been for a massage this morning at a nearby hotel. The massage was booked before their arrival in Iceland as they knew there would be tried muscles to ease after trekking. I was surprised to hear they'd retired to bed even earlier than me last night because the Swedish half of the contingent needed to be up early this morning to catch their flight home. I also suspect the contingent was still feeling the effects of overdoing it on the first night.

I share the details of my evening in Reykjavik adding in Christina's version at the end and what I'd done this morning. Coming back from the Sun Voyager Sólfar sculpture, Christina and I had run into Terri and Elissa close to the hotel. They were feeling the effects of too much alcohol and not enough sleep. They'd missed breakfast and were desperately in need of food and coffee. Because her flight is scheduled to leave later this evening and it was nearly lunchtime, Christina said she would accompany Terri and Elissa on their mission to find somewhere to eat. We exchanged goodbyes and arranged to keep in touch. My tour concluded. Now, as if on cue the shuttle bus arrives. In the course of the homebound journey, there will be plenty of opportunities to reflect on a successful and pleasurable trip.

Part 2

Ancient and Modern

The Day of Rest

In life, there is always a particular thing you want to do. For instance, this could be jumping out of a plane and parachuting back to the ground, or driving at high speed on a racetrack in a Ferrari or Porsche. Alternatively, it could be seeing the Grand Canyon in Arizona or visiting the Taj Mahal in India. My thing is to visit Cairo and see the ancient pyramids of the Egyptian pharaohs. So here I am, in early November, in a dark-brown box-shape estate car travelling westbound on the ring road approaching the east bank of the River Nile. The driver (and host for the week) is Maryanne, an expat of North America who's been living in Cairo for over 25 years. Our progress is unhindered as there isn't a lot of traffic at this hour: close to 7:00 am on a Friday morning. Maryanne explains Friday in Egypt is a religious day like Sunday is in the UK. Even though traffic is extremely light on the carriageways (mostly cars with an occasional truck) a display of driving Cairo-style is demonstrated by drivers opting to use whichever of the three lanes they so wish and passing either by overtaking or undertaking.

Our journey had started at Cairo International Airport. Just as the first rays of sunlight touched the desert horizon, my Egyptian Air flight made its descent and landed. I'd found it amusing how the only white western women present somehow managed to miss each other amongst the gathering of middle-aged Egyptian men in the arrivals hall; many of who were dressed traditionally in white galabeya (an ankle-length loose shirt). We'd found each other using our mobile phones. I had sat on a seat at the edge of the crowd to make the call. Maryanne, a healthy and stout sixty-something with short-grey hair and a friendly welcome-to-Cairo' smile emerged from the crowd like a long-lost friend. Dressed in a white shirt and cotton trousers, she looked relaxed and unruffled by the busy arrivals hall.

Keen to ensure I get the best experience from my stay, Maryanne enquires: 'What sights do you want to visit?'

'Definitely the Great Pyramids at Giza and the Egyptian Museum. Then, I'm happy to go with the flow. I'm not the type of tourist who arrives at a destination carrying a long 'shopping list' of sights to be ticked off each day. Ultimately, I'm here to relax and enjoy the riding.'

The ring road artery goes through the urbanised neighbourhoods of Cairo on an elevated section above the streets giving motorists and their passengers a good view of the buildings upper storeys. The tallest buildings are between 10 and 12 levels and are constructed using red or brown brick or sandstone. Nearly all have a flat roof. A few have a balcony. There are no neat rows or perfectly formed blocks. I get the impression land is built on without any planning on how a neighbourhood should look. Maryanne picks up on my observations, 'There are no planning permission regulations in Egypt equivalent to the laws in the UK. If you are an Egyptian national, you can pick a piece of land and build on it. If you own a property, you can extend outwards or upwards for the price of the material and construction only.'

There are a number of the buildings with partly built walls and window panes still to be installed. These high-rise building sites are presumably family homes. The new floor will be for a son or daughter with, the parents and grandparents' homes in situ at the lower levels. Because there are no design controls or restrictions, the city's structures and skyline sustain an organic look without regulated conformity.

We travel across to the Nile's west bank using the multiple-lane Moneeb Bridge. Below, the Nile is broad enough to accommodate an island that temporarily splits the river into a fork. There is an absence of painted lines to assist and funnel drivers. Vehicles move freely forwards and crosswise, and somehow there is always just enough of a gap to prevent an accident. An inferior central reservation separates the southbound and northbound traffic. Reassuring to a point, since it would be easy for a vehicle to cross the reservation and join the traffic going the other way. Maryanne points out the streetlight-lined pavements alongside the bridge's green-metal railings. The pavements are wide enough to park a car on. She tells me later today many people will use the inside lane for a different purpose. They will park their cars and set up stalls and seating on the pavements for the length of the bridge. By doing this, they establish a recreational zone to escape the torrid streets. At this hour, there is just a broken-down vehicle: an old white car in the same mould as a 1980s Skoda.

After the bridge, the west bank offers a continuation of high-rise apartment buildings. Though, it is the beginning of the end to the urbanized streets. The fertile west bank is in use to cultivate crops. As the journey advances into Giza, Maryanne and I discuss my riding experience: 'What type of horse do you ride?'

'A quiet, well-schooled and well-behaved mare who is about 15.2 hh [1.57 m].'

Without hesitation, Maryanne responds, 'I have the perfect mare for you. Her name is Jameela [pronounced 'Gah-meela'], which translates to 'beautiful' in English. She is an Anglo-Arab and the politest horse I have ever met. She came to me from a riding school, so she is used to the English-style of riding. Jameela takes care of her rider. On desert rides, she always checks her rider is ready to gallop by only responding to the second ask.'

'She sounds perfect. I look forward to meeting her tomorrow.'

In spite of the sunny morning. When we leave the ring road to join the southbound carriageway on the Mariotia Road, my first glimpse of the pyramids at Giza gets thwarted by a shroud of thick haze concealing the famous structures from our roadway viewpoint. Instead, I have to be content with watching urban transfigure to the countryside as the car moves in the direction of Al Sorat Farm, Maryanne's home, and the nearby Sakkara Country Club where I will be staying for the week.

Just after 9:00 am the next morning, Maryanne arrives at the Sakkara Country Club to pick me up. We exchange waves with the two security guards sat in their hut at the side of the unclosed main gate as the car trundles through the gateway and takes a right onto the Sakkara Tourist Road. Al Sorat Farm is situated southeast of the country club. To reach the farm, we have a five-minute drive along a straight concrete-laid roadway with the severest speed bumps I have ever encountered. A central reservation lined by tall palm trees separates this side of the road from another carriageway. Set back from the roadside are grand villas partly obscured by high-stone walls and security gates. There is no traffic apart from a middle-aged man riding an undersized-skinny-white donkey. The man's skin is dark and sun-wrinkled, and his light grey gallibaya is grubby and well worn.

Maryanne is as mellow as she was yesterday: 'How was your rest day? Do you like the hotel?'

I recount how I'd spent the hours that followed the airport pick up.

◆ ◆ ◆

In a surreal lack of sleep state, I take a shower and then get into bed. A couple of hours later and significantly fresher, I wake to find myself under crisp-white sheets in a double bed placed in a cool-dark cave. On finding the switch to the bedside lamp, the cave illuminates into a hotel room. There are a door and a heavy-curtained insufficient window at the front end and an ample in-built dressing table and mirror at the back. To keep the room cool there is, an air-conditioning unit, a ceiling fan above the bed, a tiled floor, and solid-stone walls. The architecture is more curves than angles. There is a red-cushion sofa at the window-end, moulded from the same pale sandstone used for the walls and ceiling; the soft lighting reflects the warm-yellow hue of the sandstone. All the fixtures and fittings are dark wood. Though, it's quiet in the room, outside isn't. Out there is loud music and the laughter of many children at play. I get up and go and investigate.

My room is one of 26 erected in rows at ground level. Outside each door are a covered terrace furnished with a table and a pair of red chairs. A dry heat greets me, maybe a few degrees below 30°C (86°F). There is no breeze. My eyes take a second to adjust to the dazzling mid-morning sun and then bring into focus the wood frame of the terrace's trellis and a climbing bougainvillea. A low terracotta wall edges the terrace. On the other side is a manicured lawn splattered by flecks of shade thrown down from a profusion of green-leaf trees and palms. Birds hop on the terrace wall and across the neat cut lawn. If they tweet, I can't hear them for a raucous of mass jollity stifles their songs. The unharmonious noise is coming from a raised patio and outdoor swimming pool area on the far side of the lawn.

The neigh of a horse draws my attention away from the swimming pools. On the east side of the property, I find a large outdoor schooling arena and horse pens of various sizes. The fencing is tubular-white-metal post and rail on a sand surface. Brick paths connect and provide access. It is a sizeable operation. Despite, the size the only occupants are five ponies grazing on hay strewn on the ground. A grey pony, I estimate to be 13 hh (1.32 m) shares a rectangle pen with a black pony of the same size. In the next pen, there is a pale palomino, closer to 12 hh (1.22 m). Two pens down from the palomino are a pair of miniature chestnut ponies. They have thick flaxen manes and tails. One has a white blaze and four white socks. The taller ponies are indifferent to my presence and go on grazing or standing quietly in the shade bestowed by a cluster of palm trees. The miniatures, however, relish in a bit of fuss and attention. I keep them company until a trio of vibrant nine-year-olds, two girls, and a boy, come racing along and take over. I then move on to circumnavigate the pool area.

The Sakkara Country Club boasts three swimming pools and four hot tubs located in a decked area sprinkled with sun-loungers, sun-parasols, and mature palms. At the accommodation end is a generous-sized paved patio full of square tables and wicker chairs. On arrival this morning, there was no sign of life, and the surface of the main pool looked as smooth and unblemished as a new pane of glass. Now there are young parents (I'm not sure if they are Egyptian) occupying every chair around tables besieged by towels and bags. As they chat, they watch their happy children play or splash in the pools. The men and children wear swimwear, shorts or trunks for the men and boys, swimming costumes for the girls. Several women wear a black burka. Though most wear cotton trousers and blouses, accessorized by a long patterned or plain head-scarf wrapped around their heads. The teenage girls wear the same style head-scarf and like the teenage boys, are in denim jeans and branded t-shirts. This latter faction, preferring the company of their peers and the shade of the trees, are gathered in sparse groups away from the poolside and the rest of the family. They sit on benches at the side of the manicured lawns, in the palm tree umbrage. In the manner of assembled teenagers everywhere, they are either in ballyhoo conversation or talk animatedly into their mobile phones.

With the poolside hubbub established, my attention shifts to finding the source of the loud music. I'm unfamiliar with the genre. My best guess is the sort of music a belly dancer would energetically gyrate her hips to mixed with a modern beat to make it current and appeal to the younger generation. The sound system booms out a bass low enough to make the earth vibrate. Most of the tracks are instrumental and reverberate from the whereabouts of something else I want to see close up. Behind the swimming pools and green lawns is the Sakkara Country Club's southwest-facing boundary marked out in part by a neat box hedge lined by palm trees. Behind the hedge are sand dunes that rise into a blue sky speckled by scant high white clouds. They are the vanguard dunes of the momentous Sahara Desert.

To reach the edge of the desert, I scout away from the vibrant families by using the driveway. From the main entrance, the driveway passes the one-level reception building and goes all the way to the back of the property. To get to the driveway, I re-trace my early-morning route pass the restaurant: a pink-tinted-stone building with a façade dominated by arch windows on the ground floor, and a long veranda on the upper storey. The vista from the veranda looks out across the length of the property, over ornamental lawns, flowerbeds, old-fashioned-street lamps beside palm-lined brick paths, swimming pools, sand-tennis courts, and out to the desert. The restaurant isn't open. Wooden double doors bar the way. Peering through the window, I see a spacious room sectioned by a vaulted ceiling with bauble lighting. Though, it is dark inside. Stone-top tables trace the outer walls and the base of the central support pillars. Chairs are dark wood and upholstered with red-cloth. The floor is pale-stone tiles. In the back corner is an empty buffet-service counter. There is no one around. Too late for breakfast and too early for lunch.

On the way down the driveway there are walled gardens of privately-owned villas on my right and on the left, is the Country Club carpark. Queued up drive side of the carpark are 15 red quad bikes. The quad bikes will be mounted by the helmet-clad riders soon to emerge from their briefing ready for their desert excursion. At the back of the tennis courts, the driveway regresses into a track and angles off to skirt a sizeable carpark where four newish air-conditioned coaches are parked side-by-side. Now I know how all the people currently permeating the grounds of the country club travelled here. At the back of the carpark, the track concludes at a barn-door-size gap in the hedge. This opening is the access point for the quad bikes to go out into the desert.

With every step forward the music increases in volume, and the source whereabouts soon reveals itself. At the back of the property is another manicured green lawn, close upon square and paddock-size. The lawn is teeming with people who gather in the midst of three massive open-sided marquees. Before I go to get a closer look though, I want to experience an uninterrupted view of the Sahara. To do this, I could use the gap in the hedge and walk out onto the sand. Instead, I opt to scramble up the sandbank at the back of the carpark so I can get a raised lookout.

As I stand on the edge of the largest sub-tropical desert in the world, a desert spanning 12 countries and the width of a continent, all I can do is gaze in wonder. I still experience tingles of excitement, despite my first unbroken view being a line of steep dunes tall enough to obscure the vastness of the desert beyond. White clouds are abundant and project shadows on the faraway dunes to make the sand there look black. In the foreground, at the foot of the nearest dunes are piles of fragmented rock and dry wood. There is a circular patch covered in ash; no doubt the remnants of a bonfire. I ponder momentarily on what is yet to come and then turn and go back down the bank.

◆◆◆

I describe in detail the trio of marquees to Maryanne. The loud music blared out from one and appeared to be the venue for dancing later in the evening. The other marquees sheltered long tables set up in an L-shape and set out using white table clothes and silver terrines. A variety of food was spread out for the guests to serve themselves buffet-style. Outside the marquees, on the lawn, were circular tables set with red cloths. Ten upholstered red-velvet cushioned chairs surrounded each table. I guessed it was a wedding reception. Maryanne thinks it was probably an embassy treating its staff and their families to a day out.

In preparation for my trip, I'd read on the Sakkara Country Club website that there are stable facilities for 90 horses. On my wanderings at the property yesterday, I'd not seen the stables; though, I did witness some equestrian activities. After a late lunch in the restaurant and in advance of retiring to a chair on the terrace outside my room to read a book, I had made a brief return to the back of the property using the route on the stable-side of the swimming pools. A solitary male rider in his thirties was schooling a grey Arab in the spacious arena. The Arab kicked up a trail of fine sand as it trotted around. Further back and adjacent to the lawn temporally accommodating the marquees is a sand-covered paddock. The black pony and the palomino, I'd seen in the pens were inside, tacked up and engaged in giving pony rides to a queue of children and adults. The palomino was having a better afternoon because the children were content to walk once around the paddock and dismount. Unfortunately for the black pony a couple of the fathers wanted to show off to their peers and raced around in canter. The men are too heavy for the pony and lacked a secure seat. They bounced uncomfortably on the back of the unfortunate animal with their hands moving up and down and held too high. It's a miracle they stayed on. I didn't stop to watch.

Maryanne explains the absence of horses: For many years, the country club was a thriving livery stable and had many clients who kept their horses there. Then there was a change of ownership. The new owners have more interest in the events and special occasion side of the business. Now the stables and schooling arena are mainly used for horse events. There are a few livery horses and the ponies used for petting and pony rides.

For the remainder of the day of rest, the Sakkara Country Club continued to be a bustling hive of relaxation and pleasure. At 10:00 pm the music stopped, and any remaining guests went home. When I left my room to meet Maryanne this morning the patio and swimming pool area was again serene and deserted.

Maryanne slows the car to allow a green truck going in the opposite direction to go by then takes a left to cut across the central reservation using an intersection. Another left turn follows to double back onto the other carriageway. While I wonder what the Egyptian 'rules of the road' are (there's an absence of any signs or road markings for directing traffic) the car cruises by the grove of tall and green-leafed trees we'd passed going the other way. I'm not sure of the types of tree, maybe sycamores or mulberries. After the grove, Maryanne takes a right down a lane bound by an extensive and cultivated garden belonging to a sizeable mustard-colour villa and a small-scale agricultural field and neighbouring lane-side villas opposite. The car turns at the end onto a narrower hard-packed dust track where a sandstone wall forms the back boundary of the mustard-colour villa. The villa is practically obscured from view by the height of the wall and the overhanging leafy branches of trees. The track continues alongside adjacent walls, fences and shrub borders that mark the back boundaries of neighbouring properties. However, these holdings will remain undiscovered because Maryanne applies the brakes and stops the car outside a mesh gate on the right side of the track. Reinforced by a rim of green-metal tubes, the shut gate hangs between red-brick gate posts set in a red-brick wall finished using a diamond-lattice effect along the apex. This boundary is lower than its counterpart across the way; though, here to branches from what looks to be a banana tree and perhaps some mulberries overhang from the garden behind. We've arrived at Maryanne's home, Al Sorat Farm.

Al Sorat Farm

The arrival of Maryanne's car at the gate triggers a wave of activity. An Egyptian man in his late teens or maybe early twenties, wearing a livery of turquoise t-shirt and denim jeans runs to open the gate. He is escorted by three yellow Baladi dogs and a Dalmatian barking excitedly. Seeing the dogs' attention is fixed on the familiar car crawling through the gateway the young man re-secures the gate with all canines accounted for on the inside.

Maryanne brings the car to a stationary position on the left side of a long and straight driveway. Out of the car, I find myself next to a diamond-lattice wire fence about 1.5 m (4.11 ft.) high bordering a neat cut lawn occupied by more excitedly-barking dogs. I mentally register a pair of Great Danes (one merle and one brindle), a second Dalmatian (this one missing a back leg), and at least five terriers (either white and black, white and tan or tri-colour). The driveway's width can cater for four cars parked side-by-side, and from here it looks as if it stops at a wall approximately 70 m (229.7 ft.) further into the property. In front of the mesh fence are a couple of young palm trees, and a mounting block close to the garden gate.

At this end of the driveway on the right is a one-level sandstone building with redwood framed windows and shallow steps going up to a redwood door. A row of shrubs is at the base of the building with a tie-post in front. As I say hello and make much fuss of the first half of the four-legged welcoming committee, three more of Maryanne's grooms appear. They're dressed in the same livery, turquoise t-shirt, and jeans, but are a few years older than the young man who opened the gate. They take instructions from Maryanne who speaks to them in fluent Arabic. I assume she's telling them which of the horses to prepare for our ride since a couple of the grooms have started to fetch tack from the one-level building.

Tailing Maryanne, I go through the gateway and onwards to the house by crossing the cut-lawn. I fall behind slightly when I pause to say hello to the second half of the four-legged welcoming committee. All the dogs are delightful and relish the pats and strokes they receive. The lawn leads to the house situated at the front of the property in the southwest corner of the farm. The house is three-storeys, constructed from cream stone, and features include tall arched windows, wooden shutters, and a flat roof. At the back of the lawn is a free-standing aviary, its tight-entwined mesh and thick stone walls hide the birds, yet do not soundproof the squawks of a macaw and the quacks of ducks coming from inside.

Behind the aviary is a ground-level annex attached to the main house to form an L-shape. Stone steps in the corner of the L go up to an entrance door that opens into Maryanne's living room. Inside, in the corner right of the door is an office space where a personal computer dominates a desk set flush against the back wall. A second desk is set out from the wall, creating another L-shape. There is a high-backed office chair pushed up underneath, and the top is a profusion of note-pads, books, and paper. Amongst the stationery is the cloth saddlebags and plastic water bottles that I will use on our scheduled three-hour ride.

The rest of the room is for relaxation. Four curvature chairs ring a circular dining table. There are a couple of sofas full of deep-orange and purple and green stripe Bedouin cushions, and dog beds scattered on a mottled-effect tiled floor. The back wall contains double doors giving access to a set of steps going down to another lawn. A flat-screen TV is amongst a selection of books housed on a tall wall-length wooden bookcase placed against the interior wall. In the middle of the ceiling an electric fan whirls at a consistent speed to assist the airflow drifting through from the exterior doors. The temperature is lower than outside, maybe 22°C (71°F). Maryanne directs me to the water cooler situated at the end of a modest corridor. Open plan to the living room the corridor provides access to the saloon-style swing doors of the kitchen, and the bathroom door. When I backtrack carrying full water bottles, I notice the unclosed door of a roomy bedroom with an aspect over the back lawn.

An Egyptian man in his late forties with a neat black beard and casually dressed in a light-green polo shirt and pale trousers enters the room from outside. Maryanne introduces him as, Mohammed, her right-hand man who assists her with running the business side of the farm. From her introduction I sense, Mohammed is a person who she values highly. Mohammed speaks no more than a couple of words of English, so we exchange a 'Hello' and smile. From the conversational tone used between them and Maryanne's subsequent translation, I perceive he is a good assistant and long-term friend. There is a brief discussion in Arabic then Mohammed goes off to the annex. I grab the saddlebags holding the full water bottles and go back outside accompanying Maryanne and her pack of dogs across the lawn and onto the driveway.

There are two tacked up horses tethered to the tie-post adjacent to the tack room. Further down another horse stands quietly tied to a vertical post outside a pen. I don't get chance to study the horses in detail, due to ardently trying on a variety of riding helmets placed on the upper step of the mounting block. Maryanne and I had discussed riding helmets in the car and concurred I would use one of her supply. I had brought my helmet made with warm lining and small air vents – the preferred choice for the cold climate back home. Comparatively, Maryanne's helmets have numerous air vents and less lining, a style more suitable for riding out in an arid climate. A groom takes my saddlebags away to attach them to a saddle. I don't notice which groom or the horse he goes to because I'm distracted by Holly, the darkest of the yellow Baladi dogs. Holly is on the top of the mounting block demanding the attention I gladly supply.

While I'd been trying on helmets, Maryanne's been instructing the grooms. As Maryanne is fluent in Egyptian Arabic, there is no requirement for any of her staff to speak a second language. The grooms know some words of English, however, added to my zero knowledge of any Arabic words, they communicate with me by pointing at things and smiling. Though there isn't a lot of speech, the grooms' mannerisms and tone are friendly, considerate and polite. Another trait is they are super-efficient. In a trice, the rejected helmets get whisked away, and a well-groomed beautiful brown horse marked by a star and stripe is led over to the mounting block. The horse is tacked up in a pale-blue biothane beta bridle and an English saddle.

'Hello, Jameela.'

I give her a pat and promptly get on. I move Jameela away from the mounting block to adjust my stirrups and wait for Maryanne to get on her horse. As I direct kind words in a soft voice at Jameela, I ponder her colour. She has a short black mane and a light-brown coat which isn't either bay or chestnut, just light-brown. I had never seen a brown horse and will need to ponder on this. Albeit an unusual colour, her summer coat is silky to touch and shines in the morning sunlight.

My mull ceases when I see that Maryanne has got on a muscular chestnut Arab gelding tacked up in an expensive-looking western saddle and a groom is getting on a bay Arab. He looks to be the tallest of the grooms, a strong, healthy young man with broad shoulders and a broad smile. He agilely swings up into the saddle from the ground. His name is Hassan. Unlike Maryanne and me who are wearing riding helmets, Hassan wears a baseball cap. We follow on behind Maryanne, who's started to walk down the driveway headed for the northeast perimeter wall at the back of the farm.

Another groom walks beside Maryanne. I gather he is receiving more instructions. His age and height are similar to Hassan's. Though he isn't as broad at the shoulders, and his facial features are longer. His name is Walid. Hassan takes up the rear on his bay Arab, so the horses are in single file. Maryanne interrupts her conversation and points out the vegetable garden on the house side of the driveway. In addition to their animal-husbandry duties the grooms tend the vegetable garden, and for their toil, they get to take home a share of the produce for their families. Relative to the size of a generous allotment back in the UK the plot looks ample enough to yield a good harvest for Maryanne and her staff. Opposite, on the right, are four sand-surface pens enclosed by a high red-brick wall at the back and lower walls supporting an uppermost layer of white post-and-rails at the sides and front. Canopies made from palm branches and dried leaves provides a section of shade at the front. Three of the pens each secure a single horse; two of these horses are grey.

When observed from the entrance gate at the front of the farm, the high wall on the far side of the paddocks gives the impression it is the end of the driveway. Not so, the driveway curves left and then right at the corner of the wall and then continues on its original orientation. We've entered the part of the farm where Maryanne keeps most of her horses. On the corner is a circular pen bound by a square pen behind. Seven or eight tall palms border the remainder of the driveway and the adjoining 20 x 40 m (65 x 131 ft.) white post-and-rail fence sand-surface arena. At the midway point on the quarter-lines is a tree circled by a low-set pale-stone wall. Inside the pens and the arena are many healthy and relaxed equines: grey, chestnut, bay, and dark bay horses and a big mule. Behind the far long side of the arena and forming this section of the farm's northwest boundary are five more pens. Canopies of tightly-entwined twigs cast shadows on stone troughs and the surrounding sand surface. A couple of the pens hold a solitary horse. The interior fences of the remaining pens are down to allow the horses in the arena to enter and shelter from the sun or drink from the water trough. I expect the loose horses are secured in the back pens when the arena is in use for lessons.

At the end of the arena, the driveway bends left again alongside the boundary wall up to the back gateway. Walid unlocks and opens the gate. As I go out, I say 'Goodbye' to him and turn right onto a single-lane dirt road bearing to the southeast. An initial border of tall conifers, high brick walls, and a massive palm tree give way to residential properties and planted arable fields. From my vantage point on Jameela, I glimpse over the walls that had I been on foot would have concealed the sizeable cream villas behind. Some of the villas are ostentatious. Characterized by double doors, decorative pillars, and multiple balconies. Roofs are a mixture of angles. A few have corner turrets; the grandest boasts an extravagant dome. Closed black-metal gates at a height to match the walls guard the thresholds. The comparison to another resident in Maryanne's neighbourhood is staggering. A poor farmer and his family are bundled together in cramped shack assembled at the roadside. The shack has been put together with whatever materials the family could find. At the side of the shack are a buffalo and pitiful skinny donkey. The animals are tethered and stand with at least one hoof in a dirty puddle.

On the approach to the end of the dirt road is a tunnel of tall trees created by leafy-green branches reaching overhead to meet and overshadow everything underneath. The trees on the right belong to an elaborate garden of a supposed unseen villa. An ornamental stone path curves away and through the garden's grove. Everything is in dappled shade. It is the perfect hideaway to escape the intensity of the sun and pass the time reading a book. Clear of the wooded garden and out of the tree tunnel, we take a right to join a carriageway split by the steep-sided concrete banks and low-lying water of an irrigation canal. Here a single-vehicle-width road bridge is used to cross over the canal before we double back and take a right at the corner of another high-brick walled property onto a dirt road, which peters into a dusty track.

Our course continues in a southwest direction going by more perimeter stone walls. Rising above one wall are twin structures that look like giant prototype 'Daleks' (Daleks being fictional characters from the BBC television programme, 'Doctor Who'). The peculiarity is these structures have multiple eye-stalks sticking out in every direction from top to bottom. Maryanne picks up on my curiosity, 'These structures are pigeon roosts.'

Soon after, she turns in her saddle to look at me again, 'Are you ready for a trot?'

'Yes.'

The horses respond. Jameela's trot is comfortable with long and rhythmic strides. Exactly what you would expect from a well-schooled horse of her breeding. There is a trot transition back to walk when a long ground-level structure made from thick mud-brick erected on the edge of a field comes up on the right. An open frontage allows you to look through the interior all the way to the back wall where a gap reveals green crops shimmering in the field behind. Clean straw covers the ground inside and out. Outside, a galabeya-clad farmer, a white cow and a grey donkey shelter from the sun in the speckled umbrage of young trees. Maryanne and the farmer exchange a friendly greeting then she looks back and announces: 'This shelter was built by the farmer for somewhere to keep his animals while he works in his fields.'

We spend the next couple of hours riding through the farmland in the fertile Nile Valley where there is a network of farm trackways edging cultivated fields and the banks of quaint irrigation canals. Fields are full of crops planted in neat furrows of lush green, corn-yellow or jade. It makes the locality look as if a striped blanket covers the level terrain. Palm trees abound the perimeters either solitary or planted in succession. Amongst the trees are a scattering of animal shelters and residential buildings. In the distance chains of electric pylons connect villages and farms. In this setting, life plays out at a slower pace in comparison to my modern lifestyle. Nonetheless, the traditional work is hard for the farmers and their success determines if their families eat or not.

All the animal shelters are smaller than the shelter seen at the beginning of the ride. The frames are made using tree trunks in a variety of widths. Roofs are a concoction of palm leaves and twigs. Strips of what could be dried palm leaves have been bound together and erected as walls. The technique used allows mottled light to seep in through slits. A few of the shelters have a low perimeter wall made from mud and stone. One contains a buffalo; it stands inside on a hard-packed mud floor sheltered from the rays of the late morning sun. The site for a shelter is carefully selected. Most are built by palm trees to utilize the natural shade. It is apparent the farmers have reached the part of the day when they take a break from their morning toil as they're either standing or sitting close to or in their shelters. Most are dressed traditionally in charcoal-grey galabeya; though, a younger chap in his late thirties has opted for a grey and white checked shirt, dark-grey trousers, and a grey baseball cap.

Eventually and still within the realm of irrigation canals and patchwork fields another structure comes into view behind the sparsely planted palm trees and electric pylons in the background. Having the desert close by brings a flurry of internal excitement. Its presence is made known by the vertexes of three Abu Sir pyramids.

The pyramids leave the line of sight after a change of direction. The track widens to a width where the horses could walk side-by-side, and a village replaces the trees with its cluster of cream or reddish one and two-floor buildings topped by flat roofs. From this distance, the visible windows look black as none have glass-panes or shutters. The lines of electric pylons congregate at the settlement to render an essential supply of power. On the point of reaching the outskirts, the noise of car and motorcycle engines replace the tranquillity experienced around the fields and canals.

The horses are bombproof as we enter the village and emerge onto a busy street. The street looks to be the hub of the settlement and the source of the traffic noise. Two young Egyptian men in their early twenties wearing logo t-shirts and jeans weave by on a motorcycle, neither of them wears a crash helmet. On the far side of a bridge, there is a grey truck parked up delivering goods to a shop. As the shop is on the route, I get a better look at it after crossing the bridge. Four or five stone steps take you from the street to the open shop door, where crisp boxes and soft drinks are piled up inside the doorway. The deliverers are two stocky Egyptian men in their early forties practically dressed in shirts and jeans. They stand at the back of the truck looking in, probably discussing the cargo.

We leave the village by turning right after the shop onto another dirt road. The noise from the main street fades away, and the village is soon left behind. This new direction leads us by more high garden walls and the ornamental iron gates of villas. Lining the edges of the walls are palms, young sycamores, green shrubs, and grasses. Here and there the private gardens and villas are interspersed by groves of date palms. In the shade of the tall date palms is a carpet of lush green plants.

Sand returns underfoot when the palms groves are behind us. Our course goes by more high garden walls until the desert wall cuts across the path. Hassan rides to the front and comes to a halt at a gated archway in the wall. He jumps off his bay horse and produces a key. I lightly squeeze Jameela with my legs. She obediently follows Maryanne's horse through the now open gateway and halts and waits patiently on the other side. Maryanne watches Hassan coming through the gateway on foot leading his bay. He closes and locks the gate then agilely remounts. I turn to face the direction of travel and become transfixed on the ridges and slopes of the dunes. This time there are no walls, or trees, or anything else standing between me and the sand. I'm in the Sahara Desert.

Pointing to the southeast, keeping the countryside boundary on the left, Maryanne and Hassan lead as we continue alongside the bottom of the first bank of dunes. The vertexes of the visible Abu Sir pyramids are on the skyline further on. They protrude up from behind a foreground dune, and from here the vertexes align north to south giving the impression the most northerly and southerly are taller than the middle pyramid. As we get closer to the pyramid complex, the lower parts of the pyramids come into sight and grow in size. Maryanne comments on the Abu Sir pyramids not being as well-known as the world-famous Giza Pyramids set behind us in the north. Though, I can see three there are more pyramids at Abu Sir, built during the epoch of fifth dynasty Egyptian pharaohs. The fifth dynasty ruled for a period of 90 to 150 years (depending on what resource you read) over 4,000 years ago. The trail reaches its closest point to the Abu Sir Pyramids when we ride parallel to the west side of the complex. The smooth surface of the ancient outer layer is long gone and the great stones beneath lay bare and crumbling. The alignment observed previously permutates. The south pyramid is now on the west side of the middle pyramid. There is no sign of movement in or close to the complex. Encompassed in serenity and a light breeze to take away the intensity of the heat, I'm captivated and content.

Leaving the Abu Sir Pyramids behind, our course curves north-westwards to continue on the other side of the dune, we'd just ridden alongside. Here, there is a long valley the width of a single carriageway. Everything already viewed is out of sight: The Abu Sir Pyramids, the desert wall and fertile Nile Valley. Nor can I see the expanse of the desert, which is obscured by the peaks of the dunes that outline the valley. At the end is another valley with an orientation running north to south. The line of travel remains the same, on a course to ascend the dune in front of us. At midway across the valley bottom there is a glimpse of distant palm trees in the fertile Nile Valley to our right, and on the left, the ground keeps a straight course until it ceases at the foot of a distant dune. Throughout the ascent, the green vista of the Nile Valley stays in view until at the pinnacle a panorama dramatically expands out from north to east.

Over the cusp, the horses obediently descend onto a broad sweep of sand that rises gradually southwards to shape a long slope. The width and length of the inclination would serve as a runway for light aircraft should a suitable surface be laid. Maryanne halts the ride. She confirms this is a safe place to gallop as the sand is soft and there are no holes or hazards. Also, the terrain is perfect because it climbs uphill and the horses know to pull up when they reach the top: 'Would you like to gallop?'

'Yes.'

We point the horses to face uphill. 'Are you ready to go?'

'Yes.'

The chestnut and bay Arabs, Maryanne and Hassan are riding take-off up the hill.

My heart is pounding. I squeeze Jameela with my legs, and she takes off in pursuit. I squeeze on the reins to ask her to slow down, and she steadies into a rhythmical gallop. I remain in balance by fixing my eyes on the Arab horses swiftly widening the gap ahead. I alternate out loud words of encouragement to Jameela and repeat in my head the words of my riding instructor: 'Keep your head up and look where you are going.'

It is an exhilarating experience galloping a beautiful Anglo-Arab horse in the Sahara Desert. Maryanne is right, Jameela is the perfect horse for me. I transition through canter, trot and walk to re-join Maryanne and Hassan, who have come to a halt and are waiting for me to catch up. Hassan flashes his warm smile, 'Jameela, she is slow.'

I reciprocate his smile and nod. Owing to the language barrier, I can't explain it was me who asked Jameela to hold back. Jubilant, I follow on behind Maryanne and Hassan down a decline to switchback behind the peak of the dune. At the bottom, we bear north-eastwards towards the Nile Valley and make our way back to Al Sorat Farm.

Lunch is served in Maryanne's garden on a table at the side of the house. The surroundings bring about a haven of peace and relaxation with nothing more than clucks, coos, quacks, and squawks coming from the aviary to accompany our conversation. The dogs meander close to the table or on the spacious back lawn bordered by young palm trees. Through the gaps in the trees, there is a sightline above the crops growing in the vegetable patch to the horse shelters adjacent to the arena at the back of the farm. At the side of the table is a closed white-canvass umbrella made redundant by a blanket of high white cloud.

Magda, Maryanne's housekeeper, places a generous plate of food on the table amongst the dishes she and Maryanne had already brought out from the house. Magda is short in height and wears her black hair secured back underneath a cornflower-blue headscarf. Her sebleh is African-violet, a colour to compliment her cheerful smile. While Magda departs past the aviary back into the house, Maryanne tells me what dish the plate holds: 'This is an Egyptian recipe of aubergines, green pepper, olives, and herbs.'

When the meal begins, the dogs in the garden settle down on the ground. Mindy, the merle Great Dane is on the lawn. Finn, the largest and palest of the yellow Baladi dogs, and the pack leader is close to Maryanne. Two of the rat-terriers are under the table watchful for a morsel of dropped food. Suddenly, there is a succession of frantic barks close to the farm's entrance gate. The dogs close by leap up and rush off to join the commotion. Maryanne yells to calm them down then says: 'It will be the village children looking in the gate and setting the dogs off. When I moved here, I chose a gate people can look through. I want the locals to see there is nothing behind these walls apart from a western woman and her animals.'

Maryanne grew up in California. She met her late Egyptian husband at university in Canada. In the late 1980s, they moved to Egypt with their two children. Although the house has three levels, Maryanne only resides on the ground floor. The upper floors are a recent addition built for Maryanne's daughter who currently lives in the USA. Maryanne is a non-Egyptian national, so cannot own land in Egypt. The farm had to be purchased in Maryanne's daughter's name as she is an Egyptian national.

Our conversation moves onto the farmers passed on this morning's ride. In Egypt, every resource available is used, re-used or eaten. Nothing gets wasted. Surplus stalks and leaves from crops are fed to the farmers' animals or used for building material. Buffalos and donkeys are essential for working the fields. Goats provide milk and meat. Al Sorat Farm nurtures a single water buffalo, who is currently heavily pregnant by artificial insemination. Maryanne hopes for a female calf. A female calf is worth more money for they serve as breeding stock. The water buffalo's previous calf was male. He was a real sweetie. At 12-months old, the calf went to slaughter, and there are still parts of him in the freezer. Maryanne is no exception she too must use every available resource. We agree I will stay at the farm for the rest of the afternoon so I can meet more of her animals.

When we finish eating, Maryanne picks up a handful of leftover food from the table, and we stroll over to the aviary. At the base is a stone wall, which supports a taught wire mesh that goes all the way up to the roof. The mesh is tightly entwined so you can't see through. The mesh blocks the sun and provides an essential cool and shady environment for the inhabitants. A cacophony of bird song greets us as Maryanne opens the door to cast a shaft of light into the interior. There are three sections housing specific types of birds: ducks, chickens, turkeys, pigeons, and doves. The ducks, chickens, and turkeys stand together on the ground. The pigeons and doves perch on an arrangement of branches. Just inside the doorway is an African Grey parrot elevated on a wooden shelf: 'This is Mona.'

Staying on her perch, Mona moves her head forward to take the first of the titbits from Maryanne's hand. Mona is lucky, for she is a pet and not destined for the dinner table.

The dogs in the garden are alerted again by the barks of the dogs on the driveway. This afternoon's expected clients have arrived. Leftover food is placed down for the other birds, and the aviary is plunged back into its semi-darkness by the closing of the door behind us. When we reach the driveway, a groom has the gate open, and a silver saloon car is crawling forward onto the drive. The car has an escort of three Baladi dogs and a Dalmatian. Barks cease, and the dogs settle down to greet the family as they step out of their car. The father and mother are a trim middle-aged couple. He is an Egyptian with an almost-bald receding hairline, and she is of western descent with cropped grey hair. The parents are calm in comparison to their four excited children: two boys and two girls. The children have brown hair, shoulder length for the girls, short for the boys. I estimate the age range to be from six to twelve years old and from eldest to youngest it goes boy, girl, boy, girl. They are in clothes made for an afternoon at the farm – jeans, trainers, and either a plain, chequered or striped casual shirt. Mohammed join's us on the driveway and directs the father to park the car in the same spot Maryanne had parked hers this morning. Mohammed must have moved Maryanne's car as it is under the carport connecting the tack room to a large pen where three alert donkeys with ears pricked forward stand looking over the gate.

While the family's car is parked, Maryanne, the mother, children and I congregate in the middle of the driveway in front of the tack room. Like Maryanne, the mother has a North-American accent. The two lady ex-pats discuss options, and the children busy themselves by gleefully patting and stroking either a rat terrier, a Dalmatian or a Baladi dog. Maryanne offers a list of activities thereon it is arranged for the children to spend time with the donkeys and goats and have a pony ride up and down the driveway. 'Do you want to ride too?'

The mother hesitates momentarily she wasn't expecting Maryanne to ask this question: 'Yes. Although, it's a few years since I last rode a horse.'

Waiting patiently close by are the grooms who scuttle off to collect tack and horses on Maryanne's order. While Maryanne oversees the start of the grooms' preparations, the mother and I wait by the pen holding the donkeys and give them a lot of fuss from over the gate. Like the dogs, they are friendly and keen for attention and strokes. Two of the donkeys are white, the third a grey. They are taller than the donkeys I had seen on the ride through the farmland. These donkeys have plenty of flesh covering their frame, round bellies, shiny eyes and glossy coats. Their alert heads are held high and their ears pricked. They are the opposite to the farmers' puny donkeys with their visible bones, bowed heads and pulled back ears.

Maryanne joins us and introduces the donkeys. The smallest is Margarita, a nine-year-old grey jenny. George is a seven-year-old and the tallest. Daisy, the white jenny is five-years-old and the offspring of Margarita and George. Maryanne uses them for donkey rides, an activity usually offered when school trips visit the farm. Parties of children are frequently brought here to interact with the animals. The school-trip offer includes a barbecue prepared and served on the lawn. George has a custom-made harness and a donkey cart. The donkey-cart is an option for non-riders so they too can explore the countryside at a slower pace. Maryanne says, George enjoys getting out and about giving people rides in his cart. Because her donkeys are so strong and healthy, Maryanne is frequently offered money for them. Her response is, she will never sell them, they're too loved and part of her family. Maryanne will never sell any of her animals. Most are rescues or strays. Some were given to her by their former owner who could no longer care for them. Apart from the horses bred at the farm, all the animals have a previous background, some from good homes and some from bad homes. Whatever their background they will complete their lives happy and healthy at Al Sorat Farm. Most of the animals here are in their late teens, or early twenties, nevertheless, they all behave like five-year-olds. Maryanne's daughter says there must be something in the water at Al Sorat Farm because living here secures a youthful and long life.

The donkey pen differs from the horse pens. Underfoot is a thick layer of clean yellow straw. Adjoining the back wall is an incapacious section partitioned off from the main pen by a wall standing at six-horizontal-bricks high. Inside this pen-within-a-pen is a brown-roof shelter comparable to a dog kennel. To the right in the back corner is a shed enclosed by a high brick wall and white-metal gate. Because of the width of the pen, the roof sunshade at the anterior has two central support poles. Donkeys are not the only inhabitants. Grazing on straw, resting, or standing on the lower brick wall of the interior pen are approximately 20 healthy-looking adult long-ear goats and eight kids. The goats are a mix of the smooth coat variety or long haired. A few have strong curve-back horns. They are a mixture of white, tan, black, white and tan, white and black, and dark-grey with black points. Maryanne opens the gate and the children, the mother and I go inside.

Though the goats are friendly, I mainly stick to patting and stroking the donkeys, administering an occasional pat for an adult goat when it shows interest. Maryanne's tan with black points billy goat is the tallest and most sociable of the goats. He applies a soft butt to get your attention. He is for sure a favourite of Maryanne's, doubtless because of his character.

The children are excited by the kids. Maryanne negotiates if they are calm and gentle, she will let them hold one. They consent and do well to remain calm, especially the younger boy who is on the verge of hyper and barely remains under the control of his parents. The children are thrilled to be experiencing this fun excursion. As we pass the time in the company of the donkeys and goats the children go in and out chasing the kids or fuss over the dogs out on the drive. Every so often Maryanne or their mother reminds a child to be gentle when they become too boisterous for the animal they are stroking or pursuing.

We slowly move over to the shed at the back where an enormous grey and wet nose pokes out over the metal gate. The nose belongs to the heavily-pregnant water buffalo who is confined to quarters for the periods when the kids are outside. She is hefty and the kids are mini. Maryanne fears the buffalo will not notice the kids and will stand on them. The kids will be put in the shed later in the day and overnight so the buffalo can join the adult goats and donkeys outside. Peering inside, I can see the water buffalo's massive frame, a frame considerably heftier than the typical Frisian cows commonly seen in the UK countryside. Her size expanded because she's in calf and is expected to give birth at any moment. Sticking out from the sides of her head are alert ears shaped like a bat's but larger-in-scale. White hairs ring big eyes as dark as pools of ink. I'm not particularly keen on the cows back home and tend to avoid them. However, this water buffalo's face is endearing and, she appreciates a scratch and a stroke.

The grooms notify Maryanne that the horses are ready for the pony rides. Leaving the pen, everyone congregates back on the drive where five Arab horses wait patiently tethered to the tie-post by the tack room. Mohammed and the father stand close to the garden fence, they've been talking while the father supervises the children at play with the dogs when they're out on the driveway.

Maryanne and I remain beside the donkeys (who have their heads back over the pen wall) watching the grooms assist the mother and four children as they select a suitable helmet. Four of the prepared horses are tacked up in padded saddle cloths: burgundy, indigo, teal, and purple. The youngest girl will ride a grey Arab. The older girl will ride a chestnut. The boys will be on a dark bay and another chestnut. The Arab horse selected for the mother to ride is a grey; tacked up using a western saddle. When all the riders are ready, they walk away from us up the driveway to the back of the farm. Individually the children are accompanied by a groom who walks alongside and leads their horse. They hold the strap at the front of the cloth to keep secure. The mother rides unaided.

Standing at the back of the pen adjoining the donkeys and goats pen is a beautiful brown horse marked by a star and stripe. Is it Jameela? On our return from the ride this morning the grooms demonstrated their proficiency equal to that at the start. As soon as I came to a halt and dismounted there was just enough time to pat Jameela before, a groom led her away for a shower with the hose. The grooms' efficiency meant I hadn't observed Jameela in detail. 'Is that Jameela?'

Maryanne confirms, 'Yes.'

Seconds later, I'm at the side of Jameela's pen. When I call her name, she walks towards me.

Her height and frame are inherited from her thoroughbred bloodline more than her Arab parentage. She has a refined head individualized by a slight Roman nose. She has sloping shoulders, a short back, and generous quarters. She is a light riding horse with a conformation for speed. When she reaches the gate, she stands quietly and lets me stroke her neck. She is a sweetie. I go back to the matter of Jameela's colour. There is no doubt she is brown, but not a brown I'd seen. A brown horse is usually dark, darker than a dark bay yet not black. Jameela's coat is a light brown and doesn't fit any of the bay horse classifications. Regardless of her light-brown coat, her muzzle confirms she is brown: soft, velvety and the colour of chocolate. Standing back from the gate, I watch her change position and put her head over the wall of the donkey and goat pen. She retains a calm and kind temperament and from my experience today, I know I can trust her explicitly.

Imagination

'Wow!'
This view has to be one of the most amazing I have ever seen. Riding Jamella, I have just reached the cusp of the highest dune in this locality. Maryanne stands close by on her chestnut Arab, Nazeer. Hassan, riding a grey Arab is again our escort. The ridge we are on is a vantage point commanding a magnificent panorama view: To the southwest and west are miles and miles of rolling dunes; though, the real distance is beyond the bounds of my eyes horizon. The visible Abu Sir Pyramids are in the east close to the border of the farmland in the Nile valley. Tracing the border further south for roughly 3 miles (5 km), you reach the Step Pyramid standing sentinel at the edge of the desert. From this distance, you can make out the pyramid's distinct six steps on the northeast and northwest corners. Beyond the Step Pyramid, about 5.5 miles (9 km) away out on the horizon, is the outline of another pyramid. It must be the Red Pyramid at Dahshur because the symmetry looks flawless.

Though, the sky above the desert is endless blue there is a haze over Cairo and the fertile Nile Valley which engulfs all but the closest villages. This haze also obscures the view of the great pyramids at Giza. Maryanne says on a crystal-clear-day, you can see the pyramids at Giza from here. I'm not disappointed… to a degree, the haze aids my imagination for I cannot see the modern-day settlement at Giza either. I imagine an era thousands of years ago when a triad of travellers from far away came to the close of their journey. After many days riding in a landscape of nothing more than sand and rock, they would climb a tall dune and check to take in the expanse of the valley. Their view would be of majestic and smooth-surface limestone pyramids, networks of lesser tombs and clearly defined connecting stone causeways all gleaming in the rays of the sun. Alas, I can merely imagine their view; however, many thousands of years later this view is one I will never forget.

To get to this spectacular lookout, Maryanne, Hassan and I rode out of Al Sorat Farm after breakfast. A direct course was taken through the local village to reach the desert gate. Desert side, we progressed down to the Abu Sir pyramids and with our backs to the fertile farmland headed out into the expanse of sand and stone. The destination was the dune we're on. To reach this spot, we'd trekked through a route of lower dunes using bursts of canter to go up and careful and slow footing to go down. Valleys with level bottoms were crossed in either walk or trot. On the way here, Maryanne revealed when she started riding in this region going out into the desert was not a done thing. But she couldn't resist the lure of the desert, and over the years, trails were gradually developed by going a little further on a succession of subsequent rides. The pyramids, of cause, are a great help as essentially, they are the main landmarks in a shifting landscape. It's time to get a closer look at one of those landmarks. We set off on a new course for the Step Pyramid.

Our descent down the dune is via the steeper south-facing slope. At the bottom, we turn left and begin a span of an extensive plain. As we progress, the lookout dune falls back in the north. To the east and west are lower dunes systems where the easterly summits hide the farmland from view. Though the terrain to reach the next dune system is broad, the pace is at walk using intermittent trots. The reason is underfoot there are a lot of fragments of stone. The horses' hooves clink and clank, as an expanse of denser fragments is navigated. It is not good ground to let a horse gallop. Apart from the clinking, there is no other sound. Much the same as yesterday the desert is peaceful with a warm breeze to take away the intensity of the sun. Since there is no sign of modern life, my imagination revisits the triad of ancient travellers riding through this valley to reach the ancient settlements on the banks of the River Nile. It is easy to put yourself in the position of those ancient travellers of old considering this whole region conveys the guise of an elaborate film set.

At the end of the plain, Maryanne points to a trackway slanting up and across the closest dune to reach the crest: 'This is a good place for a short canter.'

'Okay.'

I ask Jameela to go at the same time as Nazeer and the grey; she responds immediately. The ridges of the dunes are used to trace a trail from west to east. The Abu Sir pyramids have come back into sight far away in the north.

79

Although we're back closer to the farmland boarder, the haze still shrouds everything but the closest greenery and dwellings. The Step Pyramid gets ever closer, its six-step contour more defined. Our trail takes us through dune systems and narrow valleys where there are many ascents and descents intertwined with riding along the crests of dunes or crossing flat-bottom valleys almost as wide as a six-lane motorway.

I've started to notice Jameela's preference of being in the dune terrain as opposed to the wide-ranging flat stretches. Jameela is less cautious in the periods spent going up, down and around dunes. But on the plains where there are clear sightlines out to great distances, she walks tentatively. Maryanne speculates it could be because she had a bad experience out in the desert before she came to live at Al Sorat Farm. Stallions are raced out here; maybe, one threw its rider and attacked Jameela. Or, it could be because of a horse's sightline. Horses eyes are on the side of their heads giving them a monocular vision range close to 350 degrees. The enclosed peripheries of the dunes may be less threatening to Jameela as here she cannot scan great distances.

It's coming up to midday when we reach the western outer edge of The Step Pyramid complex at Sakkara. The furthest point on today's trek. The sun is close to its highest point in a blue sky touched by wisps of high white cloud. In the foreground waves of sand ripple upwards. At the highest point stands the impressive Step Pyramid. In closer proximity, the majestic smooth-limestone surface pictured in my imagination is, in reality, present-day crumbling stone. There is scaffolding encompassing the sixth, topmost step and where the third and fourth step adjoin. Maryanne announces, 'This is Djoser's Step Pyramid, built in the third dynasty [c. 2650-c.2575 BCE]'.

'Why is there scaffolding?'

'For restoration work. The stone on the pyramid is being restored to preserve the distinctive six steps.'

From this distance, the complex of The Step Pyramid looks relatively inactive. I can make out a couple of miniaturized-by-distance figures moving close to the base of the first step. There may be a roadway and carpark if there is neither is visible from out here. Nor can I catch sight of the farmland because the rise of the land and the pyramid are high enough to block out everything behind. We're far enough away to maintain the stillness of the desert. From here, the complex emanates as an archaeological site as opposed to a popular tourist location. In advance of travelling to Cairo, I learned that Djoser's Step Pyramid was the precursor for all the Egyptian pyramids. Until yesterday, I wasn't aware of the Abu Sir Pyramids. I was aware of Djoser's Step Pyramid. This monument is believed to be the first of the ancient Egyptian architectural superstructures to be built using stone. Even though reading about ancient Egypt is fascinating, no book or photo can emulate seeing the real thing. Djoser himself was the third dynasty's second king, who is understood to have reigned for in the region of 19 years. His life on earth is the equivalent of a blink of the eye in comparison to his pyramid, prevalent here for thousands of years.

I will come here again later this afternoon on foot to get a closer look from within the complex. Maryanne has arranged for me to spend a couple of days in the company of a guide. There is an opportunity to go inside a smaller pyramid not visible from our ride because of advanced decay. I'm advised to go inside the pyramid at Sakkara and not go inside the pyramid on the more renowned Giza Plateau. The reason for this is everything found inside the pyramids was removed long ago leaving the interiors to be nothing more than dark and cramped voids and chambers. Because the pyramid at Sakkara is small-scale, you don't spend so long inside, and it isn't as crowded. This reasoning appeals to me. I'm not keen on dark and cramped spaces and prefer to be outside in the extensive desert and its seemingly endless prospects of sand and sky. For me, going into the Sakkara pyramid is good advice.

Leaving the Step Pyramid behind us in the south, we turn the horses homebound and follow the border of the farmland northwards. Jameela celebrates the beginning of the return journey by having a transient jog. Maryanne says she always does this and it hints at her appreciation of her current home.

Not long after, the ride reaches a labyrinth of squat sand mounds where there are fragments of pot densely scattered amongst the sand and loose stone. Despite glimpses of terracotta here and there, the pot is predominately white or light-grey. Leading the way, Maryanne chooses her line carefully treading clear of most of the debris. She divulges that this vicinity was a dump site for the Sakkara pyramids. All the sand mounds were raised by man. There is a momentary halt after Maryanne points to a chunky piece of human bone lying on the ground. I hadn't noticed the strewed pieces of bones; though, it shouldn't be a surprise to find human remnants since the belt of land from the Abu Sir Pyramids in the north to the Dahshur grouping in the south is an extensive burial ground and bones are what you find in burial grounds.

After clearing the sand mounds, the fragments of stone and pot reduce in number until there are no more as the area of bones is left behind. We're now riding at the foot of the first dunes close to the bordering farmland. From this bottommost position, nothing but the palm groves and lofty villas can be seen. In certain spots, the palm groves look to be outlying oases. Is this what the triad of imagined ancient travellers would have seen thousands of years ago, or this close to the fertile land would there have been more occupied land? Maybe there were construction workers at the Abu Sir Pyramids or Step Pyramid complexes going to and from their labour.

As Maryanne leads us through stone ruins interspersed across a dune on the east side of the Abu Sir Pyramids, I contemplate on what this site would have looked like in its prime. It's difficult to identify what the ruins were as the only recognizable structure is a partly submerged ancient wall in disrepair. As we go by the Abu Sir complex, the trail emerges on level terrain. Here there is a vista out to the west into the expanse beyond. It is a brief glimpse before going behind the most northerly pyramid and a delightful diversion from the walls of the villas on the right. Being close to the Abu Sir pyramids means the desert gate is nearby. However, instead of continuing to the fertile land, Maryanne says there is time for a gallop. Obediently, the horses divert to the northwest and make for the 'runway' where we'd enjoyed a gallop yesterday.

Inside Ancient Tombs

It's mid-afternoon when I find myself glancing at a tourist information board outside the mastaba tomb of Ptah-Hotep and Akhti-Hotep. The tomb is west of Djoser's Step Pyramid in the ancient complex at Sakkara. On the board are two diagrams and text written in three languages: English, Egyptian Arabic and another. I'm not reading the board. I'm listening to my guide, Magdy as he informs me this tomb belonged to a family of high-ranking officials and is a double tomb shared by two family members: Ptah-Hotep and Akhti-Hotep.

Just after, Maryanne, Hassan and I arrived back at Al Sorat Farm from our morning ride out in the desert lunch was again served outside in Maryanne's well-kept garden. Today, Magdy and a driver joined us. The driver is a tall, stout man in his early forties who knows the same amount of English words that I do Egyptian Arabic. Magdy is an intellectual, an Egyptologist by profession. He speaks fluent English. He's a small man, maybe in his early fifties with black hair and a hawk nose. Both men looked uncomfortable whenever a dog came too close. Our main discussion had been on what tourist sights I wanted to see. We arranged that I would visit the Egyptian Museum tomorrow and the Giza pyramids the morning after. There was a lot of enthusiasm for me to visit the Sakkara complex and in particular, the bas-reliefs in the mastaba tomb of Ptah-Hotep and Akhti-Hotep of which, Magdy had declared are the most detailed bas-reliefs in Cairo.

Past the information board, broad steps of white stone descend into a sunken courtyard. At the top of the steps, the exterior walls of the mastaba are roughly 1.5 m (4.11 ft.) high and two-hand-lengths wide. Down in the courtyard, the walls are taller and stand at roughly 4.5 m (14.9 ft.). The walls beside the steps are in excellent repair. I suspect without validation; these walls have been re-built in modern times. However, there is no doubt that the courtyard walls are 3,000 years old. Every block of stone varies in size and has four near-to-perfect 45-degree angle corners. The assembly would have been like matching 3-D jigsaw pieces. There is a light covering of sand on the steps and deeper drifts in the courtyard. A hint at how easy it is for breezes and winds to re-bury this ancient site. A site only revealed in recent history during excavations in the 19th century. Though the sun is behind a blanket of high-white cloud, the south-facing walls still cast long shadows across the courtyard.

The entrance to the mastaba is on the south-side. Here the wall is ancient and shows the passage of time. At its centre are a recess and a tight doorway pronounced by a pair of empty stone plinths standing at over a meter on either side. Stood close to the entrance are two local men in their fifties with short black hair, trimmed beards and dark leathery faces evidencing long periods of sun exposure. They both wear white galabeyas. One wears a black skull-cap. As we walk the length of the courtyard, we pass an unused entrance in a recess on the west wall. This entrance has a frame of square pillars, and there is damage to the lintel made from white-stone blocks edged with Hieroglyphs. At the entrance, Magdy speaks briefly to the men and hands money to the man wearing the black skull-cap. I don't notice the amount for my attention is on a rectangular plaque above the doorway that provides information in various languages. I don't read the plaque because I have a guide and he has just passed me and entered the tomb. So, I follow.

My eyes take a few seconds to adjust in the dim light as we transverse a cramped ingress into the entrance hall. The dimensions of the hall look to be about 7 x 2 m (22.11 x 6.6 ft.) and in comparison, to the heat outside the space is cool. There are uniform carvings of ancient Egyptians all down the long sides. Though, some are mere outlines. We don't stop in the entrance hall. Magdy leads on straight through a doorway in the south-west corner and onwards through another passage to enter a large chamber. The chamber is the central hall; approximately 8 x 6 m (26 x 19.8 ft.). At the centre are four floor-to-ceiling rectangular pillars made from roughly-finished white stone. Natural light spills in, and the chamber is well ventilated. On the far side is a doorway, yet we don't cross the hall. There is another doorway on this side in the south-east corner, and it is where Magdy exits. Following him, I step down into an antechamber at the exact moment a young trendy Asian couple in trainers, jeans and logo t-shirts enter from the far end. While I wait to let them pass, Magdy goes through the doorway from where the couple just came. Another step down, and I find him standing in a room almost entirely decorated with bas-reliefs. Magdy is in his element when he announces, 'This is the Chapel of Ptah-Hotep'.

The chapel is small-scale, maybe 5 x 2 m (16 x 6.6 ft.). The entrance is in the north wall and looks down the length of the chapel to the south wall. The walls are nearing 4 m (13 ft.) high. Where the south wall joins the ceiling, there is a vent spanning three-quarters of the wall's width. It provides ventilation and fills the chapel with natural light; aided by a second vent on the east wall. The vents function well and assisted by the high ceiling create a light and airy atmosphere. I'm astonished when Magdy points out the outline of the ceiling. In comparison to the decorated walls, the ceiling is plain, painted a dark reddish-brown and grooved. What is remarkable is the ancient Egyptians only used two enormous stones to form the ceiling.

Starting at the east wall, we step back to take in the ancient two-dimensional drawings skilfully carved into the smooth greyish-white stone. At the centre of the bas-relief and equal in height is a detailed carving of a man in profile. He is wearing a loin-cloth and ample necklace; unfortunately, the paint has perished to lay bare the grooved white-stone of the wall. The man's skin fares better: painted a reddish-brown marred by a few sporadic spots of bare stone. His black hair in the outline of a rock-climber helmet has faded. He holds his right arm away from his body. In his hand is a long staff. His left arm is down straight at his side with the hand turned outwards clasping what looks to be a piece of cloth. Magdy lowers his voice and points to a section of hieroglyphs: 'These hieroglyphs tell us the man is Ptah-Hotep. He was the highest ranked official second only to the King.'

We marvel at the detail of Ptah-Hoptep's fingers and toes. The skilled carver had only flint tools at his disposal to etch the outline of the nails. Aside Ptah-Hotep's dominate image are male figures, who stand at the height of Ptah-Hotep's knees. One figure is in the foreground the other behind Ptah-Hotep. These men are thought to be the sons of Ptah-Hotep and other high-ranking officials. In spite of their dwarfed stature their depicted presence evidence that they were eminent men in the life of the tomb's owner.

To the left of Ptah-Hotep is a tier of seven sections depicting assorted groups of carvings. 'Each of the seven sections is a 'register' representing daily life. By carving scenes from Ptah-Hotep's life in his chapel, the ancient Egyptians believed he would take everything represented with him to his eternal life. The registers read from right to left.'

The seven registers are a third of the size of the figure of Ptah-Hotep. The difference in scale is to emphasize the owner of the tomb's importance and rank. Most of the seven registers have lost their paint, but the carvings are clear and detailed. I stand in awe of the ancient craft men while Magdy chronologically narrates what the registers picture. There is a herd of oxen fording a river and men collecting or carrying bundles of papyrus. Illustrated are the different stages of winemaking: crews of men in loincloths tend a vine, pick ripe grapes, and use tools and the techniques for wine pressing. A hunter and a pair of dogs stalking wild animals and a subsequent scene where a hunter's dogs have caught a gazelle. In others, a fisherman prepares his catch and men use nets to trap birds and put them in cages. There are wild animals on the prowl: a lion firmly clasps the head of an unfortunate ox in its mouth. A few of the registers portray boat building: craftsmen assisted by boys, understood to be their sons, work at the different stages of boat building and further carvings show men using boats to transport animals, poultry and produce. Away from the daily toil are young men exercising or playing an active game, their youth identified by the fact they are naked. A couple of the figures sit with their legs straight out in front of them and arms stretched, so their hands touch their feet. I smile, 'Ah, a yoga pose I do nearly every week.'

The registers are a fabulous insight into the daily life of the ancient Egyptians. Already I have discovered a breadth of enterprise from Ptah-Hotep's era, and we've only examined half of the bas-relief on the east wall. On the right, mirroring the position and measurements of the middle carving is another multi-coloured picture of Ptah-Hotep facing seven more registers. The main difference is this depicts him having long hair and a beard, and there is a lone miniature-sized man at his feet believed to be his son.

Apart from the uppermost register depicting youths wrestling, the final set on the east wall illustrates domestic and wild animals. A hunter accompanied by four dogs; six men escorting gazelles; and four men dragging a sledge carrying stacked cages – one contains a lion another a leopard. Three registers are of men tending to or driving cattle. The bottom register depicts flocks of birds: cranes, geese, ducks, swans, and pigeons. Magdy's enthusiasm increases as he points to a tiny carving at the side of each type of bird: 'This represents a number. The register is a bird inventory and the numbers engraved suggest hundreds of thousands of birds.'

We move onto the south wall. Narrower in width, the south wall reflects the east wall with most of the carvings devoid of paint. The exception is the carving of a seated Ptah-Hotep in the bottom right of the bas-relief. Magdy's points of interest here are the offering table at the feet of Ptah-Hotep and the seven registers illustrating part of the preparations involved to produce the funerary meal offerings. He tells me this is the purpose of the chapel, a place where offerings can be brought to the deceased after he had departed to the eternal life. Because the higher up registers have faded, I learn what is there via my knowledgeable guide. Magdy identifies outlines of pottery vessels in a variety of shapes and sizes, plates of fruit and possibly containers of wine. These items have to be visualized more in my mind as there isn't a lot to see on the wall. The next two registers are equally faint and sketch women carrying offerings in containers balanced on their heads. The accompanying text reveals the women represent the domains of Ptah-Hotep and the locations of these domains. I can make out the outlines of a number of the women. The lower of the registers is damaged where the carved stone had fallen away to expose the undecorated stone behind. To the left of the carving of Ptah-Hotep seated at his offering table are the lower registers. The bottom doublet is depictions of men bringing the prepared meal offerings to the table. The highest depicts the royal butchers preparing meat for the feast.

Magdy and I take a step back so we can get a full overview of the chapel's west wall. What is striking on this wall is sections of the bas-relief remain painted, albeit patchy and faded. There is another enlarged, and colourful carving of Ptah-Hotep sat on a chair. He is wearing a greyish-white robe fashioned from the skin of a big cat. The tail of the cat drapes down the back of the chair. His face, neck, lower legs and arms have reddish-brown paint. His long hair and neat beard are black.

'This carving represents him in the eternal life. His offering table is full of the offerings we've seen pictured on the previous walls.'

The offerings are plentiful, and the pile reaches above the height of Ptah-Hotep. In his left hand, he holds a vessel close to his nose and mouth. 'This contains a liquid said to regenerate Ptah-Hotep as he takes in its scent.'

Magdy points to four columns of hieroglyphs above Ptah-Hotep's head. 'This is a list of the positions he held in life and his high-rank duties.'

To the right of the central bas-relief are four registers. Three portray high-ranking officials bringing offerings to Ptah-Hoptep in his eternal life. The highest is of priests carrying out a ceremony. Magdy summarises the hieroglyphs carved above: 'These are lists detailing the ceremonies and offerings.'

Again, I rely on Magdy's knowledge because the hieroglyphs are difficult to examine in detail owing to their high locality and aged state.

The remaining registers bring a glimpse of what the chapel walls would have looked like in sublime fresh paint. There are more priests and high-ranking officials, portrayed with black hair, cream loin cloths and reddish-brown skin painted against the remnants of what looks to be a dark-grey background. Animals and offerings brought by the officials are a vivid-cream.

On each side of the central bas-relief is a false door covering the height of the wall. The door on the left has an outer frame decorated with hieroglyphs and carvings and topped by a cavetto cornice. There are more hieroglyphs on the thinner inner frame cut back into the stone of the wall. Inside the inner frame is a deep-carved and inexact 'doorway' roughly 1.5 m (4.11 ft.) high. The lines, angles, and curves of the entire doorway look symmetrical. Pointing to the relevant hieroglyphs, Magdy explains the purpose of the false door is to allow Ptah-Hoptep to enter the living world and participate in the ceremonies detailed on the central bas-relief.

On the right side is the second false door. It has the same design as the other door yet there are no decorative carvings. The broader outer frame has a vertical red and white stripe design. A central square above the 'doorway' displays the same stripes only reduced in size. Another difference is there isn't a cavetto cornice. In its place, there is a simple design of vertically carved sections. Because there are no hieroglyphs or carvings, the purpose of the door can only be speculated. 'The presence of a second door is an unusual feature for a mastaba.'

Magdy goes on to divulge when archaeologists first discovered the chapel it displayed vivid artwork. The dry heat and being buried under sand for aeons had preserved the vibrancy of the paintings. Unfortunately, in the early days succeeding discovery, the preservation techniques fell short, and most of the paint got removed when the archaeologists of that time took wall casts. I expect I would be looking at a more vibrant display had this find happened a millennium on using the modern archaeological techniques available today.

There are two bas-reliefs carved on the north wall. The biggest fills the section left of the entrance and the second covers the entire width of the wall above the entryway and the bigger bas-relief. On the principal part of the wall, there is a tier of four registers all uniform in height and width. They display carvings of ancient Egyptians in the act of preparing or giving offerings. In the lower sections men are cutting up dead oxen, and a man is presenting an oxen leg to a priest. The upper registers depict a procession of eight men carrying offerings: a game bird, an animal, a tray of food or cloth. The registers background is back to bare stone; whereas, the pictures of the men have kept part of their paint albeit somewhat faded. They have reddish-brown skin, cream loin-cloths, and black hair. I cannot make out the detail of the higher bas-relief due to its lofty position. What I can survey is another inflated carving of Ptah-Hotep on the right above the entrance doorway. In attendance are the pint-sized carvings of servants carrying out grooming duties such as attending to his hair or applying ointment to his feet. He is seated facing four registers. Magdy says these registers display musicians playing harps and a type of flute. They entertain the aggrandized image of Ptah-Hotep. Accompanying the musicians in the uppermost register are four dwarfs who are assembling jewels and pampering items. A couple of the registers illustrate officials knelt down in Ptah-Hotep's presence. In the bottom, right corner under the chair where Ptah-Hotep sits is a servant holding the leashes of three dogs and a monkey. Because the monkey is carved flush to the top of the entrance door, I can see the remnants of blue paint on its back and foreleg.

On the way, out of the chapel, there are more carvings. Eight vertical registers carved to cover the thickness of the doorway and a further four on each side. They portray men carrying an offering of a goose, a duck, a deer or a tray of pots. The upper register on the west side of the doorway displays several types of birds: 'Here the hieroglyphs carved above defines the type of bird… duck, goose, pigeon and so on.'

The carving high up on the east side of the doorway is of an ancient Egyptian leading some oxen.

Ptah-Hotep's chapel is a marvellous introduction to this ancient civilization. I can understand why Magdy was so keen to bring me here, and I'm glad he did. Backtracking through the antechamber, I notice a shelved recess in the west wall: Magdy explains, 'This is where the artists stored their paint.'

I'd missed this feature earlier because I was moving out of the way of the young Asian couple. Back in the chamber with the four central pillars, we aim for the doorway in the centre of the west wall. Behind this doorway, there are more bas-reliefs to behold in the chapel belonging to Akhi-Hotep.

After 90 minutes inside the mastaba, it feels good to get back outside and gaze out onto the desert as it sprawls unbounded to the north, west, and south. The wisps of cloud have built up and now block out the intensity of the sun. In the northeast on the distant horizon are the Abu Sir Pyramids. Eastwards from the pyramids, I can make out a palm grove on the edge of the Nile Valley's fertile land. To the west of the Abu Sir Pyramids are the long and planar crests of three high dunes. The most easterly looks to be closest as its outline is more defined and it has a steep ascent on its west side. I wonder if this is the dune, Maryanne, Hassan and I rode up this morning to take in that incredible panorama view. In the foreground are the convex crests of shallow mounds. The closet mounds reveal pieces of pot and stone scattered in the sand. Buried beneath each one could be the bones of an ancient Egyptian. Over the millenniums, the desert had claimed most of the ancient burial grounds and what lies beneath this part of the Egyptian Sahara is hard to imagine. Behind the mounds are the dunes and valleys I had ridden through to reach the Step Pyramid this morning. I scan the landscape, but there is no movement apart from the delicate breeze.

'Are you ready?'

Magdy's voice breaks my fixation. I turn to walk alongside him to where the white MPV we are using is parked.

We're driven eastwards, back up past the north side of The Step Pyramid. 'Do you want to visit another mastaba?'

'No, my curiosity is satisfied, and you've shown me the best bas-reliefs in Cairo.'

After Ptah-Hotep's chapel, we'd looked at the bas-reliefs belonging to Akhti-Hoptep. The designs and layout are similar to the bas-reliefs in Ptah-Hotep's chapel. However, many of the carvings are unfinished or damaged. Where the carvings are intact and completed the detail is as precise.

On the way out of the tomb, Magdy showed me the unfinished work of the ancient craftsmen in the entrance corridor. The east wall displays the carved outlines of approximately 15 to 20 women carrying baskets on their heads. A woman at one end has carved facial features (eyes, ears, mouth, and nose) and long black hair. There is no more detail on her or any of the other women. For whatever reason, after the craftsmen cut the outlines of the women and offerings, they didn't return to complete the work. Above the woman with the facial features is another incomplete section of the bas-relief, which demonstrates a different stage of the creative process. Drawn on the wall in ink are the outlines of a pair of substantial storage vessels. There are men at the sides of the vessels pouring wine into containers. It was fascinating to observe the distinct stages used to complete a bas-relief. At the time, Magdy had mentioned this was part of the reason why the mastaba of Ptah-Hotep and Akhti-Hotep is his mother's favourite place to visit. Neither he nor his mother tire of visiting the tomb and spend many hours marvelling at the level of detail on the beautiful carvings etched by the ancient Egyptians. If Magdy and his mother endorse the bas-reliefs I have just seen to be the best in Cairo, I do not need to look at anymore.

The MPV had travelled roughly 6 m (19.8 ft.) when Magdy instructs the driver to pull up at a crossroads. After jumping out, I wait for Magdy and the driver to confirm a rendezvous point. The MPV then trundles away, southbound. Mine and Magdy's course is northwards down the approach into the pyramid complex of King Teti. A man on a camel is by the junction, he is wearing a white uniform, and a black beret-style hat. Magdy confirms, 'He is an officer of the tourist police.'

I'm surprised at how tall the camel is, specifically its long legs that leave an ample gap between the ground and its underbelly. The camel makes a good vantage point for the officer to patrol the site and watch the tourist activity.

A walkway of wood slats aids our stroll down to the bottom of the hill where the track curves 90 degrees to the right in front of a windowless stone structure displaying smooth walls and a rough roof that blends into the desert. As we approach, Magdy reports, this mastaba belonged to a high-ranking official who was in service during the reign of Teti, the first king of the sixth dynasty (c.2325-c.2150bc).

Around the corner, we enter a throng. There are 30 or more men, and women of various ages in groups, some are accompanied by a guide. Nearly all are western tourists identifiable by loose trousers and shirts, wide-brim hats or baseball caps and carrying backpacks. Local men in light-grey galabeyas and white turbans sit outside the doors of more ancient officials' tombs, ready to collect entrance fees. The quietude of the desert gives way to the movement and voices of a closely-scattered crowd. In amongst the tourists and guides, we go by the first mastaba. The outer layer of dried mud on the façade has crumbled away in places to leave exposed stone blocks. Its entrance fares a little better: narrow, roughly the height of two men and decorated by an ancient Egyptian guard holding a long staff on either side. A border of hieroglyphs adorns the entrance, though the highest have almost perished. To reach the entrance of Teti's pyramid we stroll beside an ancient wall, close to 2 m (6.6 ft.) high, using pavements of rough-cut white stone partly revealed by the careful work of archaeologists and their support workers.

Unlike the Step Pyramid, Teti's pyramid had lost its original appearance to become a high steep-sided dune littered with pieces of stone. At the base, old walls lined with stone benches funnel you to the pyramid's entrance – a tight rectangular hole shaped by massive pale-grey blocks. A middle-aged western lady sits watching her husband remove a camera from a backpack and move into position to take her picture. On the bench, closest to the entrance is a local man in a light-grey galabeya and a white skull-cap. He watches the tourists and their guides going in and coming out of the pyramid in single file. Magdy speaks to a leather-faced local man in a slate-grey and well-worn galabeya then he turns back to me, 'I cannot go into the pyramid.'

He makes a gesture towards the man in the slate-grey galabeya: 'He will be your guide inside. I will wait here for you.'

With the pyramid guide leading, I advance to the entrance. At the point of entry, he looks back at me and with a smile baring a set of blackened teeth and a heavy accent, he cautions: 'Mind your head.'

I grab the wooden handrails fixed to the walls and descend into a claustrophobic shaft: steep, roughly square with smooth angles and a low ceiling. To descend, I have to bend my head, neck, and back forward and steady myself by running my hands down the rails. The pyramid guide moves swiftly in the dim light, and I'm grateful for the anti-slip boards fixed to the floor.

At the bottom, another pyramid guide in the company of a couple tagging behind in single file crosses our path. This guide is also moving quickly, and the tourists rush to keep pace. My pyramid guide points up: 'Mind your head.'

Bending my head, neck, and back forward again, I trail along behind at speed through a stunted tunnel and into a dim chamber. Thankfully, the chamber has a high ceiling so I can stand upright. For all that the ceiling is high, the chamber is still cramped and the air stale. Daylight seeps in from somewhere to provide enough light to make out the walls. My pyramid guide directs the light from a torch he is holding onto a wall. The beam illuminates' ancient hieroglyphs carved symmetrical and uniform in size. There is no evidence of a colour enhancer just simple horizontal ancient Egyptian text. My pyramid guide says something to me I don't know what and then we're off again through another tunnel. 'Mind your head.'

Two western tourists and I exchange a smile as they rush past me behind their pyramid guide. In the next chamber, the pyramid guide shines his torch to pick out the white outlines of star shapes on the ceiling. These shapes cover the enormous slabs of stone that slant to meet at the apex of the ceiling. The points of the stars are close to nearly touching. To me, the stars bear more resemblance to starfish than twinkling stars in the sky. My eyes follow the torchlight in its movement from the ceiling to the back of the chamber where it illuminates a wall covered with hieroglyphs. I don't linger. My pyramid guide is off again at speed through another tunnel. I've no idea of the direction.

An empty sarcophagus placed on stone mounts is the main feature of interest in another chamber. At almost the same width of the chamber and waist height, the stone sarcophagus is smooth and the colour of charcoal. Capping the sarcophagus is a damaged lid carved from the same smooth stone; though the damaged half bares rough edges. Two men and a woman stand in an unhurried manner discussing the sarcophagus. There is no sign of their pyramid guide. Like the previous chamber the slab ceiling is pointed and covered with stars; though, these exhibits are worn. The presence of the sarcophagus equips the chamber with a 'chapel' aspect. I don't get to mull on this. My pyramid guide says more words I don't understand then repeats his mantra: 'Mind your head.'

He ducks down into another tunnel.

At the end is the bottom of the entrance-shaft. My pyramid guide has stopped to talk to another guide who is alone; perhaps, he is the guide who the tourists in the sarcophagus chamber have abandoned. I've had enough of this dark, cramped and stale place, and want to get back outside. I leave the pyramid guide to his conversation and climb back up the shaft where I find Magdy sat on a stone bench looking at his mobile phone. He stands when he sees me, 'Did you not like the pyramid? You were very quick.'

'It was okay, but as you mentioned there isn't much to look at.'

Downtown Cairo

It is mid-afternoon in downtown Cairo. Magdy and I are feasting on a late lunch in the Felfela Alaa El-Din restaurant. Today is our second day together, and we've just spent four hours two blocks away in the Egyptian Museum of Antiquities.

The Felfela Alaa El-Din restaurant is a refuge away from the hot, dusty and busy street outside. Designed to keep the sunlight out and the restaurant a pleasant temperature a limited amount of natural light seeps in through the facade windows. The interior design resembles a paved a garden. Green high-back wooden chairs and bistro-style tables occupy the space between the walls and a centre aisle made up of a variety of stones in various shades and shapes laid into the concrete. Behind me, five steps go up to another seating area where red paving slabs form a central walkway. In places, beside the rough-cut red block walls, there are wood sculptures carved to represent tree trunks. These 'trees' reach up to a trellis on the upper part of the wall. Artificial green vines cover the trellis and ceiling beams. Completing the garden theme are tropical-fish tanks to represent garden ponds.

Although technically lunchtime had passed there are other diners filling up the tables close to us. Most are Egyptians, men and women in their twenties or thirties casually dressed in loose-fitting shirts and jeans or trousers, many of the women wear a head-scarf. They enthusiastically greet each other on arrival and embark on a lively conversation of catching up and no doubt gossip. Magdy's brought me here because the menu includes a good selection of vegetarian dishes. A bowl of delicious lentil soup and a selection of tapas-style dishes are put on the table: koshary, vine leaves, bread, and baba ghanoug. Magdy seems more relaxed today. He mentions he lives a few streets away from Felfela. He is in his comfort zone in downtown Cairo as opposed to the countryside and being amongst the animals at Al Sorat Farm.

Today's excursion started after Magdy, and our driver picked me up from the Sakkara Country Club after breakfast. Initially, the route taken was the same one Maryanne had used in the latter stage of the airport pickup: Setting of northbound into Giza where again my first glimpse of the Great Pyramids was impeded by a blanket of sunken white cloud. After the Moneeb Bridge, our course continued north following the east bank of the River Nile. The MPV made slow headway through the dense morning traffic on the Al Kasr Al Aini Road. While horns beeped and vehicles crawled slowly forward, I'd looked lazily out of the back-seat window.

As the MPV limped forward getting ever closer to the Egyptian Museum of Antiquities, our conversation had broached the matter of the world-famous Rosetta Stone. The Rosetta Stone is considered to be the most important discovery in the matter of understanding ancient Egyptians. The reason for this is the Rosetta Stone is the only artefact in existence engraved with ancient Egyptian hieroglyphs and two other scripts: demotic and Greek. The different scripts repeat the same decree inscribed on the black granite. At the time of discovery, hundreds of millennia had passed since the last hieroglyph has been scribed and any translations were assumed lost. It is the presence of the demotic and Greek scripts that equipped scholars with the translation they needed to unlock the meaning of Egyptian hieroglyphs. Magdy's tone of voice had changed from the informative guide to disdain. It is the same tone he uses when his ex-wife is brought up in conversation and is always accompanied by him pulling a face and looking down his nose at you: 'The Rosetta Stone, viewed by many to be one of the most important artefacts of ancient Egypt is neither exhibited at the Egyptian museum nor is it exhibited anywhere in Egypt… Because the British have got it.' He emphasizes the 't' and second syllable in 'British.'

'Where is it?' I innocently enquired.

'On display at the British Museum in London.'

I perceived this is a sore point for Magdy, who probably reflects the opinion of a large percentage of the Egyptian population. While the British Museum exhibits the real Rosetta Stone, the Egyptian Museum suffers a life-size picture displayed at the top of the steps in the entrance hall. In my thoughts, I'm sympathetic. It does feel more appropriate for the Rosetta Stone to be at the Egyptian Museum. Conversely, my thoughts went on to question if the Rosetta

Stone is safer under the guardianship of the British Museum, away from the undercurrents of protests and political instability in present-day Egypt.

Sitting in Felfela, our conversation touches on last year's uprising. Magdy's daily life primarily plays out in the handful of blocks connecting his home and the Egyptian Museum. Because he lives close to Tahrir Square, and the streets where the battles took place, Magdy and his daughter got caught in the gunfire on the first day, and Magdy got shot in the lower leg. He says since the uprising, all political material gets censored in Egypt. Egyptians have to rely on the international press, and websites to keep up to date with what is happening in their own country. Despite Egypt's first democratically elected president being in office since June, there is still a sense of distrust in the governing political party. I sense the election did not produce the outcome required for the forward-thinking and economically-focused section of the Egyptian population. The tour of the life and possessions of ancient Egypt this morning had been touched by the recent events and struggle of modern-day Egypt.

World famous and situated in downtown Cairo close to the frequently newsworthy Tahrir Square, the Egyptian Museum is a two-level neoclassical-style building, which opened to the public in 1902. Flaunting a frontage that wouldn't look out of place in either Athens or Rome, the museum's famous pink paint takes on a dusky-tone in the light of an overcast sky. At the centre of the façade is the stepped entrance flanked by white-stone pillars. High-up, on either side of the entrance there is a sculpture of an ancient Egyptian goddess. I had read somewhere that the Egyptian Museum holds over 120,000 ancient Egyptian artefacts. As I trod on the heels of Magdy, past guards clutching machine-guns and went through the robust black security gates into the museum's garden, I felt satisfaction and excitement because, in my opinion, I was at a must visit tourist sight.

Before I arrived in Egypt, I knew the Egyptian Museum was the most vulnerable to cancellation because of its proximity to Tahrir Square. As we drove through Tahrir Square a few minutes prior, Magdy pointed to a street where the six-storey and ten-storey buildings on the corners are battle-scarred, black and empty. The street was where some of the heaviest fighting occurred during the uprising in January and February last year. An uprising that succeeded in the removal of Hosni Mubarak, the then Egyptian president who had held power since 1981. In consequence of the uprising, the military had taken control of the country in the lead up to the presidential elections in June this year. Through the period of military leadership, protests continued in Tahrir Square and only ceased at the end of June.

Today, Tahrir Square was relatively empty with a handful of tourists taking photos and locals going about their everyday lives. Most of the noise and motion was out on the thoroughfare where there is a constant hum of traffic. Peeps, toots, and honks accompany the vehicles that arrive from all directions, and partly circle the square and then exit down a different feeder street. Had the Egyptian people chosen to protest this week, the square would be a changed setting and a different atmosphere, and my visit to the museum cancelled.

The noise of the traffic outside the museum gates was mostly drowned out by the disharmonized voices of a sizeable crowd interspersed throughout a modestly-sized enclosed garden. At the centre is a rectangular ornamental pond where thin jets of water spurt upwards then fall back down to hit water-lilies floating on the surface. On either side of the pond is a small-scale statue of a sphinx sculpted from grey-stone. Pathways link raised lawny beds planted with young trees and tall palms. The beds are framed by a wall at the perfect height for tired tourists to sit on. Exhibits grace the space: great statues of ancient Egyptians, head sculptures, and vessels. Some bare damage. Mostly to facial features where noses are missing.

It warmed my heart to see western tourists amongst the throng. The largest group had surrounded their guide who stood at the side of a colossal statue of an Egyptian king seated on his throne. Out on the desert ride yesterday, Maryanne spoke of the decline in tourism as a consequence of the political instability in the country. Western tourist numbers have dropped significantly enough to be a real problem for the Egyptian economy. The most noticeable absentees are the North Americans who are currently being advised not to travel here. I'm sure the visitor numbers at the museum today fall woefully below the required amount to support a healthy economy.

On my tour of the museum's ground floor, Magdy pointed out the alleged location of where looters entered the museum during the uprising. At the time it was well documented in the world media that looters had broken into the Egyptian Museum and stole over 50 artefacts. Magdy disclosed there are many theories regarding the looting. A popular rumour is it was not merely a random act of mindless vandalism, but planned as ancient Egyptian artefacts can sell for high prices on the black market. The main reason for suspicion to fall onto a more organized offense is the looting befell in different zones throughout the museum. This theory suggests it was the work of an organized gang 'looting to order', taking specific artefacts from across the two floors. Another 'looting to order' theory goes on to imply senior members of the museum staff were involved. A third theory is the looters were organized to cause as much damage as possible. This theory does not manifest to be as plausible considering the scattered positions of the damaged and stolen artefacts. Many of the stolen artefacts have been recovered. Though, fatefully a few of the artefacts are so damaged they may never get restored back to the original state. There is another twist to the 'loot to order' theory, maybe the original artefact was swapped with a fake? The suspicion fell when some artefacts were found close to the museum with no attempt to hide them. Magdy said it is hard to prove if a recovered artefact is a fake or the real thing.

After we'd concluded the tour of the ground floor and preceding going upstairs to look at the infamous Tutankhamun exhibition and royal mummies' room, we'd briefly gone back outside to indulge in a Turkish coffee at the museum's coffee shop. Sheltered by an umbrella from the early afternoon sun breaking through the cloud, Magdy drew my attention to a neighbouring building on the west side of the museum. The building used to be the headquarters of the National Democratic Party. It is an ugly 1950s concrete office block standing at 15-storeys to dominate the skyline. Unattractive in its prime and even uglier at this time because during the uprising the building was set alight. Burnt out windows are without panes leaving the interior exposed to the elements. The outer walls of the higher levels are charred black from soot and smoke. The structure is declared unsafe, its future undecided.

With lunch finished, we decide to have a coffee at an alfresco café nearby. My eyes take a second to adjust from the dimly lit interior to the brightness outside in the transition from restaurant to the street. I don't know the direction we walk in along crowded pavements, where in places there is a need to step into the roadway or weave amongst the handcarts of street-sellers laden with merchandise from piles of vegetables to varieties of fabric. There are parked vehicles to negotiate as men unload white mini-trucks outside shops. The majority of the populous out on the shopping streets are Egyptian. The difference with downtown Cairo, comparatively to the countryside, is how the city dwellers dress. Men wear western-style trousers or jeans and loose shirts or t-shirts. Even though the temperature is a pleasant 25°C (77°F) most of the older men have added a light jacket – well it is mid-autumn in Cairo and no doubt to them it feels cool. Others have draped a scarf over the crown of their head. By far fewer in number are women, who favour loose or tailored shirts and cotton trousers accessorized by a headscarf wrapped around their head to frame their face. The men are all ages whereas the women are young, maybe within the demographic of 20 to 40 years old. As for the minority of women hidden underneath black burkas, their age will remain unclassifiable.

I'm enjoying the ramble in this part of the city and feel quite at home in these familiar-looking streets. This familiarity is because the seven and eight-storey buildings have 19th-century European architecture. When I look up higher than the heads of the people I can easily imagine I'm walking down a Parisian street. Aside from the people and language, the difference between Cairo and a European capital city is the dry climate and the light covering of sand and dust.

We step away from the crowds into a side alley. The café is halfway down on a corner at the end of an arcade. Alfresco tables and chairs are in an L-shape, several are on the alley's pavement, most are on the arcade side outside a glass-façade café. We seat ourselves at a four-seater table on the alley's pavement. Magdy orders a Turkish coffee and tea from a prompt young waiter dressed in black trousers and a clean white shirt, who takes our order across to the other side of the alley where a middle-aged Egyptian man stands behind the counter of a kiosk rapidly exchanging orders with waiters. The café is crowded and noisy as a result of many animated conversations going on at once. There is one other woman a young Egyptian sat beside her boyfriend. The rest of the clientele is male, ranging from young men in their twenties to pensioners, some share a hookah – a table height smoking pipe comprising of orbicular water chambers and a long mouth pipe. Noticing my interest, Magdy discloses the café is reputed to be a favourite watering hole of Cairo's free thinkers, artistic types and maybe some revolutionaries. I wonder if the more ardent conversations where heads are close together are plotting another push towards becoming an economically strong Egypt.

The efficient waiter comes back and politely places the drinks on the table then goes again.

'Do you want sugar?'

Magdy isn't used to a European who likes Turkish coffee. Earlier at the museum café, he ordered my coffee to come with sugar. I hadn't minded as Turkish coffee is extremely bitter and therefore drinkable sweetened:

'No, without sugar is fine.'

Magdy talks about his family. His deceased father was Muslim his mother is a Coptic Christian. A worldly coupling, which goes some way to explain how Magdy gained his educated and open-minded character. He talks dearly of his mother, who I perceive as a strong woman, the matriarch of the family. He might not admit it if asked, but I reckon Magdy likes strong women. For instance, I discern his disdained ex-wife is a strong woman even though he no longer speaks of her fondly. I regard his daughter a fortunate young woman as she has the support of a strong mother and grandmother and a broad-minded father.

With the drinks finished we take our leave from the pipe smokers and 'plotting revolutionaries' via an arcade of knick-knack shops, which funnels us back amongst the traders and shoppers on another broad and traffic-filled shopping street. I don't attempt to get my bearings. I'm happy to walk beside Magdy as he picks a route through the crowds. Our pace is faster than the slow-moving traffic supplying exhaust fumes to the sand and dust mix. Frustrated drivers add a sporadic chorus of calls to their percussion of honks and peeps.

The street ends at a square where there is a central statue of a smartly-dressed man standing on a white-stone plinth holding a scroll in both hands.

'This is Talaat Harb Square.'

Talaat Harb Square is square in name only for it is circular with a perimeter of curved colonial four-storey buildings. At street level, the shops display colourful awnings. In an attempt to protect the pedestrian from the continual flow of traffic entering and exiting from six feeder streets, zebra crossings connect pavements lined with colonial-era streetlamps. As the zebra crossings are the exclusive road markings the traffic manages itself as it enters, passes-by the statue (the plinth's flimsy protection is a low-hung chain supported by four intervening ornamental metal posts) and then exits. Interspersed amid the hum of cars, trucks, and motorbikes going by are erratic peep peeps and honk honks. A small number of the pedestrians take their chances and dodge the traffic opting to ignore the outer pavement and make a beeline through the square. We too aim for an exit on the far side of the statue; though, our passage uses the pavements and zebra crossings.

From Talaat Harb Square the afternoon amble continues down another busy shopping street where there is a bounty of aromas, exhaust fumes, dust and wafts of coffee and spicy food as we go by the open doorways of cafés and fast-food outlets. When I'm not dodging pedestrians, I glance into shop windows displaying laden mannequins, rows of shoes, shelves of cloth or free-standing furniture. Along the kerbside are market stalls where young Egyptian men in jeans and baseball caps sell sunglasses displayed on carousels and old men with weather-beaten faces sit on crates at the side of wooden tables holding neat piles of cloth. Interspersed with the stalls are parked cars and delivery vans. Most of the people walking up and down the pavements or dodging the slow-moving traffic as they cross the street are men. Though, we do come across a trio of young women in their early thirties, smartly dressed in loose trousers, blouses, and pale headscarves. They are peering at a shop window dressed with mannequins. They seem to be having an enthusiastic discussion about the clothes on display. Further down the street, I have to sidestep to avoid a woman in her forties and her husband as they step out onto the pavement from a shop. I spot a solitary westerner: A bearded middle-aged man dressed in loose cargo trousers and blue shirt. He looks comfortable in this setting, and I presume from his appearance, he is well travelled.

Magdy is impressed with how quickly I have taken to crossing the street 'Cairo style' (this involves weaving through traffic with the aim of not getting peeped at or hit), I even take off in front of him at the busier side street junctions. I reveal I had worked in Central London for five years. Though the traffic in London is more orderly, there is still an element of traffic dodging, especially when dashing to arrive at a meeting on time.

We turn into a dual-lane street where we have to dodge the traffic to get to the pavement on the other side. On the side of the street we cross from, there are modern boutiques set back on a wide pavement bordered by a curb-side railing. Pedestrians are dispersed making it easy to notice a trendy young woman in smart attire: black trousers, shirt and carrying a handbag on her shoulder. We cross over to where stall holders and parked cars squeeze pedestrians onto a crowded narrower pavement. At a stationary handcart piled full of vegetables, Magdy waves to acknowledge someone ahead. It is our driver stood by the white MPV he has somehow managed to park amongst the stalls and other parked vehicles.

The street the MPV was parked on is close to Tahrir Square. Our driver makes slow headway as he exits and steers across many lanes of traffic to reach the carriageway that runs along the side of the river. At this junction, there is an attempt to assist the congestion. A man in uniform stands in the centre and periodically stops the traffic travelling north to south to allow the northbound traffic to proceed and the traffic flowing from the street where we've come from to join. Even with this assistance chaos reigns with vehicles bumper to bumper and three or four simultaneously moving forward side-by-side.

The slow-moving spectacle presents a young woman wearing a long headscarf and fashionably large sunglasses driving a new saloon car; white vans and old blue 4x4 vehicles moulded using sharp angles; white taxis with yellow roof signs marked by a thin black-check strip beginning at the headlights and ending at the rear. The young woman is not the only driver in a new car. Amongst the older car and van models are newer saloon cars: Audi, VW, etc. Magdy informs me car finance is cheap in Egypt nowadays and this has led to an influx of new cars on the streets of Cairo. Access to cheap car finance has enabled many more Egyptian people, and in particular the young, to own a car. The flow of the traffic quickens on joining the southbound lane. In the fading daylight, the interior lights of high-rise corporate office buildings intensify on the citified side of the street. I lean back and reflect on the fascinating glimpses of ancient and modern Egypt revealed by Magdy and downtown Cairo today.

When we left the Egyptian Museum, Magdy had awarded me the accolade of 'second-longest tour of the museum he had ever guided.' My four-hour tour is beaten solely by a Swedish party who clocked up five-hours inside. I was extremely pleased with this news as it meant I hadn't squandered my time escorted by an Egyptologist in a museum packed full of ancient Egyptian artefacts. That said there were a couple of exhibits in the museum where I went in alone for the reason they require an extra cost, so guides tend to wait outside. The first of these exhibits is the heavily-secured and dimly-lit room where the treasures of King Tutankhamun are on display. The centrepiece is the infamous Gold Death Mask in a reinforced-glass case. The mask is a beautiful object and well worth seeing. The second exhibit is the mummies' room.

On the first floor in the south-east corner of the museum is a modest room sectioned off away from the noise and crowds of the grand central galleries. I was unsure about visiting the mummies' room and had tentatively entered a subdued environment of low lighting, and glass display cases laid end-to-end in the centre. Straightaway you know you are in the presence of 11 of the long-deceased Kings and Queens of the New Kingdom. An eerie atmosphere commands quiet contemplation. Although the mummies are in temperature and humidity control glass cases, there is still the faint musty scent of the long-dead. A wooden walkway follows the perimeter of the room giving you access to peer inside each case in order. The mummies are displayed so visitors can observe various stages of preparation. One is wrapped entirely in shredded-linen cloth with just the mouth and teeth visible. Some are inside wooden coffins; perhaps, they are too fragile to display in their entirety.

I had not lingered long in the mummies' room as I don't have a great interest in the remains of the dead no matter how noble or ancient they are. My uncertainty didn't dissipate in the act of peering inside the glass coffins, and I'd questioned: Is it appropriate for the remains of the ancient Egyptians to be on display for the world to gawk at or would it be more appropriate to display replicas and rebury the real mummies? An ironic twist is these ancient kings and queens of Egypt had their bodies prepared for the eternal life, and maybe by being on display, their lives at least are remembered thousands of years later.

Darkness cloaks the city. The MPV moves undeviating in the traffic underneath the glow of the streetlights. I look out the window and try to catch glimpses of the ink-black water of the River Nile as my thoughts go back to the Rosetta Stone. I sneak a smile. Earlier, as we'd entered the Egyptian Museum, Magdy had pointed out the picture of the Rosetta Stone on display at the top of the steps inside the entrance hall. We hadn't stayed looking at the picture for long, just long enough for Magdy to pull his 'ex-wife' face and change his tone of voice to emphasize: 'It isn't here because the British have got it.'

Rested from the break at the museum's outdoor coffee shop, my tour moved up to the first floor to the well-visited east wing where the contents of King Tutankhamun's tomb are on exhibit. In the act of perusing the many treasures of Tutankhamun, I had picked out an exquisitely decorated wooden chest on display in a glass cabinet at the centre of the gallery. Exhibited beside heftier treasures the chest appealed because of its scale and design: symmetrical patterns carved into panels of wood using gilded gold and framed with carvings of hieroglyphs. Light-heartedly I had commented, 'That chest would look nice in my living room. I think I will take it home.'

Magdy laughed, 'What will you exchange for the chest?'

'Ah, the Rosetta Stone. I will be in London the weekend before Christmas. If you hear of a break-in at the British Museum get the chest packed up as I will have the Rosetta Stone to trade.'

I think Magdy appreciated the joke.

Giza Plateau

It's about 10.30am when the white haze that's masked the built-up district on the River Nile's west bank clears to reveal a cloudless blue sky. From my elevated viewpoint, I look out over the upper storeys and flat rooftops of the dense urban sprawl of Giza and briefly appreciate this setting of modern-day life. However, I'm not at this spot to gaze at modern civilization. I turn to look southwards to where Magdy is walking and where the outlook is of enormous rough-edged stone blocks stacked side-by-side and upwards to roughly 140 m (459 ft.). A width and height that blocks out the sun. Not for the first time this trip, I'm hit by the feeling of satisfaction as I look up and across the immense structure. Namely, The Great Pyramid of Khufu, the second king of the fourth dynasty. I can fully appreciate why this monumental and majestic pyramid is one of the seven wonders of the ancient world and of cause, where there is a wonder to behold there will be many tourists present to gaze at it.

Meandering in pairs or groups, most of the tourists at the base of The Great Pyramid are young Egyptians. A fashionable twenty-something man is taking a photo of his girlfriend who poses at the base. Momentarily I recall the first holiday I took at their age in the company of a past boyfriend, and I wonder if this is their first holiday together. In this area is a scattering of young-teenager girls who must be part of a school trip. They're in an assortment of colourful long-sleeved tops and pattern head-scarves. Akin to most teenage girls, they giggle and converse excitedly in their friendship groups. Three of the girls have climbed up the pyramid to the fifth tier of blocks and stand taking pictures of each other. One waves down to four friends who stand close to where I am. The girls below wave back, shout and then jog to the pyramid. I'd presumed tourists would not be allowed to climb onto the pyramids. As I watch the girls climb up the blocks using the route previously taken by their friends, I can see my presumption was wrong. In the process of the girls joining up, a man in a tourist police uniform moves towards the girls already on the pyramid and asks them to make their way back down. Magdy explains, 'Tourists may climb to where the man in uniform is and take photos. But they're not encouraged to stay on the monument for long.'

Over 2,000,000 stone blocks with an average weight of two-and-a-half tons per stone were used to build Khufu's pyramid. Its colossal size was a beacon for looters. In all likelihood, looting is responsible for why there is an inadequate number of known ancient antiquities to evidence the existence of King Khufu. Yesterday, on my tour of the Egyptian Museum, Magdy purposefully led me by many large god-status statues of kings, queens, and noblemen before coming to a halt by a glass case elevated on a plinth in Room 32. Inside the glass case is a tiny statue no higher than 8 cm (3.1 in): 'This is the only complete statue known to exist of King Khufu, second pharaoh of the fourth dynasty.'

Carved from ivory the statue is of Khufu seated on a throne. His right arm crosses his chest and he holds a flail in his hand pointed towards his left shoulder. His left arm is at his side, and his hand rests on his thigh. Khufu's eyes, ears, mouth, nose, chin, and jaw are visible. On his head is the crown of Lower Egypt. Magdy had pointed to the cartouche on the statue that identifies it to be of Khufu: 'Some experts say the statue was carved later than in the reign of Khufu. Because the style of the throne and flail is associated with the later Middle Kingdom of ancient Egypt and not the Old Kingdom when Khufu reigned.'

There is an irony to the king who owned the most prodigious of all the pyramids now being represented by the littlest statue. Especially stood in the Egyptian Museum amid hundreds of colossal statues and grandiose artefacts.

Magdy makes a gesture towards the pyramid and the path the teenage girls used: 'If you go up onto the pyramid I will take a photo of you from here.'

I hand over my camera.

At the base, I join on behind three middle-aged Egyptians. The men have thinning-grey hair and the woman a black headscarf. They all wear jeans and pale shirts. The way upward cuts across the lowest levels. I assume it has been purposely selected as a safe passage for tourists to walk amid the enormous stone blocks. Keen to get the photo session done with, I peel off at the fifth tier to take the place of a young Chinese couple, who've vacated a pathway that goes behind several of the blocks, thus leaving the middle-aged Egyptians to continue onwards and upwards to where the tourist policeman stands. This spot will do nicely for a photo opportunity, and without any consideration, I sit on the edge of the block and look down at Magdy, who snaps the photo. Oops, I'm being shouted at by the tourist policeman. I can't hear what he is saying for he is too far away. Though I deduce from his hand and arm gestures, I'm not allowed to sit on the block. I make my retreat back down the levels pausing briefly for another photo on the next level down. I remain standing up for the second photo.

Back at ground level, the tourist numbers are increasing. There are tightly-knit bands of chattering girls and boys, and well-off middle-age western couples in pairs or quartets carry backpacks and expensive cameras. Amidst this substantial crowd are two Giza people who are working hard to convince the westerners to purchase their wares. The Gizas, as they are collectively known locally, are scrawny men in their late twenties characterized by dark-skin faces aged more than their years – a combination of too much sun exposure and a hard lifestyle. Magdy had warned me about the Gizas. They were the topic of conversation before getting out of the MPV at the entrance gate close to Khufu's Pyramid. There is a general dislike of the Giza people as they can be pushy and unpleasant to tourists. He warned me not to acknowledge any of them for the reason once they have your attention they will not leave you alone until you buy their souvenirs: 'Do not make eye contact. Completely ignore them.'

I could tell Magdy found it hard to relay this message since it is human nature to acknowledge fellow humans. I had made light of the seriousness of his words, mostly to make him feel better: 'Oh that's easy. I'm English. Plus, I commuted on the tube in London for years. No one acknowledges or speaks to anyone on the tube.'

Magdy had given me an appreciative smile.

Back amongst the scattered crowd, I pass right by a Giza. Thankfully, there is no pretence needed since he is engrossed in trying to persuade a pair of western men to buy his merchandise. Just as I re-join Magdy and take back my camera, the Giza fails to make the sale. To his credit, he does not pursue his goal, he leaves the men and walks away making a beeline for another set of tourists. Magdy indicates for us to move on.

Away from the crowd, beyond the northeast corner of Khufu's Pyramid, an unattended single-hump camel has laid down in front of a wall of rocks. On its back is a red-carpet seat spacious enough to carry two people and decorated with black tassels. Knowing most tourists are eager to get on a camel, Magdy dutifully asks: 'Do you want a camel ride?'

'Oh no. Camels don't look comfortable to ride.'

I repeat the comparison of driving a dumper truck or a Ferrari to the riding of a camel or a horse previously discussed with Maryanne. The camel being the dumper truck and the horse the Ferrari. This characterization is a little lost on Magdy as he has no interest in riding either animal. The camel has an equestrian companion, a skinny dark bay horse, saddled up with a mini version of the carpet-seat. It looks overworked and stands with its head bowing close to the ground. During my first lunch at Al Sorat Farm, Maryanne reported, she used to ride to the Giza Plateau many years ago. However, she stopped this riding excursion when her horses became unsettled and anxious as they verged on the plateau. Perhaps it is because there are too many tourists and coaches. Or maybe the horses became sensitive to the stress of the overworked animals and could smell the rotting carcass left on the spot where an animal had dropped dead from exhaustion. The dark bay is a wraith in comparison to the healthier and relaxed horses back at Al Sorat Farm. Maryanne's own experience of the Gizas was also unfavourable. Always keen to broaden her grooms' knowledge of their heritage, she had ridden to Giza accompanied by a groom who had never visited the plateau. When she went to pay at the kiosk the groom was refused entry just because he is from a different neighbourhood.

Giving the camel a wide berth, we emerge out of the shadow of The Great Pyramid into the intense and close to midday sun pouring down from a perfect blue sky to drench everything in brilliant light. I'm grateful for the dark-lensed sunglasses and peaked cap I'm wearing. Even more so now a Giza advances, a man wearing a long white scarf wrapped around his head and a determined look on his face. He carries a bag on his shoulder and something in his hand. Magdy and I put on an act of being in a deep conversation. The Giza is undeterred and walks up to me making his pitch in Arabic. Magdy and I remain focused on our conversation. Ignoring a person speaking to you from a step away is hard. Nevertheless, the performance works, and the Giza continues on his course.

We've moved into the eastern cemetery where immense stone blocks overspread the ground. The blocks are uneven because the ancient Egyptians had just stone available to chip out the edges. Magdy quickens his walk as he picks out a route and, in my pursuit, I have to take care where I put my feet.

Climbing up a high bank of blocks, I notice that a reasonable amount of unpopulated ground has opened up between us, the pyramid and the crowd of tourists and I wonder where we're going. When I step up onto the uppermost layer of blocks I see Magdy has come to a standstill, he has his back to me, gazing to the south. I adopt his sightline, 'Wow!'

Looking pleased with himself, he declares: 'This is my favourite view. Few tourists wander up here because they stick close to the pyramids.'

There are no people close by, just the company of the breeze. We take a couple of steps forward to get a better outlook.

On our level, in the foreground is the eastern cemetery. An area of stones, brick walls, sand mounds, and mastaba doorways bedecked with lintel stones. The cemetery ends at a cliff edge commanding a spectacular viewpoint. Out to the east are the upper storeys and flat rooftops of modern-day Giza sprawling out to meet the horizon. To the south is the side profile of the head of the Great Sphinx – the rest of this historic statue is out of sight in its dugout ditch. Beyond the Sphinx's head is a row of tall conifer trees – an unusual sight in a locality of stone and rock. Maybe the trees were planted to mark the edge of the plateau for behind the trees is nothing but rolling dunes, which fade to silhouettes on the faraway skyline. On this occasion, the Sahara holds my gaze momentarily for my eyes are drawn westwards to where five pyramids align and form a mini-manmade mountain range that extends out into the dune system from the edge of urban Giza. Close by is the Great Pyramid of Khufu, the prodigious of all the pyramids. On its sunlight drenched eastern side are the ruins of three satellite pyramids known to be the tombs of ancient Egyptian queens. The northmost is a flattened pile of rock and sand. The middle has merely its lower tiers intact. The third and most southern remains a pyramid, its outline is rough and jagged, and at this moment there is a modern-day invasion taking place. A couple of unidentifiable by distance men have climbed six tiers up on the pyramid's south-east corner to look out at the desert. It is this third pyramid for a queen that forms the second peak in the illusion of alignment. It looks to be half the height of Khufu's pyramid and three-quarters of the height of the next in the line: Khafre's pyramid. Khafre, the fourth king of the fourth dynasty, is the son of Khufu. His pyramid is referred to as the Middle Pyramid and is famed for having most of its limestone outer casing intact to render smooth sides with just the upper tiers and peak revealing the lighter stone underneath. South of Khafre's pyramid is the Little Pyramid of Menkaure, Khafre's son, and the fifth king in the dynasty. The Little Pyramid being much further away looks from here to stand at a third of the height of its Middle Pyramid neighbour. At the Little Pyramid's south-east corner is an even smaller pyramid, roughly a quarter of the height. This pyramid is one of a trio of south-facing secondary pyramids. From this distance, the Little Pyramid and secondary pyramid give the illusion of perfectly formed smooth sides and pointed vertexes. A background of blue sky completes the panorama. In my opinion, anyone who has the resources to bring about the opportunity should stand on this spot at least once in their lifetime.

To gift me a moment of solitude and rarely found stillness on the Giza Plateau, Magdy walks on while I absorb the spectacular view. To catch up, I pick my passage along the ridge of a burial mound to join him at the southern tip of the eastern cemetery. Had he been looking straight ahead he would be admiring the Middle Pyramid. Instead, he looks downwards onto the road linking the south-side of the Great Pyramid, the north side of the Middle Pyramid and the Sphinx. I too look down: 'Ah, that's where they are. I was wondering where all the tourists had gone.'

The roadside below is littered with people, camels, and horses. From our elevated overlook, it is a parade that plays out in miniature. There are bands of tourists riding horses and camels led by persuasive or persistent Gizas. Intermingled amongst the animals are friends and relatives on foot wielding cameras. At the west end and bookended by a pair of horses and a camel is the largest crowd espied in Cairo so far. There must be 40 to 50 people. Magdy breaks his gaze from the mass: 'Do you want to go to Khufu's Boat Museum?'

Tempted though I am to remain in the undisturbed eastern cemetery, the momentary spell of isolation is already broken by viewing the crowd and it is time to get back in amongst them.

In the early 1950s, Khufu's solar boat was found buried in a pit on the south side of the Great Pyramid. Subsequently, this became the site of Khufu's boat museum. The boat's purpose was to be used by Khufu in the afterlife. For this purpose, the boat was dismantled and placed in the pit carved out of the plateau by the ancient Egyptians and closed using an air-tight seal.

The boat museum is a modern two-level building fronted by pained windows and pale walls. To me, the building design resembles a boat in dry-dock. While Magdy collects tickets from the kiosk at the museum's entrance, I wait further back amongst the congregation of Egyptian, Western and Asian tourists. The school children are here too; though now there are more boys and girls. They are with their teachers, who are trying to install some order in the mass of excitement and giggles. The children are an assemblage of colour against the pale stone of the Great Pyramid sky-scraping overhead.

As Magdy returns from the kiosk five of the schoolgirls, all in the region of 12 to 13 years old, break away from the main party and talk purposefully to him in Arabic. After the brief exchange of words, Magdy relays: 'The girls asked if they can have their picture taken beside you. Do you mind?'

'No, not at all.'

Though I can't imagine why?

He nods to the girls and immediately I have five almond-skin faces adorned by big brown eyes wrapped in autumnal-colour headscarves at my side. Amid massive smiles, jostling for position and darting to and from Magdy, the newly recruited photographer, the girls take it, in turn, to ask: 'Where are you from?'

Each time, I reply 'England' there is great excitement, and 'England' gets repeated amongst themselves. With the photographs taken, Magdy and the girls exchange final words, and we leave them to go inside the museum.

There are benches in the entrance hall where you can sit to pull on the obligatory hessian overshoes. In the process of putting on the overshoes, Magdy chats about the five school girls. He found out they are from the Nile Delta in the north of Egypt, a region on the Mediterranean coast, and are on a school trip to Cairo. 'Egyptian children love meeting people from different countries. Especially people from English speaking countries because they like to practice their English.'

'I found them endearing and appreciate their enthusiasm for meeting someone from another country and culture. Something, I would never discourage any child from doing.'

With overshoes secured we enter the ground floor exhibition room; a light and airy gallery providing a welcome respite from the midday sun. Sets of tourists talk amongst themselves as they move around the exhibits displayed on plinths in the centre of the room. Before I join them in perusing the accomplishment of finding an ancient Egyptian boat, I briefly recall the long-forgotten memory of the parquet floor in my infant school's assembly-room. A memory jogged by the museum's parquet floor. I remember the assembly-room floor was particularly good to skid across just after it was polished. This day, decades later, I find myself resisting the temptation to skid across the length of the exhibition room, and opt to shuffle my hessian-clad feet, so I slide slightly further than my usual walk and at the same time suppress a mischievous grin.

The exhibition room's length is owing to its main exhibit: The boat pit. My untrained eyes see a long definite dark hole carved into bedrock and partly covered by eight substantial lintel stones placed at intervals. Essentially, the perfect size for a dismantled solar boat. Most of the displays focus on the how the boat was excavated and restored using photographic and written records. Magdy's pick of 'most interesting and relevant exhibit' is a miniature model of a cross section of the boat's hull. The model showcases how parts of the boat are held together by rope and the type of knot used. My favourite is a pile of frayed rope that had come out of the excavated pit and is now jumbled together inside a glass cabinet. What amazes me is despite being millenniums old the rope would not look out of place in the present day on the harbour walls in the traditional fishing villages close to where I live. It is a unique piece of archaeology considering rope does not generally preserve for thousands of years, and this rope is the only example of the skilled work of the ancient ropemakers on display.

At the west end of the room is a modern staircase going up to the upper exhibition room where Khufu's solar boat is on exhibit. It takes me longer than Magdy to ascend the steps because every time I lift my left foot the overshoe falls off and I have to stop and reattach it. Full-length glass windows monopolize the north and south walls and flood the room in daylight. At the centre of the upper room is the boat, elevated by many supporting white posts and fenced in by suspended wooden walkways. With a length of 44 m (144 ft.) and a width of 6 m (19.8 ft.), the boat resembles a Viking longboat with a sharp angular bow and stern. Close upon centre and at the lowest part of the boat are ten long wooden oars: five port (left side) and five starboard (right side). The outboards of the oars point downward to reach beneath the bottom of the boat. The inboards point upwards and cross above the deck. Behind the oars close to the bow is a rustic rectangular cabin assembled from wooden panels framed by tree branches. Because the wood is a relatively good condition it is believed, the boat was either not used or used once to serve as Khufu's funerary boat. If the latter did come to pass, his body would have been laid out in the cabin as the boat carried its human cargo down the Nile. Wood preserves better than rope and consequently, the intricate knots holding the boat together today are reconstructions. The modern rope's pale tinge stands out against the ancient dark wood.

For the first few minutes of leisurely moving along the higher walkway, taking in the boat from its port side, we are in the quiet company of an

Egyptian couple who are close to the bow, and four young adults of oriental origin who stand on the lower walkway looking up at the boat's starboard side. Suddenly the calm ambiance erupts into much chatter and excitement. It is the school girls from outside, but now their number has increased to 12. They ask via Magdy if they can take more photos. Magdy is again the photographer. He directs us to stand in front of the walkway railing, so the boat is behind us in the photo. I'm at the centre of the back row flanked by the taller girls. The shorter girls form a front line. It is a gathering of bright colours, smiles and jostling whenever a girl leaves the array and hands Magdy a camera thereon quickly regaining her place. Some of the girls also take pictures. The shyer girls stand at the edge looking on with awe at meeting a foreign woman travelling alone. There are many repeats of, 'Where are you from?'

'England.'

Again, this triggers excitement and a plethora of chatter amongst themselves. When every girl is satisfied, she's acquired a photo the posse of noise and colour, ignore the boat and exit down the front staircase. The noise level returns to the quieter individual conversations of the adult tourists. Magdy expresses concern that I may have found the girls a little overwhelming: 'Did you mind having your photo taken with them?'

'Not at all. Their enthusiasm and fascination are charming, and something I will never forget. Though when I picture their homecoming and their parents ask: 'What did you see in Cairo?' I'm concerned the girls won't mention the pyramids, Khufu's boat or the Sphinx, they will reply: 'We met an English woman travelling on her own, I have photographs of her.' And I expect my description will have changed to an American woman by the time that conversation takes place too.'

Going down to the lower walkway, I fall behind again. The overshoe has fallen off my foot, and I have to stop to put it back on. After I repeat this action a third time, Magdy suggests I take the overshoes off. For all the fun it's been to slide along the overshoes are starting to annoy me, and I don't hesitate to take its partner off and carry them in my hand. The lower walkway offers a starboard view underneath the boat. It is here you can see the scaled-down twin oars at the stern for steering, and you can appreciate the wonder of the ancient craftwork. The knots and wood fittings are so precise the boat would float if launched today.

Back downstairs we offload the overshoes and go back outside into an atmospheric wall of heat and dust – compliments of the midday sun and desert. There is brief respite when a shortcut is taken using a shady passageway (enclosed by the west wall of the boat museum and another modern building where chefs in their whites are busy at work in a fitted cafeteria type kitchen) to emerge amongst more ancient ruins at the side of the road previously observed from the eastern cemetery. For the length of the thoroughfare, there is a continual stream of tourists, vendors, camels, and horses. Most of who walk westwards towards the Great Sphinx. On the other side is a broad stretch of sand where the ancient causeway of Khafre is positioned to join his mortuary temple on the west side of the Middle Pyramid and his Lower Temple on the south side of the Sphinx Temple. Walking on the ancient causeway is a tiny fraction of the number of tourists who walk on the modern-day road. The main reason for this is a massive carpark situated close to the north-east corner of The Middle Pyramid. Joined to the road the carpark is clogged up with long rows of air-conditioned coaches, white MPVs, black-saloon cars, and taxis. Recently alighted from these vehicles are groups of up to 40 or 50 mainly western-looking tourists who are accompanied by their tour guides, coach drivers and infamous vendors. What is worse is our set course is aiming for the hordes of people and vehicles. On the way, I voice my observations, 'Tourism doesn't look too hard hit for there must be hundreds of people in this vicinity.'

'The coaches are from the cruise ships. They're hired to collect the passengers and bus them in on mass to the most popular tourist sights. The itineraries are so specific and tight, the passengers only have a short stint at any one location and are swiftly moved onto the next place of interest. Because of this, cruise ship passengers do not spend money at the local businesses that rely on tourism. The beneficiaries are the cruise-ship companies and to a lesser extent the site owners via the entrance fee.'

In the carpark, we weave around groups of cruise-ship passengers who congregate around their guides. As we dash between the coaches, care is taken to dodge the vendors until our driver is spotted waving beside the MPV. The encounter isn't through sheer luck. Magdy had phoned him after we left the boat museum, so he roughly knew where to find him. Planned or unplanned I'm thankful to be back in the MPV and closing the door behind me. While, Magdy instructs our driver all eyes are on a Giza, who hinders a middle-aged couple as they alight their tour coach. In a pushy manner, he puts a tacky white scarf on the man's head and demands payment. The tourist attempts to take the scarf off. The Giza is persistent and uses his hand to prevent it from being taken off while relentlessly demanding payment. Disgusted, Magdy swivels in his seat to look at me, 'Now you can see why people dislike the Gizas as this is how they greet tourists.'

With the chaos of the carpark behind the MPV turns north then west at the Middle Pyramid and onwards using a level-surface brick road edged by white-brick pavements. I marvel at the pyramid's smooth outer casing and try to conjure up the image of the Giza Plateau in its youth. The detour takes us through an expansive landscape where the terrain inclines subtly upward and spans out. Traffic is light with the odd vehicle going by. Here and there a car is parked up, and the disembarked occupants stand on the pavement taking in the view. Up ahead where the road bends to the southwest, there is another populous carpark. Thankfully, Magdy asks our driver to pull up in advance of the bend, and we step out of the MPV.

I stand in awe of the setting for the second time today. There is a ridge behind us in the northwest. It obscures the settlement of Giza, so it appears like there is nothing here except for the six pyramids that dominate the skyline. To the north are the Great Pyramid and the Middle Pyramid. Because of how the land lies the Middle pyramid looks to be higher than the Great Pyramid by cause of the latter's lower tiers being out of sight. A substantial gap divides the Middle Pyramid and Little Pyramid where a single-lane track drops out of the foreground leaving a vista to the distant and practically cloaked in haze urban sprawl of Giza on the east side of the plateau. The urban sprawl extends behind the Little Pyramid, and it's three side-by-side satellite pyramids at the base of the south face. If you travelled north through the desert from the Abu Sir Pyramids, it is the Little Pyramid and the three satellites that you come to first.

Apart from the crowded and I expect noisy carpark the vicinity is sparse of human activity. Wrapped up in peace and brushed by a breeze, I pick out the movement of people going about their day. In the foreground, there are four pedestrians, men making their way to the cusp of a dune on a direct course to the entrance gate we'd used to get onto the plateau. A white minibus follows a 4x4 travelling slowly on a course to the Little Pyramid. I use the zoom on my camera to watch them advance down to the base of the Little Pyramid where I pick up a pair of camels and their riders, dwarfed by the pyramid's size and miniaturized by the distance. I can make out a rider dressed in white and another in black. The third man wears white he walks at their side. My camera zoom reveals a detailed view of the satellite pyramids. The first two are worn to crumbled ruins and no longer hold the true pyramid shape.

With the sun past midday, Madgy reminds me we need to stop for lunch before I'm taken back to Al Sorat Farm for a late afternoon ride. There is, however, another great monument to visit on the Giza Plateau. Back in the MPV, our driver turns the vehicle around, and we go back in the direction of the pyramids and the Great Sphinx.

Our progress slows down when the MPV reaches the cruise-ship coach carpark and joins the flow of pedestrians, vendors, camels, and horses all going downhill past the back of Khufu's solar boat museum and the ridge of the eastern cemetery. Nearing the bottom of the slope the upper half of the Great Sphinx comes into view: The side profile of a king's head and the long back of a lion. After passing the colossal statue, our driver mirrors the actions of the two vehicles in front and pulls over onto the roadside. Magdy and I jump out and our driver, drives onwards to modern-day Giza where the vanguard of the urban streets is less than 200 m (656 ft.) away.

We are at the top of a drop which ushers pedestrians down to Khafre's lower temple and the Sphinx temple. Because the plateau's eastern entrance is close by there are tourists everywhere: sitting on stone walls at the roadside or walking back up to the road. We join fellow new arrivals going down to the temples. The outer wall of the Sphinx temple is a ruin featuring gaps where the passage of time has left a higgledy-piggledy outline. Vertical-bar railings at the height of the lowest part of the wall take the place of the razed ancient wall. They peer into the interior at the chest and face of the Sphinx pointed to the east posed to greet the sunrise. At about 8 m (28 ft.) high the entrance to the temples looks to have fared the aeons well. Access is via an ancient causeway made from large stone blocks. Stalls line the causeway presenting an orderly offer in the sale of souvenirs. There is no hard sell by these vendors, who are happy to leave the tourists to browse and choose for themselves. The smaller-scale vendors who perch by the entrance mirror this amicable trading style.

Inside, we advance through an enclosed passageway where the space between the floor and ceiling is roughly 14 m (45.11 ft.). At the end of the passageway, a vendor sits bathed in sunlight beside a modest display of tourist tat. Movement through the temple is via a network of passages and doorways fashioned by huge pieces of stone. Some of the walls are smooth, and some have crumbled. There are more vendors, who sit with their back against the wall in a roofless section. They too are content to let the tourists amble by or browse their goods freely. In spite of the temple being a ruin, there is enough structure to make you feel you're walking back through time. More so in the pillared hall where sandstone pillars stand 4 m (13 ft.) high and have a thickness of at least a 1 m (3.2 ft.). Every pillar supports one or two weighty lintel stones. The smooth-surface pillars have fared better than the crumbling outer walls of the hall, probably because the walls provide the necessary protection to slow down the erosion of the interior. With no roof, the floor of the hall is dazzling-white in the early afternoon sun.

We emerge from the temple close to the right paw of the Great Sphinx. The sculpture, possibly the biggest ever made, is carved out from the rock. Its lion body supports a regal human head that looks forever eastwards. Experts say the face of the Sphinx is that of Khafre as it is Khafre's name carved on the stone adjoining the sculpture's giant paws. Furthermore, Khafre's mortuary temple and pyramid align with the Great Sphinx and the rise of the sun in the east.

A wall cuts off the ditch of the Sphinx from the Causeway of Khafre. On the north side of the wall, a walkway gives access to the right side of the Sphinx. Although there is a sizeable crowd of tourists armed with cameras gathered on the walkway, Magdy manages to find a gap in the mass where there is a clear view of the magnificent beast.

I'd read the Sphinx is carved from limestone and is said to have been built in the same period as Khafre's pyramid, 4,500 years ago. A shortcoming of limestone is it erodes rapidly. There probably wouldn't be much of it left today for us tourists to gaze at and imagine it in its original splendour if the desert hadn't concealed it for most of its existence, the full excavation of the Sphinx was in the 1930s. Despite erosion, the royal head retains its fourth dynasty, Old Kingdom-style triangular headdress and most of its facial features the exception is a missing nose. The broad and flat crown of the headdress is the highest point at 20 m (65 ft.). If there were once curves shaping the lion's body, they are no more. Instead angled steps go up to a plane back. Colossal forelegs and paws stretch out from the chest of the lion. A tail curves around the right-hind leg ending at a tip pointing skywards. The measurement from forepaw to the rear is 73 m (239 ft.).

After retracing our steps back through the temple, we head to the eastern boundary of the plateau via a raised white-stone causeway set in an area of strewn blocks. It isn't a long causeway on the account it ends at a low-set dune.

On the brow of the dune I look back at the temples, the Sphinx, and the majestic Great Pyramid and Middle Pyramid towering up behind on the higher terrain against a backdrop of blue sky. Modern day life quickly snatches away the ancient past as I turn back on course and skim the outer edge of an ample outdoor seating area with row after row of empty chairs. Multitudes of tourists will sit here tonight and watch the 'Pyramids Sound and Light Show.' At an hour-long, the show uses the Sphinx in the role of narrator and chronicles the history of Khufu, Khafre and Menkaure.

A band of sand no wider than a cove beach is all we have to span to reach the sandstone-brick boundary wall. Behind the wall, there is a rank of white MPVs and tourist minibuses parked parallel to the forefront of the modern-day buildings. These multi-storey buildings are densely packed and come with a flat roof, enclosed balcony, and a satellite dish. Forming part of the facing row is a dominate glass-facade building placed so you can't miss its globally recognizable white letters on red background signs spelling out KFC and Pizza Hut.

Vet Clinic

It has gone 3:30 pm when Magdy, our driver and I arrive at Al Sorat Farm and find Maryanne and her grooms outside the farm gate and to Magdy's relief the dogs secured on the inside. There is no barking or fuss. The pack is settled somewhere behind Finn, who is lying down watching the action through the mesh. A white-plastic garden table temporarily occupies a spot by the high garden wall of the large villa. On top of the table is a plastic container full of medicines, wound dressings, hoof trimming tools and other resources needed for this afternoon's vet clinic.

One patient remains, a dear little jenny donkey stands untethered close to the low brick wall of Al Sorat farm. Her stance is stiff despite standing square. Her vertebrae, ribs, femur, and humerus are all visible through her pale-grey coat. On her head is handmade headcollar made from rope and a grubby sheep-skin noseband. A clean blue fly fringe has been put over the headcollar; probably by a groom. Years of hard work and ill-fitted tack are evidenced by white hairs that have eradicated most of the black hairs that form the horizontal part of a grey donkey's inherent black cross. Maryanne and the vet are discussing the treatment and care arrangements for the donkey. The vet, a man in his thirties, is most likely from an affluent background. He has neat black hair and is kitted out in the standard on-call vet attire of jeans and a casual shirt. While Magdy waits to speak to Maryanne, I introduce myself to the mother and daughter who are assisting at the vet clinic. Unlike the vet who looks to be local, the women are expat North Americans. The daughter is in her early twenties and wears the same style of clothing as her mother, cargo trousers and a vest top. They report on the donkey's plight as they help the grooms pack up the items from the table and coax the donkey to eat the armful of green leaves placed on the ground. She belongs to a local farmer who brought her to the clinic so the vet could treat a wound on her right-fore hoof. The donkey has received treatment, and her injured hoof has a neat and secure-dressing, but her wound has a severe ramification. The unfortunate donkey has tetanus.

The vet puts his veterinary bag in the back of his 4x4 and departs. Now I must say goodbye to Magdy and his tour of discovery and learning about a minuscule part of the ancient Egyptian treasure trove. Simultaneously, I'd welcomed the opportunity to gain an understanding of modern-day Cairo and its ongoing struggle to obtain unity, opportunity and economic growth.

During the drive from the Giza Plateau to the restaurant where we had lunch, Magdy's curiosity couldn't be contained any longer: 'What religion are you?'

I had been waiting for him to ask me this question.

Yesterday evening, he went to visit his mother. They'd discussed his day, and I had become a topic of conversation. His mother asked him the question then, and he could not answer. Magdy, like his late father, is Muslim. His mother is a Coptic Christian. For families living in modern-day Cairo, these types of mixed religion unions have the potential to cause issues. For Magdy, being brought up in a household where choice is accepted, and part of everyday life has provided a bedrock for his liberal attitude to global life. This same attitude meant he hadn't flinched when I gave him my answer: 'I don't practice any religion.'

Initially, he was speechless as he absorbed the words. Out of the possible answers I could have said it was apparent he didn't expect this one. Mindful that I'm in a country driven by religion, I broke the silence by recalling memories from my childhood. My mum is a practising Methodist and attends chapel every Sunday morning. She is a long-serving member of the congregation and is involved in the choir and most of the endeavours that help secure the chapel's continuation. My dad was christened Church of England, albeit non-practising. His favourite pastime on a Sunday morning was a round of golf. When I was a baby, I was christened a Methodist and used to attend the Sunday school at the chapel for most of my early years. I don't remember my exact age when the choice to opt out was presented, maybe around 10-years old. There was no hesitation in my decision to cease and spend more time in bed every Sunday morning. A practise I kept up for many subsequent years. Magdy then threw me a curveball, he had not heard of Methodism. Eek, my experience was many decades old, and I had not thought about this subject since. It was Magdy's mother who came to my aid as I explained Methodism is a Christian faith and thus mirrors many of the values and lessons his mother practices. I had tried to recall a couple of the well-known stories but, Magdy using his superior knowledge of Christianity had filled in the cavernous holes of my memory leaving me to say: 'Yes, that is it, I remember now.'

I believe, Magdy was semi-satisfied I wasn't a complete lost soul on the grounds of early childhood exposure and my upbringing where Christian values were successfully installed. With his curiosity satisfied the conversation moved onto another subject.

Magdy and our driver get back into the MPV and me and Maryanne wave them off as the vehicle goes around the corner heading back to the main road. Our attention moves to join the expats by the poorly donkey. Maryanne is concerned, the next 24 to 48 hours are critical for the donkey. Walid is dispatched to persuade the farmer to leave the donkey in the care of Al Sorat farm at this critical point. Not an easy task for a farmer's animals are his livelihood, and without them, he can't feed his family. Because of this farmers are always reluctant to let their animals go.

Maryanne fears the donkey's tetanus has spread beyond treatment and with every beat, it gets closer to the donkey's heart. Any sign of hope is clung to the donkey's pricked ears, her willingness to eat the green leaves and then tuck hungrily into the bran mash Hassan puts down in a tin bucket. Walid returns accompanied by the farmer, his wife, and young children. Maryanne, Walid, and Hassan update the farmer on the donkey's plight and persuade him to leave her. Their success means the family goes home without their donkey. With the clinic finished and the equipment packed away the expats say goodbye and take their leave.

The excited dogs greet us on the inside of the gateway. Hassan and Walid are assigned to put the donkey on a patch of grass adjoining the vegetable patch and give her plenty of green leaves and another bucket of feed. As we cross the lawn and enter the house, Maryanne tells me the farmer and his family live nearby. She knows where the donkey is kept and is not surprised the jenny has tetanus. Previous attempts to raise the family's education in animal care and the ramifications of keeping an animal in poor conditions had been unsuccessful. Unfortunately, the family is poor and do not have a lot of options available to them. Just getting the farmers to bring their animals to the weekly vet clinic is considered a breakthrough.

Maryanne is passionate about the vet clinic. Not only does it treat the animals of the local farming community it also, strives to raise the education of good animal husbandry. Patients are mostly goats, donkeys, horses, and water buffalo. The most common treatments are hoof trimming, worming, tick removal and tending to and dressing wounds. The clinics are also used to increase the animal care skills and knowledge of the grooms who have learned how to administer basic-level care and treatment. The grooms are pivotal in delivering the good-animal husbandry message to the local farmers. Maryanne is a shrewd woman and knows what avenue to take: 'It's important the grooms take on this role. The local men and farmers are going to listen to them as opposed to me, an expat North-American who's moved into their neighbourhood.'

For the third time since I arrived in Egypt, Jameela is groomed, tacked up and handed to me by Hossam, another of Maryanne's grooms. Hossam is the groom who helped me choose a hat at the start of my first ride. He attaches my saddlebags, helps me mount and checks the tack. On my return, he removes the saddlebags for me and takes care of Jameela. In the manner of all the grooms, he is polite and professional. The best thing about the grooms, apart from them all being handsome young men radiating friendly smiles, is they love their work.

It feels good to be riding again after sightseeing. Maryanne is back on Nazeer and Hassan is on a small bay Arab. Evening draws near as we ride through the back gateway of Al Sorat Farm passing the neighbourhood villas and onwards through the arable land. On the main road, a young man and woman ride by on a motor scooter. Neither of them wears a crash helmet or any protective clothing. He wears a patterned shirt and jeans. She has sat pillion, and because of the length of her navy-blue dress she sits side-saddle; a precarious position to be in for a person whose head is protected by a yellow headscarf and has sandals on her feet. Maryanne points to a grey donkey toiling on the opposite side of the street. Upon its back are a blanket and dual side-hung wicker basket. Undernourished, it has a black aloft mane and a brush of black hairs at the tip of its tail. On its head is a tatty red-cloth headcollar. There is no human in attendance, essentially it knows its task, and where it's going.

Back out in the fields, on the dust tracks alongside the irrigation canals there are plenty of opportunities for trot, and canter. The farmland of the Nile Valley and its grassy canal banks and sporadic palm tree borders has come to be a familiar sight. In the fading light, the canal water changes from dark green to a shiny black reflecting grasses and trees on the surface. A farmer rides by on a donkey followed by a loose buffalo with a pair of loose goats bringing up the rear. Other farmers roll by on their full wagons. They are all on the way home after a day's graft.

As we enter the desert, the sun is low enough in the west to cast shadows on the east side of the dunes and elongate the silhouettes of horses and riders on the sand. The fading light creates an enchanting prospect by lavishing the Abu Sir Pyramids and surrounding sand with an orange tinge. Out on the eastern horizon the blue-sky transitions to a darker tone. Similar to the ride a couple of days ago, our course curves to the southeast away from the Abu Sir Pyramids to point to the distant Sakkara Pyramids. The Step Pyramid is more sunlit than the trio recently passed. The terrain here is expansive, and there aren't as many high dunes in its proximity to block the light; although, the east side of the pyramid is in shadow, and the sand has an orange tint.

Though I've only been here a few days, I'm already smitten with this environment. A constant feature that is always present is the sun, and until this ride, it has been high up in the sky; essentially, undertaking a support role in a setting of pyramids, dunes, and blue sky. For the following 20 minutes or so the sun takes centre stage for today's swan song of dropping beneath the western horizon. Every time we reach a crest or transverse a valley, the sun is seen sunken further down and its light transitions from intense to an easier-on-the-eye glow. Preparatory to dropping out of sight it reveals its true sphere. In this micro version of its magnitude, it brings to mind the glow of a red spotlight. A yellow and orange hue frames the dark-grey haze on the horizon. Overhead the sky fades from blue to grey.

We arrive at the start point of the 'runway' gallop at sunset. There remains enough light to see the gradual rise of the ascent and the surrounding dunes. Maryanne looks back from her saddle, 'Are you ready for a gallop?'

'Yes.'

I'm getting used to riding at speed, and I know Jameela isn't going to do anything I don't want her to do. All I have to do is remain in balance and enjoy. Nazeer and Hassan's horse take off. I let Jameela go with them, yet I don't ask her to emulate the pace of the Arab horses, and a gap between them and us grows. My heart thuds less than on the first gallop, yet the elevation and excitement are the same. I remind myself to keep my head up and look where I'm going. Just as I reach my waiting companions, Hassan smiles, 'Jameela is slow.'

I pat Jameela, 'Good girl.'

She listens to and takes care of her rider.

With dusk upon us, the horses are pointed to the north-east to pick up the route back to the desert gate. When back in view, the white of the gate and the adjacent cream buildings are distinct from the sand, which is now a tone comparative to if it is sodden. Desert shrubs and countryside trees are black silhouettes. Sprawled out on the other side of the desert fence is an array of faint orange and yellow lights in the inhabited countryside. The lights are sparse where the grander villas reside, and gleaming clusters in the more-populated villages. The Muslim 'call to prayer' leaves the speakers of the local minaret and drifts out over the rooftops. Out in desert the resound magnifies and induces the sensation of tingles down my spine. At this moment, I can't think of anywhere else I'd rather be.

Day Ride to Dahshur

The following morning, I am again in the company of Maryanne. We're in the porch on the east side of the aviary. Just after, Maryanne, Hassan and I arrived back from the ride yesterday evening, Maryanne and I enjoyed a barbeque accompanied by salads and beer. Last night the porch was lit up by an outdoor lamp and citronella candles. This morning the roof is a welcome sunshade. I sit with my back against the side of the aviary facing into the garden. Pippin the one-eyed rat terrier is on my lap. Maryanne is opposite and has two doting rat terriers lying at her feet. A chorus of clucks, coos, and quacks celebrate the early morning light. There is optimism in the air since the little jenny donkey diagnosed with tetanus made it through the night. On the drive from the Sakkara Country Club, Maryanne reported the news and added the jenny had broken her tether and raided the vegetable patch in the night. Maryanne is pleased. This raid evidences there is still spirit in the donkey, and considering the jenny's current condition, Maryanne is happy to sacrifice a portion of her and the grooms' vegetable crop.

Today the ride is to Dahshur. It is the longest ride of the week taking approximately six hours there and back, which includes a lunch break at a villa owned by an expat American friend of Maryanne. Maryanne hasn't ridden to Dashur for a while, and because of the infrequency she's invited her riding trainer, Zurab to join us for breakfast and the ride. It will be Zurab's first time on this ride.

'He is from Jordan and lives in Cairo with his wife. She is a Dutch national who works at the Dutch embassy in downtown Cairo. Zurab is a qualified equestrian instructor who's been giving the grooms and Al Sorat Farm's regular clients' lessons to improve and polish their riding skills.'

Zurab arrives and sits down at the end of the table on my right. He is dark skinned with short black hair underneath a tan baseball cap He isn't a tall or broad man. However, he does have an athletic frame and is the perfect-size jockey for Maryanne's horses. He looks the part too in a red polo shirt, grey britches and long black riding boots. His English is excellent. Over breakfast, conversation falls onto horse riding in England. Zurab was once based on a country estate in the Home Counties. He praises the English equestrian scene for its facilities and competitions. He doesn't miss the inclement weather.

With breakfast finished, Maryanne and I collect our gear from the house and go back to the driveway where the horses are tacked up and ready. In advance of joining us for breakfast, Zurab had prepared the horse he will be riding. Hossam attaches my saddlebags to Jameela's saddle and holds her reins while I get on using the mounting block. I move Jameela close to where Zurab stands beside a grey Arab making final tack adjustments. When he's satisfied with his checks, he gets on the Arab from the ground. Zurab knows Maryanne's horses and comments: 'Jameela, she is beautiful.'

'Yes, she is beautiful.'

Maryanne is the last to get on her horse, Doobie the grey with the dark mane and tail. After mounting, she finalizes arrangements with Mohammed and two of the grooms. Mohammed and the grooms will drive the lunch provision for horses and riders to the villa, in Dahshur. Hassan is chatting to Tamer, a stocky oval-faced young man and another of Maryanne's grooms. They are on two bay, Arab horses. To my unfamiliar eye, the two bays look the same except for Hassan's horse has a red-bridle and Tamer's horse has a blue-bridle.

Happy and relaxed the ride sets off down the drive to the back gate. Maryanne and Zurab are side by side leading the way, Hassan and Tamer are together in the middle, and I'm at the rear. As we go by the cream villas and fields of Maryanne's neighbours the motor of a chainsaw and the subsequent noise of metal cutting through wood gets louder and louder. A trio of men are at work in the tunnel of trees, they have felled a tree which now blocks the lane. The instant the men notice the horses they silence the chainsaw. Maryanne talks to the men and then relays their instructions in English. We are to detour through the elaborate garden of the unseen villa. The road runs parallel to the villa's northeast boundary so riding through the garden will take us to a point not far from the junction on the canal road.

In the garden, an ornamental-stone path subtly arcs through a grove of tall green-leaf trees. The highest branches of the path-side trees reach to touch overhead, underneath everything is in dappled shade. I certainly feel privileged to be riding through this enchanting garden. The chainsaw starts up behind, but the noise gradually fades. Maryanne explains animals aren't usually allowed in the garden, so we're lucky to get permission to ride through. The mature trees clear to allow daylight to spill down onto a potting area of soil beds supplied by a variety of pots and a semi-coiled hose. The clearing looks like the kind of patch you will find at a nursery.

Leaving the garden, we emerge onto the canal road close to the concrete bridge. The clip-clop of the horses' hooves on the hard surface of the bridge makes our imminent arrival at a cluster of houses know to a trio of women who sit on a pale rug in the shade of a tree. They chat and supervise three young children playing close by. The women look to be three generations of the same family, daughter, mother, and grandmother. They all wear long black headscarves. The older women are in traditional dark abayas. The young mother wears a blue-and-green-striped loose shirt and navy trousers. Her children play in jeans or flower-pattered trousers and yellow and red long-sleeved cotton tops. The women smile and greet Maryanne in Arabic. The oldest child, a girl who looks to be six-years old, repeats 'Hello' several times. Her face lights up whenever I reciprocate the greeting.

Clear of the local village, the trail enters the familiar surroundings of dirt trackways crisscrossing the farmland and date-palm groves in the Abu Sir region. An area where there are lots of enjoyable canters and trots along the banks of irrigation canals. Soon after leaving the village, we encounter a considerable puddle engulfing the width of the path. The only way forward is through the puddle as there is a hole in the bank on the left and a high fence on the right. Doobie and Zurab's grey aren't keen on the idea of getting their hooves wet. It looks like Egyptian Arabs prefer the dry sand. Hassan is called forward on his bay, Wadi. Wadi is happy to take the lead through the unexpected obstacle and as herd animals, the rest follow in succession. I reckon Doobie became more concerned with his status as the lead horse as he miraculously forgot about his earlier resistance and splashed through the puddle without hesitation to get back to the front of the ride.

Beyond the fields behind the desert boundary, are the Abu Sir pyramids, elevated to dwarf the first band of dunes and the highest treetops growing on the farmland and in neighbourhood gardens. At the Abu Sir pyramids, the course remains southward riding close to the desert boundary through countryside no longer familiar. Not long after, another village is ridden through. The village is a settlement of two and three-floor houses assembled using handmade red bricks. Many of the houses are a pastel shade of paint. Windows either have panes or shutters. Roofs are flat. The houses are not in uniform linear rows; instead, the properties contour the dirt road as it snakes by garden walls, palm trees, and old sycamores. Women sit on the front steps watching their children play. Older women are in black sebleh and have long-black scarfs wrapped around their heads. The younger women and older children wear abayas: white, green or turquoise, plain or patterned. The boys play in t-shirts and three-quarter-length jeans, girls in floral-print summer dresses. Although this village is unfamiliar to me, I can sense we're still in Maryanne's local district by the manner she greets the women and children. A man, older than Hassan and Tamer is securing a tarpaulin onto the back of a flatbed vehicle parked at the roadside. Hassan and Tamer engage him in a brief conversation. I perceive the man is a familiar face to them. There is no other traffic in the village. As we pass, the children run at the rear of the ride for a few strides animatedly repeating, 'Hello.'

For an hour or so the trek rambles through subsequent villages and along quiet roads to traverse the fertile farmland close to the desert boundary. Houses in the villages are grey-stone or dry-mud painted either mustard, brown, turquoise or blue-grey. Doors are panel wood and painted light-green, white, yellow or orange; a few have patterns made from wire. Several houses have an overhanging upper floor; others have an entrance opening straight onto the street or have steps, the width of the façade, going up to the door. There are long one-level homes and three-storey homes where laundry drapes over the sides of the first and second-floor balconies. In the villages, women and children sit on rugs placed on the top step outside their front doors. There are more women in abayas, young girls in jeans and summer tops and boys in short-sleeved polo shirts and mud-splattered trousers.

Outside of the villages, the route takes us along canal paths shaded by tall palms and green-leaf trees. In places, palms growing on the banks extend over the canal to touch the other side. Away from the farmland the trees and grasses grow wild and dense and proffer cool patches of places to rest. Intermittently there are stone footbridges supported by bankside walls where the height and density of trees and bushes on the far bank virtually obscure the buildings further back. A pair of unattended water buffalo grazes lazily in a coppice of thick-trunk trees, relaxed and content in the natural sun shelter. It is incredibly peaceful by the canals, breezeless with just the clip-clop of horses' hooves and the tweets and chirps of the birds.

On the outskirts of a particular village is a cluster of dry-mud-wall animal shelters covered by roofs of dried leaves and twigs. The roofs may have recently received maintenance because there is material scattered on the road. Close to the shelters are a couple of stunted trees, which look like a bush stuck on a stick. Here the canal bank is fractured by diamond-shaped concrete structures protruding out into the water. Most of the diamonds are hollow in the centre, though a few are full of mud and bricks. Because there are no trees the yellowing grass is as trim as a newly cut lawn, there are spindly bushes, and plants are sparse of leaf all effects of the harsh sun.

It is past midday when the road emerges out of the trees and villages and into an expanded outlook close to the desert boundary. Just as my seat bones and legs begin to ache, the Bent Pyramid comes into view to distract me from the temporary discomfort. The pyramid is beyond the boundary of palm trees, behind the first ridge of dunes out in the desert. From here, the Bent Pyramid looks smooth-sided and its outer casing intact. The east side presents a pyramid vertex; however, at two-fifths down the angle steepens and thus gives the pyramid its bent form.

The Bent Pyramid does not stand alone in this locality. Its companion is the Pyramid of Amenemhat III, also known as the Black Pyramid. Unfortunately, the Black Pyramid has not fared well. It brings to mind a child's crude sand castle on a beach late in the day amid water rushing to reclaim the exposed wet sand as the tide comes in. The first of the waves have hit the sides, and the water gushes to encircle the base. Sides crumble, and the upper part collapses to leave a curvilinear nipple no longer in the same mould as the bulk of the sand sculpture.

The pyramids belong to the Dahshur group the most southern grouping in the pyramid fields from Giza to Dahshur. If you set a course to the Giza Plateau 20 m (32 km) in the north, keeping close to the desert border, you will happen by many pyramid complexes including the pyramids at Sakkara and Abu Sir. The belt of the desert from Dahshur to Giza is an extensive ancient burial ground of visible pyramid complexes and undiscovered secrets buried beneath the sand.

The presence of the Dahshur pyramids coupled with Jameela's quickened walk of her own accord makes me conclude the lunch destination is nearby.

There is an ample grove on the east side of the roadway with villas set back in a sea of palms ensconced in sunny plots. We take a left off the road onto a track going up through the grove that provides access to two of these homes.

The horses are brought to a halt at the back of a two-story villa with dark-wood arched-framed windows, shutters and doors, and washed with Persian-orange. Mohammed's car is parked outside, and Mohammed and the grooms are there to greet us. Amongst the exchanges of Arabic and action of five riders dismounting, Jameela is led away down the north side of the villa by a non-riding groom. Maryanne suggests I go inside and make myself comfortable and directs me to the bathroom and then the balcony on the first floor where we're to eat lunch. The villa belongs to an expat American friend of Maryanne's and is primarily used for a weekend residence as its owner is an academic who works and lives in Cairo during the week. On entering the villa, Maryanne and Mohammed peel off into an open-plan kitchen where they stand at a central kitchen island and unpack the generous supplies Mohammed has transferred from Al Sorat Farm. I take the stairs beside the back wall of the villa up to the first floor where I find a sitting room beautifully furnished with colourful cushions and decent-sized rugs. Stone archways fitted with wooden doors lead to elsewhere in the villa. My mind leaps back to yesterday because the villa's architecture makes it a perfect location to display the arts and crafts I'd seen at the Ramses Wissa Wassef Art Centre in Harrania Village.

After the Giza plateau yesterday, another stop preceded lunch. At Maryanne's request, Magdy took me to the Wissa Wassef Art Centre. The founder of the arts centre was a local architect called Ramses Wissa Wassef, who in the 1940s helped local children possessing no previous skills or education to master a craft and develop into professional weavers. An ongoing project was initiated based on Ramses Wissa Wassef's philosophy of if given the tools and opportunity children can tap into an abundance of inner creativity to produce outstanding arts and crafts with little or no assistance from an adult. To start the project was set up in the Wissa Wassef family home. Then in the early 1950s, the land for the arts centre was purchased. When the project moved to the new premises in Harrania Village the original set of children, now older, became the teachers, and the children from Harrania Village joined the project.

It had gone past 1:00 pm when the MPV rolled to a standstill outside the arts centre's east-perimeter wall close to the main gate. Our driver had selected a spot underneath the overhanging branches of trees growing behind a high stone wall. I stepped out of the MPV, into an ambiance of quiet and rest, a far cry from the coach loads of tourists and peddlers back at the Giza plateau. At the arts centre, the chirps of the pocket-size birds produce the bustle as they went about their business. Then the sweet chirps were temporarily drowned out by the barks of two pint-sized brown mixed-breed dogs. The dogs were just inside the gate on the left bouncing to and fro in an exercise run, which forms part of a kennel enclosure. Magdy strode happily by knowing the dogs could not get to him. Friendly wagging tails and excited dog faces soon settled.

We'd entered a garden where stone paths lined by wooden benches wend around raised beds planted with shrubs, palms and spindly trees. On both sides of the entrance gate were partly- hidden-by-foliage clusters of single-level buildings shaped by smooth-stone walls with either a flat or domed roof and featuring a mixture of arched or rectangular windows and doors. Up in front was the Wissa Wassef family home: A grand villa built using a darker-tint of sandstone in comparison to the other buildings and characterized by a partly-domed roof, balconies, verandas, and wooden window frames and shutters. Alongside the villa were shrubs, flower beds, and potted cacti and plants.

At the villa, we'd turned right to arrive at the entrance of a single-level building where we'd entered a long windowless gallery fashioned by a curved ceiling and alcoves. Thick stone walls kept the room cool. Lights installed lengthwise in the apex of the ceiling supplied illumination. It is the tapestry and batik gallery and as the name suggests is where the tapestry and batik pieces decorate whitewashed walls. At the end of the gallery was an archway leading through to another exhibition room. An Egyptian man, about the same age as Magdy, yet taller, broader and unable to hide a rotund belly beneath his shirt, was stood talking to a grey-haired middle-aged European couple. I couldn't hear what they said for they were using hushed voices, but I got the inclination the couple was soon to depart. As the couple left the room, Magdy and the Egyptian man exchanged greetings in a manner implying familiarity. I said, 'Hello' and then took myself off for a tour of the tapestries while they remained at the entrance and conversed. Many of the exhibits on display used the local villages and countryside for inspiration. There were depictions of houses, trees and mosques, and factions of villagers and marketplaces. The countryside landscapes included farmers escorting their cattle and goats amid canals, palm trees, cacti, and desert. There were also pictures of wild birds and fish. The detail of the pictures and patterns were brought to life by the use of dyed natural materials to produce several shades of green, blue, red, yellow, pink, brown and cream. Each thread is expertly woven. The result: a beautiful and vibrant piece of artwork.

When I returned to the entrance, Magdy finished his conversation. We left the Egyptian man behind and went back outside and entered a modest courtyard that gives access to a spacious workshop where the stoneware gets produced. The interior walls of the workshop were high and had curved recesses. Daylight spilled in from windows set into all four walls. At the front of the workshop was shelves adorned by neat rows of completed pieces of glazed vases and jugs in a variety of shapes, sizes, and colours: patterned, two tones, pale green, cream or dark blue. In the middle and at the back of the workshop were a mix of stone and wood workbenches. Unglazed pots waited on the surface of the benches ready for a decorative design or stain to be added. To the contrary of order and stillness dust floated in the shafts of light.

Back outside, we ventured deeper into the cluster using a passageway and more courtyards. As we moved through the cluster of buildings, it became apparent the workshops are where all the exhibits get created. Magdy halted outside a closed door, knocked twice then opened it wide enough to put his head around. Words were exchanged, with the occupant thereon the door was opened wider and he signalled for me to stand beside him inside the doorway. Sat on the floor and working a broad wooden loom was a young teenage girl. A long scarf was draped around her head and shoulders and cascaded down her colourful abaya. She greeted me with a warm, shy smile and turned back to her work. The workshop was modest and airy. Daylight flooded in through the windows set in the back wall. A rotating standing fan and thick stone walls ensured the room remained cool. The girl skilfully threaded the strands of wool through the strings on the loom using her fingers and a hand tool. The frame clanks to signal the completion of a line. I briefly pondered on this way of life as it no longer exists in my society back home – a non-mechanicalized industry sent off to the museums and historical archives before I was born. Whereas here it is a way of life and a lifeline for the girl and her family. Magdy and I thanked the girl for letting us encroach on her day's work. After we left, Magdy dutifully closed the door behind us.

Aside from being smaller the weekend villa at Dahshur has the same architecture to the Wissa Wassef-family villa. The sitting room has access to the southeast corner terrace, furnished by a glass-top wicker table and matching faded-viridian wicker chairs seating up to seven people. At the back are wood-slat cabinets and a wooden staircase going up to the roof. A wall supports an upper layer of thin-wood post and rails to form the balcony's south and west side. Down below amongst the palm trees is the track we'd ridden down and a neighbouring villa flaunting manicured lawns flooded in sunlight. Closer still, and to my delight is Jameela. The groom has tethered her to a palm with a thin trunk close to the house. Untacked and secured using a blue headcollar and lead rope she is being hosed down. The groom takes the hose away and comes back carrying an armful of green leaves for her to eat. Jameela is in the front garden an allotment of sand for soil and tall palm trees. Five of these trees have a horse tethered to the trunk. The palms yield enough shade for the horses to cool down and relax.

After the horses have been hosed-down, fed and watered, Maryanne, Zurab, and Mohammed join me on the balcony. They have come laden with freshly prepared food from the Al Sorat kitchen. Mohammed goes back downstairs and joins the grooms who stay with the horses. Maryanne, Zurab and I sit down and feast on a delicious lunch.

An hour later everything is packed-up and in Mohammed's car. The villa is left neat and tidy – the same as how we found it. We're on the horses going back through the palm grove. At the road, our troop turns to the south for a few minutes keeping the palm grove and villas on the left, east side. Dahshur Lake is in the foreground, and the pyramids and desert are the backdrops. The area oozes tranquillity. A shallow canal runs alongside the road. A green carpet of wild grass and shrubland spans out to meet the first low-lying ridges of dunes. Behind these ridges is the Bent Pyramid, and the Black Pyramid set against the clear blue sky. On the south side of the Bent Pyramid is a satellite pyramid a fraction of the size of its neighbour. Set back in the desert to the northeast of the Black Pyramid is the perfectly-formed Red Pyramid, its base tucked out of sight behind another ridge of dunes.

Our return journey northward begins at the southeast corner of Dahshur Lake where a narrow bridge of stone straddles the canal and deposits us onto a track overshadowed by an alignment of tall green-leaf trees on the south side of the lake. The lake splits the dunes from the fertile valley giving it the appearance of an oasis. Today, the lake is scaled down to a river meandering through grassland where six donkeys graze on a patch as slick as a golf-course green. A small herd of white sheep lazes in the shade close to the bridge, several have a black face or have black spots on their coats. The perimeter is a mixture of thickets of wild shrubs and tall trees cloaking everything underneath in shadow. Maryanne informs us every autumn the lake is flooded using the water from a canal connected to the River Nile. As this is the first week of November, she wonders why it hasn't happened yet.

On reaching the desert side of the lake, our course bends northwards through a sprawl of long coarse grasses, and thereupon the plant life ends. The terrain rises onto a plateau and leaves nothing but the crowns of palm trees in the grove visible. The direction is forward to the Black Pyramid, and the pull of the desert takes my attention away from the countryside. At the closest point, Maryanne announces the Black Pyramid belonged to Amenemhat III, a twelfth dynasty Middle Kingdom pharaoh who is estimated to have reigned between 1818-1770 BCE. I've already had an introduction to Amenemhat III, for Magdy and I discussed his blighted pyramid on Wednesday morning at the Egyptian Museum.

After we'd passed the picture of the Rosetta Stone in the Egyptian Museum's entrance hall, I found myself at the top of a staircase looking down through a cavernous gallery of exhibits. It is a long room with a three-level-high ceiling. Monumental stone pillars support a second level balcony, which encircles the perimeter of a central atrium. Multiple skylights and windows contributed to the light required to illuminate the immense space. At the back of the atrium, raised on a platform were the colossal statues of Amenhotep III and his favoured wife, Tiye, seated side-by-side on thrones. The height of the statues reached to just below the balcony. I'd questioned, 'How did they get the statues into the museum?'

'I don't know.'

The exhibits are Magdy's area of expertise and not the engineering techniques used to move monumental objects. The zone connecting the statues and the staircase in the entrance hall displays statues, sarcophagus and pyramid capstones raised on wooden or stone plinths of various sizes. A capstone of a pyramid is called a pyramidion, and it was a particular pyramidion that Magdy had singled out to be the first exhibit he wanted to show me amongst the thousands on display. In the thick of tourists, we descended the steps, ignored the first band of exhibits and came to a standstill at a central plinth supporting a black pyramidion. The sides of the pyramidion were as smooth as marble where there was no damage. Magdy informed me the material used was granite. There were ancient inscriptions carved on all four sides. Magdy pointed to the hieroglyphs that identify who the pyramidion belonged to Amenemhat III. Although it was unearthed close to Amenemhat III's Black Pyramid in Dahshur, there is no proof it ever crowned the ruined pyramid. Experts can only speculate this based on its proximity to the pyramid when found.

In this spot beside the Black Pyramid, only the Bent Pyramid is in sight due to the rise and fall of the dune system obscuring the other pyramids. From this angle, there is the illusion the Bent Pyramid is the perfect shape, as nothing but the vertex is visible protruding up from behind a raised gradient. This illusion shatters when the first clear view of the Red Pyramid materializes. In the distance to the north and secluded by an expanse of mounds and rolling dunes, the Red Pyramid is flawless. Two sides are in sight: the shaded east-face and the red-tinged south face. The pyramid is so beautiful my eyes are only averted away from it when our direction briefly diverts westwards to allow for a closer look at the Bent Pyramid.

The Bent Pyramid belonged to Sneferu, the first king of the Old Kingdom's fourth dynasty, who is believed to have reigned between 2575-2465 BCE. Sneferu is understood to be the father of Khufu, the owner of the Great Pyramid at Giza. There are theories on how the pyramid became to be bent. The most common theory is Sneferu's death was imminent so the design was changed to a steeper angle so the project wouldn't take as long to complete. Essentially, this theory says it was a rush job. From closer proximity, the full shape of the Bent Pyramid and its abrupt change in angle is clear to see against the blue sky. The satellite-pyramid is also misshapen as it no longer has a capstone and all that is left is a level surface.

With the sun on its descent in the west long shadows of horses and riders are cast onto the ground. Our visit to Dahshur is drawing to an end. Ten minutes on from the Bent Pyramid, we're at the closest point of the ride to the Red Pyramid. Also, built by Sneferu, the Red Pyramid is known to be the first true pyramid to be successfully symmetrical and was the 'blueprint' for the pyramids at Giza. This pyramid is my favourite. As we ride away from the Red Pyramid, there are just over two hours until sunset. The dwindling daylight changes the tone of the Red Pyramid every time I turn back to snatch another look.

Suddenly, I find myself following my fellow riders over a railway track. To me, the rails are a strange sight as I'm used to railway tracks on high and stony embankments protected by fences, walls or dense thickets of holly and brambles. This railway line comes out of the countryside and continues out to the western horizon in a straight line. There's a section of infrastructure further out in the desert where the middle of a substantial dune has been cut out to allow the rails to run through. It is the Cairo to Fayoum railway line; a useful marker in the sand to tell me we're leaving the district of Dahshur and the southern pyramid group.

With the countryside on the eastern flank and the expanse of the Sahara to the west, the return journey takes us up and down dunes where there are many opportunities for a short gallop. Trot is exercised to cover the long flat-bottom valleys and gravel plains where a shimmer of white haze decorates the horizon and disconnects the sand and vast blue sky. The only sounds come from the occasional conversation of the riders and hooves clinking against pieces of stone.

On the descent of a steep dune, Maryanne halts the ride midway. In front of us is a level-bottom valley with another steep-sided dune on the far side. There is a thin trackway running sideways up the dune to reach the brow. 'We will gallop across the valley and up to the top of the hill. Make sure you go up the hill in single file.'

Primarily this brief is for Zurab, Hassan and Tamer. As afterward, she looks directly at me and in a quieter voice and accompanying smile, she concludes: 'I don't see this being a problem for Jameela.'

At the bottom of the dune, Maryanne checks everyone is ready, and thereupon the Arabs fly. Jameela waits for my signal and then takes off in pursuit. Because I'm straggling behind, I get to watch, Maryanne and the boys make their transition from the valley to the side of the dune. Maryanne is in the lead as Doobie ensures his lead-horse status remains intact. The boys arrive at the foot of the hill together and quickly sort themselves into a single file. There is a clear run up the side of the hill when Jameela and I reach the bottom.

Since we left Dahshur, there have been occasional glimpses of the Sakkara pyramids out on the horizon. For the most part, this is the upper layers of the Step Pyramid easily visible in the course of riding on a ridge or across a plateau. With every elapsed minute, the Sakkara pyramids get closer and heighten. It is coming up to 4:30 pm when the trek reaches Sakkara South. There is a ride-by the most southerly Sakkara pyramid to mark our arrival. On a higher gradient than where we are, the pyramid is compact, rough-sided and decayed. Its upper part precariously holds on to a pyramid form its bottom is squared. At the base are scattered pieces of stone and derelict ancient walls. In places, the wind had blown sand to create drifts against the side of the pyramid and walls; a sign of how easy it would be for this invisible force of nature to rebury the lower structures. What we see today is presumably the work of the archaeologists who conserve this once buried and forgotten pyramid complex. Maryanne calls back, 'The pyramid of Pepi II.'

Pepi II was a sixth dynasty king (c. 2325-c2150 BCE) of the Old Kingdom.

Further, into the Sakkara grouping, there are three pyramids, smaller-scale and tumbled-down. These pyramids are overshadowed by another, which commands the skyline and draws your attention away. We are back in the realm of the Step Pyramid.

I'm back in familiar territory on the north side of the Step Pyramid complex, and it's not long until the first and last pyramids of today's ride, the Abu Sir grouping, is in sight. Shadows of horses, riders, and plants grow longer. The horses are still willing when asked to canter on the planar of sand linking the soaring Abu Sir pyramids and the desert fence. For a short time, the route stays close to the fence line with a slight deviation to go around a gang of 12 boys, aged between eight years to young teen. They have entered the desert through a gap in the fence and have set up a mini-football pitch on a piece of level ground. There is the standard childhood improvisation of jumpers for goalposts, and they have organized themselves into teams. I'm not sure if there is a referee, but the boys politely stop their game until the horses have gone by.

Before we reach the desert gate, there is another detour back into the desert. There's to be a final gallop of the day, and the location is the 'runway.'

This time I ask Jameela to go on the tails of the other horses. She is ready and willing and takes off in close pursuit. There is no thump of the heart today. I relish every second as this wonderful horse keeps up with the other horses all the way up the hill. It must be the best place in the world for a gallop. When I reach the end and halt, Maryanne smiles: 'Not so far behind this time huh.'

She knows her horse, and she knows I've been asking Jameela to take it steady while I re-oiled my rusty gallop skills.

The Sarcophagus and the Felucca

It's late afternoon on the day after the ride to Dahshur. I'm sitting at the table in Maryanne's living room with Pippin, the one-eyed rat terrier on my lap. Maryanne stands by her desk in front of the open doorway. We're watching Nadim, Magda's toddler, practice standing and walking. Whenever he momentarily wobbles he uses one of the taller dogs as an aide to balance himself. Nadim is adorable with thick black curly hair and large brown eyes. Maryanne tells me that Magda doesn't earn enough money to purchase baby formula, so she had paid for all the baby formula for Nadim. Children born to poor parents get fed what the rest of the family eat. The consequence is they miss out on the valuable nutrients needed for brain development. Magda wasn't working for Maryanne when she had her older child, and this child missed out on the formula at the early development stage. Maryanne's determination to get Nadim the best start in life is evident. Though he isn't talking yet, Maryanne speaks to him using English and Arabic. Showing great affection for the toddler Maryanne forewarns: 'When that kid starts talking, he isn't going to shut up. He is going to drive us nuts.'

She repeats the sentence to Nadim. Magda comes through the swing doors of the kitchen simultaneously to, Mohammed entering the room through the outside doorway. As they discuss Al Sorat business with Maryanne, I relax in the chair and think back on the events that happened earlier today.

This morning, on the drive from the Sakkara County Club to Al Sorat Farm, Maryanne delivered the sad news that the little grey donkey had not made it through the second night. She had lost her fight against tetanus. Upset by this development, Maryanne had described how the grooms found the dead donkey and their journey at first light when they had transported her corpse into the desert and buried her. I'd tried to administer comfort by saying at least the donkey was comfortable in her final hours relishing regular meals and afforded the opportunity for a night raid on a well-stocked vegetable patch.

My ultimate ride had a late start, and it was close to 11:00 am when I got on Jameela. Our constant riding companion, Hassan wasn't riding today. Instead, Maryanne and I were accompanied by Walid, who kind of drew the short straw for this week's share of the riding. A consequence of the long ride to Dahshur yesterday is my riding muscles are tired and sore. Therefore, we had mostly walked with a few trots only. Considering, all the exciting gallops Hassan had enjoyed throughout my stay, now it was Walid's turn he had to escort a close-to-broken rider. Maryanne made me feel better by confirming she felt sore from yesterday's ride too. In spite of riding most days, it had been many months since she had ridden down to the lake at Dahshur.

Jameela was impeccably behaved, as always throughout the ride. Nazeer, Maryanne's chestnut Arab, wanted to run and where he felt was a suitable hill, he held a beautiful outline with his muscles flexed ready to take off at speed. As for Lily, the bay Arab expertly ridden by Walid, Maryanne said it was a good lesson for her to complete a slow desert ride.

Though sore and mostly at a walk, we made it to the northern edge of the Dahshur district and back again. The destination was a red sarcophagus Maryanne found a few years back not far from the section of railway crossed yesterday. Aware it was my final ride in the desert on the beautiful Jameela, I'd entered determined to soak up the scenery and ignore my aching muscles. My pleasure was supported by another perfect day for riding out, uninterrupted blue sky and an ever-present breeze. The route was similar to the inbound trail ridden yesterday, close to the west sides of the Abu Sir, Sakkara, and Sakkara South pyramid complexes. There was a second opportunity to get close to the pyramid complex of Pepi II. This morning, we'd arrived from the opposite direction. From this approach, the pyramid looked bigger and had a more distinctive pyramid look. Continuing on we again crossed the railway line. Today, I'd noticed the sand and stones encompassing the tracks were stained black and grey. Situated at the base of a minor dune not far from the railway was the sarcophagus. Though intact, the sarcophagus is lidless, and whatever colour it may have been had faded to match the sand. It was also on its side so the hollow middle faced forward and the bottom was the back. Maryanne must have been in full exploratory mode when she found the sarcophagus seeing it's in an area of shallow dunes and therefore not an object you can spot from a distance.

On the return leg, there was a wide berth away from a steep-sided dune with an occupied watchman's hut sited at the top. The hut is square with no distinguishing features except for a flat roof. I have no idea what the men are watching for out here. Maryanne preferred to steer clear of the hut and by doing so our presence upset a wild dog. Light-tan and the size of a terrier, she guarded a hole dug into the side of the dune and barked at us with intent. Maryanne suspected there were puppies in her den. Not wanting to upset her more the horses were steered by at a distance.

After three hours of riding, we arrived back at Al Sorat Farm. I dismounted from Jameela and gave her lots of pats. She has been the perfect horse for me to ride on this trip. Jameela is and always will be a horse I could quite happily take home. Be that as it may, she wouldn't flourish in the climate. It would be too cold and wet for this desert dwelling steed.

Back in the living room at Al Sorat, I say goodbye to Mohammed and Magda, and thank them for their warmth and assistance. To compensate for the language barrier, I express the words in a way to mirror the warmth and friendliness they have shown me throughout my visit. The food Magda prepared was always well presented, fresh and delicious. Throughout the week Mohammed had shared the task of collecting and dropping me back to the Sakkara Country Club with Maryanne. Having completed their day's work, Magda scoops up Nadim from the floor, and the three of them depart through the doorway and down the steps towards the aviary.

When we'd returned from the final ride, Maryanne and I had showered and changed clothes ready for a trip to Maadi, one of Cairo's eleven suburbs. Maryanne has booked a Felucca (an Egyptian sailboat) for an hour at dusk to watch the sun go down on the River Nile. Before we leave, Maryanne makes a pizza and beer order using the telephone on her desk. We will collect the order in Maadi on the way to the Felucca jetty.

I have gained many memories this week that I know will always bring a smile to my face on recall. Because I have felt so at home here, it feels a strange concept to be walking down the house steps, pass the aviary and through the garden gate for the last time. As we get into Maryanne's car, a groom who is yet to leave for home opens the gate. The car pulls out onto the track where the little grey donkey received her initial treatment and takes a right onto the lane leading to the Sakkara Tourist Road. Earlier today Maryanne and I discussed the possibility of a revisit. Al Sorat Farm is a special place and I know

I'm always welcome, nevertheless and in Maryanne's own words: 'I guess there are too many other places to see.'

She is a wise woman who not only knows her employees, and animals, she understands her guests too.

The sun had dropped beneath the horizon as I follow Maryanne down the wooden jetty to where three feluccas are moored together port side. Maryanne apologized for having to watch sundown from the car on the ring road coming into Maadi. I reassured her the delay wasn't a disappointment for me, for she cannot control the traffic. It was not the first time in my life congested traffic caused me to be late and nor will it be the last. Traffic delay is part of modern day life, and you have to stay relaxed about it. At the beginning of the journey, we'd made good progress through the countryside. It was on joining the main flow travelling into the city centre when the traffic slowed to a sustained crawl all the way into Maadi. Because every lane was bumper to bumper and moved no quicker than 5 miles (8 km) an hour, all the exertion came from the un-harmonious peeps and honks of many horns surpassing the hum of engines. Much the same as my previous experience of being stuck in Cairo traffic, vehicles had appeared from and disappeared in every direction managed by limited traffic lights and scarcely any signs to guide drivers and navigators. Amid this exhibit of Cairo's traffic chaos, Maryanne informed me world experts had carried out various studies on how to improve this modern-day problem, and still, no person has identified a better solution than: 'Cairo traffic manages itself, and somehow most of the time it works.'

Situated on the River Nile's east bank, Maadi is a suburb comprising of skyscrapers, offices, shops, cafes, and residential streets. So, another somehow is the availability of a kerbside parking space outside the pizza shop and another close to the felucca jetty. Out of the car, on foot, there is an advantage of crawling traffic. Though a little deafening, the stationary bumpers make it easy to cross the road next to the river.

At the bottom of the jetty, the noise of the traffic fades away. We swiftly board the first felucca and cross its deck to board the second and then board our vessel moored up alongside. The captain, a young Egyptian man in his early twenties and sole sailor, prepares the boat and casts off. The felucca is a wooden sailboat the size of a sailing yacht characterized by a spacious passenger deck. Taking up most of the deck is a fixed broad-wooden table painted pale blue. Surrounding the table are upholstered cushioned seats in striped or floral patterns and shades of brown and cream. A frame encloses the passenger deck. Maybe the frame is there to attach a tarpaulin as a sunshade or a makeshift-sleeping quarter for people who want to venture away from the city on an overnight river tour.

Maryanne and I stand on the starboard side of the deck taking in the panorama view. The Nile's rippled surface mirrors the sky: dusky-shades of grey and dark blue encased in an orange hue, the remnant of the today's sunlight. Across the expanse of water is the less urbanized west bank where there are patches of silhouetted trees. Where there are clusters of buildings, the dwellings are just low-rises made know by interior lights. With the felucca slowly gliding out into the river comes a better view of the east bank. The taller buildings of Maadi begin to lose detail and glass panes, balconies and stone morph into silhouettes against the close-to black sky. The suburb lights reflect on the surface of the river as twinkling strips of white, blue, green and orange. What is incredible is the felucca remains close to the main thoroughfare alongside the east bank, and I can't hear any of the mayhem we just weaved through. Out on the majestic Nile, the din of the city is replaced by the lap of water against the hull and the occasional tug of rope by the quiet and discreet captain as he steers his course.

The River Nile flows northwards to reach the Mediterranean Sea. Boats heading downstream get propelled by the current. To go upstream sails are hoisted to catch the southerly wind which powers the boat against the current. Right now, the sail is down leaving the felucca to float downstream drifting silently on the slow current. After dusk becomes night a felucca in full sail, glides swiftly by, propelled by the southerly wind. Hardly visible and noiseless this felucca looks like an apparition against the night sky. Its silhouette reminds me of the yachts back home where white sails are a common feature out on the edge of the bay throughout the summer months, especially on clear and breezy days. More feluccas glide by. This section of the Nile is wide, so there is plenty of water between us. Absorbed by the calmness out on the river, Maryanne and I sit back on the cushion seats, eat pizza and drink a can of beer each. She reminisces about the years her family lived in Maadi as it is here where her children had grown up. When her daughter was old enough to go out on her own, she and a gang of friends would hire a felucca and spend an hour or more at the weekend relaxing and gossiping on the cushion seats.

I don't wear a watch, and on holiday I don't give much attention to the clock on my mobile phone. In general, I have a good perception of how much time elapses without the need of a device. I know the sail on the felucca takes an hour, and I estimate our drift downstream to have been about 45 minutes. I raise this with Maryanne, 'How is the felucca going to get back to the jetty in 15 minutes when it's taken 45 to get here?'

'Ah, wait and see.'

As if on cue the captain starts to move about on the gunwale, he hoists the sail and turns the felucca around. The moment the boat faces upstream the sail catches the wind, and we go from a slow-leisurely drift to speed with a purpose. Water splashes against the bow and gentle waves cascade out from behind as the felucca rapidly glides upstream.

It's magical being out on the Nile at night with reflections of the city lights dancing on the water, the wind in the sail, and the sound of water splashing against the felucca. All too soon the captain drops the sail and expertly docks the felucca without even the slightest bump. I thank Maryanne for the perfect end to an unforgettable week. After traversing the moored feluccas onto the jetty, we walk back into the noise and mayhem of the busy Maadi streets. Maryanne knows of a nearby coffee shop that serves a delicious chocolate cake.

Part 3

Twenty-seven Miles Southwest

Wheal Buller Riding School

The county of Cornwall has wallowed in a couple of months blessed by plenty of sunshine and warm days to get outside and appreciate the beautiful and rugged landscape. I know this because Cornwall, the most south-west peninsula of the UK mainland is where I live. Yesterday was Saturday and the last day of August. Last night, I'd closed my bedroom window for the first time in the evening since June. In contrast to the warm summer evenings of July and August, the drop-in temperature after the sun went down had been low enough to leave a chill in the air. It was the first sign of the seasons on the change.

An hour ago, I left home and drove southwest bound on B-roads until joining the A30 dual carriageway, the main artery of Cornwall. I exited the A30 when it reached the outskirts of Redruth. There I'd taken the slip road and proceeded southwards through the town and out into the country lanes of Bucketts Hill and Buller Hill to arrive at my destination: Wheal Buller Riding School where I will be spending the next five days. Wheal Buller Riding School is at most 1.5 miles (2.4 km) south of the centre of the town of Redruth – a commercial town with a population of approximately 12,500. The settlement of Redruth is in a part of Cornwall historically known to have expanded because of the mining of copper ore in the 18th century.

Indicating right, I steer my red Toyota Yaris of the carriageway on Buller Hill where sizeable signs announce you have arrived at the riding school. The car judders over a cattle grid onto a single-lane track going north-eastwards until rounding a bend to face the southwest. On the left, after the bend is a high grass bank. Behind the bank is the post-and-rail long side of an outdoor arena, set up with brightly-painted show jumps. On the right, a rustic two-plank fence bounds a large grazing field where I count four cross country jumps. The field descends to further fields rolling out to the northwest. Thick high hedges border fields in a landscape of telegraph poles, hamlets, and white farmhouses interspersed with derelict engine house chimneys – relics from Cornwall's 18th century past. In the background is a township and I conclude it is the community of Pool. Roughly 4 miles (6 km) on from Pool, as the crow flies, is the coastal town of Portreath and a glimpse of the Celtic Sea.

At the gate end of the arena, I pull up aside four cars parked in a slapdash row in front of another high bank with a field over its crest. It's 1:00 pm, my expected time of arrival. Continuing on foot, it feels strange to be in jeans again having spent the last couple of months wearing shorts and summer dresses. Yesterday evening's chill had persuaded me to ditch the shorts and pack jeans. I will wear jodhpurs in the daytime, so now the evenings are cooler, I believe jeans will serve me well. Thankfully, t-shirt weather still prevails in the middle of the day, and I'm appreciative of the additional warmth when the sun pops out from behind a white cloud that had drifted to block out its rays. The track continues by a pale-grey modern detached house with a porch. There is the distant noise of cars passing back on Buller Hill. Songbirds tweet in the hedgerows and the whirl of a mower carries across the valley on the breeze.

After the house is a pair of attached stables constructed from corrugated metal, cream-painted concrete and wood-plank bottom doors. Suddenly a clamour of eight children scurries out from a dark-wood cabin up ahead on the right. They go across the track to sit on a long bench in front of a cream-painted outbuilding. The rabble is a mixture of boys and girls whose age range from eight-years-old to early teens. In an array of colourful jodhpurs and t-shirts, there is chatter and jostling as they settle down on the bench to consult and discuss the contents displayed on their tablets and mobile phones. Despite the peacefulness of the afternoon being interrupted, I can't help but smile and recollect when I was their age and the long summer holidays spent at my childhood riding school. My riding buddies were roughly the age of what they are now; though, back then there weren't any tablets, mobile phones or Wi-Fi.

A trim lady of early middle age with short hair wearing riding clothes rounds the corner of the building where the children sit. 'Hello, I'm Rachel. I'm staying here until Friday. I was told to arrive at one.'

148

She amicably replies, 'Hello, I'm Linda. I'll grab the paperwork you need to complete and take you to your accommodation. Have you come far?'

I reply as I accompany Linda back to where she had just come. The cream-painted building is the yard office. Inside there is a computer on a desk and pigeon holes containing an assortment of forms. Though it is a cramped space with just enough room for two people to work in, it keeps all the administration requirements to organize a riding school. Thus ensuring the strict rules and regulations enforced and inspected in the UK are adhered. Linda picks up a pen from the desk and takes the required form from a pigeonhole. We leave the office and enter the main yard where a perimeter of stables, outbuildings, and accommodation surrounds a grooved, and immaculately-swept concrete quadrangle.

The office is in the north corner at the lower end. At the lower end, situated north to south is a block of six concrete stables painted cream with wood plank bottom doors and bridle hooks and tie rings fixed to the wall. On the opposite side are a confined outbuilding and a parked horse lorry set apart by a gap wide enough for a horse to walk through. Next to the lorry is a static caravan, then a grey one-level building with a flat roof, generous windows and a post-and-rail fence alongside a concrete ramp going up to the door. On the office side of the yard, and where we pass, is a standalone metal-panel outbuilding displaying a selection of girths and numnahs draped on the uppermost planks of a two-part fence outside the open doorway; these items have been left to dry out in the sun.

Our destination is a bungalow at the higher eastern end of the yard. The walls are granite, windows double glazed, there is a tiled pitched roof, and a central gable-roof porch. From its raised setting on a granite veranda enclosed by a rustic wood fence, the bungalow overlooks the setting. On the north side of the yard, partly behind the metal-panel outbuilding is another block of eight stables. The stables match the lower block with an added feature: top doors secured to the wall by hooks. Not quite in the centre, yet away from any of the buildings is a stepped mounting block. Because the mounting block has been set against the slant of the yard the height varies depending on what side you stand. As we take a direct route between the stables and the mounting block, Linda reveals another guest is booked to stay for the week. A lady from the Greater London area, who has already arrived.

To the right of the bungalow's porch is a gap in the fence where uneven horizontal stones make steps up onto the veranda. Yard level, at the side of the steps, is a strip of mowed grass where a large piece of granite has been set down at the edge; perhaps an alternative mounting block for use when the yard is busy. Beside the stone is a dark-wood rail the height of a car bonnet possibly used as a temporary saddle rack. On the way up the steps onto the veranda, I receive more instructions, 'Cars aren't allowed on the yard. You can park your car here to unload your things. Then you will need to take it back to the carpark.'

In the interior of the porch is a white-PVC framed door (more pane than plastic) that opens into a sizable sitting room with framed pictures hanging on mustard-colour walls, and brown-leather sofas and matching chairs shaping a semi-circle completed by a cabinet supporting a flat-screen television. Central to the furniture is a sturdy wooden coffee table with piles of magazines and books on a bottom shelf. In the back corners are interior doors. In the right-front corner are a dining table and four high-backed wood chairs. A wood cardholder containing locally-made postcards is on top of a draped tablecloth. Each postcard is made up of a photo taken of a resident horse or pony. Treading on a circular pattern brown carpet, I follow Linda through the doorway in the back-right corner into a hallway where there are two closed doors on the left and right and another at the end. The first door on the left is pushed open, 'This is your room.'

After a quick peek, Linda closes the door, and we move on. The next door along is a PVC framed glass-panelled door that takes us back outside.

At the back of the bungalow is an enclosed barbeque area of terracotta and cream chequer flagstones set out with white-plastic garden tables and chairs beneath a Perspex roof. An ornamental wall and trellis separate the barbeque area from the garden where there are more white-plastic garden sets placed on a raised deck also furnished by a covered hot tub, rotating clothesline, a shed the size of a summer house and planters full of flowers at the base of the bordering Cornish hedge. A row of tall conifers at the southern end of the garden provides shelter and privacy.

Sat chatting merrily around the closest table on the deck are two men and a woman, they all look to be in their younger years of middle-age. Linda and I go up some steps to join them. We exchange greetings and names, and I learn from the trio, who travelled down from the London area this morning, that it is solely Jill who is staying at Wheal Buller. The men will leave soon to embark on a week of driving around Cornwall to visit old haunts from a holiday taken in their youth. Dressed in branded surf tops and baggy jeans and touring in a camper van, they are certainly going to fit in with a proportion of the locals. Their voices are slightly jaded as a result of an early start and a long car journey. But having arrived at their destination, and at the start of their holiday, they are eager to get going. Jill too is dressed ready for her holiday in a short-sleeve sports top and jeans. Her loose long straight hair is the palest blonde; also, apt for the Cornish surf lifestyle. Revealing a slightly nervy character on meeting someone new, she mentions this is her fourth holiday at Wheal Buller. Good to hear. Repeat visitors are always a good sign of a well-run holiday.

Turning away from the deck, Linda concludes my tour at the back of the bungalow in a white PVC conservatory accessed from the garden by the use of a passageway. The conservatory is where Jill and I will have our meals. It is a light and airy room with a wood-pattern lino floor and walls painted light-grey and magnolia. Everything else is white: fittings, shelves, plates, bowls, and mugs. There are curvy-chrome chairs neatly arranged around two circular tables set with patterned easy-to-wipe covers. In the back-right corner is a fridge supporting two drinks machines that make continual whirling noises as one mixes orange juice, the other chilled water. At the fridge-end, another exterior door provides access to a concise courtyard monopolized by a long picnic table. This door remains closed as our attention shifts to the contents of the fridge. Amongst the many items, there is yoghurt, cheese, and milk. The fridge door is closed, and Linda points to the relevant shelf or container: 'There are biscuits, cereal, bread, and crumpets. Please help yourself. Breakfast is self-serve, and Terry will prepare your evening meal. Let Terry know later if you require anything specific.'

It is time for me to collect my car, unpack and get changed into my riding gear. Steps are retraced through the bungalow and out on the yard. Linda and I part at the office after I receive a final instruction to be back here at 2:00 pm for a riding assessment.

With the car unloaded and back in the carpark, I go to inspect my room. Moving my recently-dropped case out of the way as I enter, I discover a medium-sized room that accommodates up to four people. The décor is chocolate-brown carpet and floor-to-ceiling curtains, mint-green painted walls, and dark-pine doors and bed frames. Being a lover of light and airy rooms, I'm just about satisfied with the amount of light spilling through the double-glazed window at the centre of the southeast-facing wall. Outside is the passageway leading from the deck to the conservatory. There are twin single beds, one pushed against the wall under the window, the other pushed against the southwest wall close to the door. The former is made up using a pattern pillowcase and duvet set in pastel green, blue and yellow.

It takes about five minutes to unpack the contents of my case. Knowing I will be the lone guest using the room, I disregard the veneer double wardrobe and a four-draw chest and opt for putting my clothes on the empty single bed. The easy-to-crease items get hung over the top rail of a bunk bed that is flush against the northeast wall. Seeing the mirror is above the chest, I squeeze my hairbrush, makeup bag, and tablet on to the surface already taken over by a portable flat-screen television and a doughnut-shaped lamp with a yellow shade. Finally, I deposit my wash bag in the snug on-suite bathroom accessed through a door medial to the chest and the bunk beds. White-tiled and compact there is a shower, a sink, and a toilet.

While I select clean riding clothes from the single bed, I study the pictures hanging on the walls above it. Over the headboard is a modern canvass depicting a winding estuary flanked by sandbanks set against the always hoped for blue sky. In the foreground is a pleasure boat moored on aqua water. The canvas is an idealistic interpretation of this part of the country. The second, smaller picture hangs on the wall above the length of the bed. Traditionally framed in wood and edged by a white border it is a print of two powerful grey horses drawn using black to outline the animals, define the features and texture the manes, tails, and muscles. The artist depicts a single body and a tail leaving the remainder of the second horse out of sight behind the horse in the forefront. The front horse flings its head skyward, its forelegs essentially in a rear. The horse behind is defined by its head and forelegs in a stance as if about to take-off over an invisible jump. Another idealistic picture in a world where horses canter free on a beach beside a calm steel-blue sea beneath a white-cloud sky. After unpacking my belongings, I change into my riding clothes and go back outside to join Jill and her friends in the garden.

Jill and I leave the bungalow a few minutes before 2:00 pm, momentarily stopping to take in the view over and above the roof of the lower stable block. From the veranda, you can see the silhouettes of the monument and castle against the sky on Carn Brea hill ('carn' is the Celtic spelling for cairn) located under a mile away as the crow flies on the far side of the valley. The monument marks the apex of the hill and from this distance resembles a rocket pointed skyward. Further along and near to the northeast-face on the left side of a saddle, I can make out a portion of the turrets atop the blackened castle. In the background, the hill ends where the sea meets the sky. I will never tire of looking at seascapes.

When I went back to the deck after I'd unpacked, Jill's friends had departed for their reminiscence tour. Jill and I stayed in the garden for a short time and swapped snippets of information about ourselves. Jill works part-time for one of the Big Four auditors based in the London Docklands office. Her home is in South East London, a cycle-ride from where the grey cob she shares with his owner is stabled. She usually holidays here in the company of friends; however, this year she was unable to get the same week off work, and they will arrive next Sunday. As this is Jill's fourth visit, she knows about how things work: 'You choose how involved you want to be. You can either do the whole horse care and riding experience or ride only. I opt for just riding because I look after a horse at home.'

The main reason why Jill comes back every year is the amount of riding on offer each day, and as she mentioned if you ride almost continuously through the day, you're too tired to do anything else.

Jill's knowledge of the resident horses and ponies is impressive. While we waited for the minutes to take us up to 2:00 pm, I'd picked up a postcard one by one from the table in the bungalow's sitting room and showed Jill the photo of the horse or pony. She told me Wheal Buller has more than 50 horses and ponies, several of whom are for sale. There are usually a lot more postcards. Jill suspects the children who stayed here over the school holidays depleted the supply. I was still impressed Jill knew the name of every horse or pony photographed. Sat on a brown-leather sofa, a couple of meters from where I held the postcard there was no hesitation on which name to call out.

Our discussion moved on to what riding we want to do this week. Jill is keen to go swimming with a horse because she has not for whatever reason done this on her previous visits. My full-length wetsuit was abandoned in a cupboard at home at the end of a couple of successive summers of surf lessons several years back. Outdoor swimming in this country is a resolute sport because the water can feel icy cold, so I leave this option as undecided for now. My list is concise, primarily I want to get out into the local countryside, and the beach ride is an absolute must. Jill doesn't want to go to the beach as she's been on the ride a few times. Her main priorities are show jumping and cross country as she doesn't get the opportunity to do this at home. I'm not keen to jump. It scares me. I've never been an enthusiast jumper, and my reluctance to go airborne was exacerbated to phobia level by a fall in a lesson

153

18 years ago. I was knocked unconscious by a jump pole landing on my head after me, and the horse parted company when I was attempting to jump a combination. As I drifted in and out of consciousness, an ambulance took me to hospital. Because I threw up in the accident and emergency room, I secured an overnight hospital stay that involved medical staff shining a torch in my eyes at regular intervals throughout the night to make sure I was still conscious. The morning after, I was a little dazed as I stood in the hospital corridor talking on the payphone to my riding tutor, a kind and caring lady who was a few years from retirement. I recall the brief yet significant conversation: 'How are you?'

'I'm okay. Did my hat fall off, because I've got a huge lump on my head?'
'No, it didn't.'

I don't remember the accident. What I do know is had I not worn a jockey skull cap, I would not be here today. Jill and I concluded our conversation by the suggestion of while I'm at the beach (an excursion that takes up most of the morning), she can have a couple of jump lessons.

With lunch finished there is a lot of activity on the yard amid the children receiving direction on what tack they need to clean or which horse to prepare for a ride. Karen, a warm, young woman with long dark brown hair tied up in a ponytail and professionally-manicured painted nails introduces herself. Karen is the joint owner of Wheal Buller Riding School, a title she shares with her mother, Janet. Aside from living in Cornwall for many years, she isn't a native the giveaway here is her North of England accent. She stands inside the threshold of the office and considers a list of names of the available horses. The plan for this afternoon is a riding assessment followed by a two-hour hack.

Jill is offered a familiar name to her: Fergie. I'm assigned, Ollie. On hearing his name, a lady with reddish-brown cropped hair supervising the children nearby points out Ollie is booked in with the farrier tomorrow morning because of a loose shoe, so cannot go out for a hack today. Ollie's replacement is, Marble. Following Jill's lead, I enter the metal building where the girths drape on the outside rail and come upon the tack room. The lady organizing the children is now inside accompanied by three of her charges. I learn her name is Ruth as she shows us to the bridle peg and saddle rack labelled with our horse's name. Carrying my tack, I go back onto the yard where James, a thirtysomething man in a blue t-shirt and jodhpurs volunteers to take me to where I can find Marble. Back past the office door, I follow James as he takes a left at the corner of the lower block of six stables into a passageway formed by the north wall of the stable block and the cabin where the children emerged from earlier. Adjacent to the north wall is a pair of timber stables with doors side-by-side. Jill is in the furthest away stable tacking up a big chestnut with a flaxen mane and tail. James opens the door of the nearest stable where a cob stands quietly on a thick bed of clean yellow straw. At approximately 15 hh (1.52 m), Marble is skewbald with black hairs in her mane and tail, so technically a tri-coloured horse. Considering her white face and the well-defined-patches of brown and white covering her body, I can see why she is called Marble. I say hello as I pat her. Seeing she's had a brush, James asks if I want any help to tack up. I take up his offer because although she has a simple snaffle bridle and a cavesson noseband, there is a breastplate and humane-girth attached to her saddle, neither of which do I recall ever fitting. Marble stands still throughout James's breezy demonstration on where to position and fit the unfamiliar tack and takes the bit when asked.

The main yard is a flurry of activity when I re-enter leading Marble. Children are busy with their given chores. Members of staff are preparing horses required for a party of adults and children who are booked in for a hack out in the local countryside. It is all 'hands to deck' as approximately eight tacked up horses of various sizes are led from stables and out onto the yard. There are inspections to ensure the tack fits correctly and the horses are well turned out. Jill and I are directed to lead Fergie and Marble into the indoor arena and wait in the middle on the centre line. Jill leads us along a level walkway bound by the top four stables in the north side block and a high granite wall in the east corner of the yard. At the end of the walkway is a right-angle turn to enter an indoor corridor where there is a stall on the left and a gate straight on that opens into the arena.

The gate is on the long side of a 20 x 40 m (65 x 131 ft.) arena in the corner between the letters C and M. The surface is dark-woodchip. Fixed to the perimeter are rust-red boards the height of a horse. At the A end are floor-to-ceiling wood-plank double doors. Opposite in the letter C end is a concrete wall. On the top of the wall, high up in the rafters is a horse-rug storage area. Above the rust-red boards are corrugated metal sheets held in place by wooden vertical beams and horizontal posts. Natural light pours in from the skylights that go down the length of the pitched roof. Connecting the rug storage area and the entrance, on the short side between C and M, is a small gallery for spectators.

With our horses turned and halted on the centre line, we're adjusting stirrups from the floor when a young woman in her twenties walks into the arena. Beneath her blue and red baseball cap is blond hair tied back in a ponytail and a bright smile: 'Hello, I'm Emma, and I will be taking your assessment.'

Her effervescent character fills the arena as she collects a blue-plastic block from a shelf hidden behind the nearest board.

Emma checks our tack, helps us mount using the blue block and rechecks the girths. While Jill and I make further stirrup leather adjustments, Emma recalls snippets from Jill's previous visits and asks about my recent riding experience. Then for the next 20 minutes, using the correct protocols set out for national riding schools, Emma takes us through a standard riding assessment. We're instructed to walk and trot 10 and 20 m circles, complete a three-loop serpentine, ride the quarter lines, trot without stirrups, and canter out of the corner on the outside track. Emma immediately picks up on my weaknesses and reminds me to sit up straight and bend with Marble in the corners. Marble has a forward going trot and canter and does everything asked of her without hesitation. To conclude the assessment, Jill and I turn in and halt on the centre line, dismount, run up stirrups and in single file lead the horses back outside.

Carn Brea Monument

As we walk down the passageway back onto the yard, Emma keeps up her joyful-chatter by letting us know we're going straight out on a two-hour ride to Carn Brea Monument. At the bottom of the yard, there are four horses tacked up and waiting: two big bays, a small piebald horse and an Exmoor pony. Using the stone mounting block, Jill and I get back on our horses and Emma re-checks our girths and tack. While we wait for the other riders to get on their horses and have their tack checked, Jill broaches on the bay horses. James, who will be leading the ride is on a young horse called Jake. The second bay, a strong-weight-bearing horse marked by a white snip on his nose is called Harvey. Jill describes Harvey as calm, trustworthy, a bit on the slow side and can be hard to get going. It looks like he's going to enjoy this afternoon's ride as a slender young-teenage girl has just got on him. Two slight girls who must be in the region of 12-years old will ride the piebald horse and Exmoor pony. Both girls have long mousy-brown hair and wear a borrowed riding school helmet. It becomes clear the latter two girls will not be joining us when James gets his ride into order, Fergie behind Jake, then Marble and Harvey at the rear.

With the clip-clop of metal horseshoes on stone, our procession leaves the main yard passing between the office and cabin. Next to the cabin is a hay store that I hadn't noticed earlier. The track widens and curves around the hay store to go behind the back of the cabin to an outer yard where there is a block of four wooden stables. On a smaller scale to the main yard, the outer yard retains the same grooved surface on a downward slant to end at a wooden gate. A closely-bound fence keeps the yard enclosed. The horses' clip-clop loudly on the concrete surface before, James opens the gate and the ride strides out onto a dirt track with hems of scrubby wild grasses. On the near side, behind a decayed Cornish hedge is a cream and barn-red bungalow set in a generous garden established with many outbuildings. To the right, in the foreground, a post-and-rail fence edges a broad field with some well-maintained cross-country jumps built inside. The closest is a low triple jump made from dark-wood tree trunks laid horizontally and tied securely to upright posts. Since turning the corner at the back of the hay store, the valley, briefly admired on arrival, is back in view. From this vantage point on Buller Hill, the vistas resemble the lowlands of a moor characterized by a patchwork of green fields, dark-green hedges, and gorse bushes infiltrated by scanty-trees and clusters of buildings belonging to smallholdings. The valley is set apart by the old-engine-house chimneys bestrewn from here to the wild patch of moorland higher up on Carn Brea Hill.

In the south corner of the cross-country jump field the track curves to face Carn Brea Hill. The incline steepens, and granite stones cover the ground. All the riders weave the same course as James as he directs Jake down the least-stony route. At the bottom, the track meets The Great Flat Lode trail, a seven-and-a-half-mile multi-use trail circling the valley from Buller Hill to the back of Carn Brea Hill. The trail is part of a network of multi-use trails totalling a distance of over 30 miles (48 km) collectively known as The Mineral Tramways Trails. This network intertwines much of the UNESCO Cornish Mining World Heritage Site and many of the trails, including The Great Flat Lode, weave by old engine houses and chimneys abandoned by Cornwall's 18th and 19th-century mining past. The closest of these relics, a chimney at the back of a paddock, reveals the detail: a stone brick flue with a black rim; probably stained by soot. Set back from the chimney and on slightly lower ground looks to be a broader version closed by a pointed cap. Thick green gorse bushes growing at the base accentuate the structure's dereliction.

James takes a right, northbound onto a straight off-road section of The Great Flat Lode sandwiched by the post-and-rail fences of fields belonging to Wheal Buller Riding School. On the lower side of the multi-use trail, there is another grassy field accommodating more cross-country jumps to complete a carefully designed course. Off the back of a dry summer, the surface of the trail is hard and has a layer of dust and tiny stones. The sky retains its mix of high white cloud and blue, and the sea breeze dilutes the heat from the sun, an excellent combination for a pleasant afternoon ride out.

Seeing the trail is clear of users, James checks everyone is ready for a brief trot. In the quicker pace, I notice an effect of Marble's humane-girth. This type of girth allows the saddle more freedom to slip, so I need to take extra care to ensure I retain an equal balance of weight. We soon clear the length of the cross-country jump fields, and James brings the ride back to walk factoring in plenty of time to tighten up any gaps in our train in preparation for arriving at the junction where the off-road trail joins Cooper Lane. There is no traffic, so the ride takes a left onto the quiet country lane and after a few strides halts at a T-junction where another off-road trail starts straight ahead, essentially, transforming the T-junction into a crossroads for horse riders, cyclists and walkers. James halts in the middle of the lane so he can watch for vehicles. Jill is assigned to lead the ride across to join the off-road section. When we're all safely off the lane, James retakes the front of the ride.

On this section, The Great Flat Lode wends northwards towards the east side of Carn Brea Hill. Long, level and bordered by grazing fields it is an ideal stretch for a canter. Marble's canter is steady and easy to control so all I have to do is concentrate on keeping my weight even. The canter is brought back to trot and then walk when James spots a couple of walkers advancing towards us. At the point of walking by the ladies who've side-stepped into a gateway, there is an exchange of hellos, and riders add a thank you. They look to be an elderly mother and her middle-aged daughter.

In the distance, high up in the sky is a pair of hand gliders. One glider has a red-sailcloth, the other a yellow-sailcloth. Watching the hand gliders silently circle above Carn Brea Hill, James comments: 'Carn Brea is popular for hand gliders because it's a take-off point for them.'

He hopes they will be gone when the horses reach the monument as he isn't sure how Jake will react should the young horse have a close encounter.

There is a brief diversion from The Great Flat Lode onto a footpath that loops through a scrubland inhabited by long-green and straw-yellow grasses, gorse bushes speckled in yellow flowers and an abundance of purple heathers. Nature has reclaimed this humble-plot of land back from the redundant mining industry. The engine house, chimney and industrial buildings are ruins in a setting dramatically changed since these relics where in use. Today, it's a place of shelter and quietude where the songbirds sing.

The Great Flat Lode is re-joined just as it tapers downward through a thicket of tall trees where in-leaf branches meet overhead and camouflage everything underneath in dappled shade. The multi-use trail ends at a lane. We need to turn left to stay on The Great Flat Lode, James takes a right, and the ride enters the rural community of Church Town.

Our transit through Church Town is shallow and fleeting. It starts with a ride by a picture-postcard church in the design of the quintessential parish church found in quaint villages and towns throughout rural Britain. Typified by a four-turret bell tower, pitched roof on the naive and a neat lawny graveyard with leafy trees dotted here and there. A high granite wall protects the graveyard from the comings and goings out in the lane. The wall's continuation is broken only by twin black-metal gates on either side of a central ornamental main gate sheltered beneath a miniature version of the turret roof on the bell tower. The white-paint lattice on the main gate is decorated in pink and white ribbons an indication a wedding took place here yesterday. Any wedding ceremonies and morning congregations have ended, and the community has moved into a lazy and quiet Sunday afternoon temporally disturbed by shod-hooved horses clip-clopping on the tarmac.

At a T-junction, there is a left turn to advance through a cluster of houses. On the way, out of Church Town, the lane is bounded by a nearside paddock and a field opposite. A lone pony occupies the paddock. It is a youngster who looks keen to join our procession, yet has to be content with poking its nose through a gap in the fence. On the right, after the paddock, there is a 1970s-disco glitter ball dangling from a low-hanging branch on a tree. Despite having a long look at this surprising object reflecting light, the horses remain calm and relaxed. The glitter ball tree is on the edge of a paddock-sized common outside the village hall. On the other side of the common is another decorated tree flaunting bunting, and sets of tables and chairs along the side of a marque. The site projects the look and feel of the morning after the night before and must be the venue for yesterday's wedding reception.

Leaving Church Town behind the ride continues through the periphery clusters of houses and out into the pasture land connecting the town to the northeast-end of Carn Brea Hill. At the foot of Carn Brea Hill where the lane meets another off-road section of The Great Flat Lode, we re-join the multi-use trail to advance southwards. We're not far from the hill's most easterly point when we turn onto a bridleway that spans the lower part of the hill's south face. The first section is level and suitable for a quick canter. On the crest of the hill are rocky cairns and glimpses of Carn Brea Castle. Down here the slope is covered in ferns, long grass, and hardy plants in yellow or pink flower. The red hand glider circles at a distance overhead. Because we haven't seen the yellow hand glider since the earlier sighting, we concur it must have landed.

At the end of the bridleway, we take a right onto the track going up to Carn Brea Castle. We stay on the track momentarily until a steep footpath that goes up to the monument comes up on the left. The horses can only proceed in single file as the footpath slices through the dense array of purple heathers, ferns, and grasses. In the places where granite stones jut out of the ground, I give Marble a long rein and lean forward so she can carefully-step up onto more even ground.

On the ridge of the hill, the terrain flattens, and stacked rock formations partly cover the trodden-down grass. The dominant feature is the monument, a granite Celtic cross standing at approximately 30 m (98 ft.) high. After a short halt to admire the view and take some photos, James begins his scan for a suitable path to make our descent. He takes a glimpse down the north face: 'The yellow hand glider is down there packing his equipment away.'

He points to a footpath following the crest of the hill on the far side of the monument: 'We will go this way… I wonder where the red hand glider is?'

We hadn't seen the red hand glider since the sighting from the lower slope.

James halts the ride on the monument's west side in between the monument's square base and a substantial-rock-formation. The monument is a landmark viewable from afar. Its base alone reaches a height higher than my head, and I'm on Marble. This immense-Celtic-cross was erected in the 1830s to serve as a monument to Francis Basset (1757-1835). Basset was a local mine owner, who carried the title 1st Baron de Dunstaville. The title bequeathed on him following his involvement in some notable events: The defence of the city of Plymouth from the French and Spanish fleets in the late 1770s, and the quashing of a miners' riot in 1785. (Riots arose in the late 1700s, and early 1800s to protest about the high cost of goods.) Though admirable, I feel these achievements are an Englishman's basic-duty to his country. For me what makes Basset a worthy beneficiary of this elaborate monument was the use of his voice when he petitioned the House of Lords to abolish slavery in the early 1880s. This monument elevated above the rooftops of the local towns and villages reminds us of a local man who achieved great things and is a legacy left to emphasize everyone must have the fundamental right to live free.

For all the years I've lived in Cornwall, I'd never visited Carn Brea Hill. At 250 m (820 ft.) above sea level, it's certainly worth a visit for the outstanding panorama view. In the foreground are the roofs of the local towns of Redruth and Camborne and the midway settlement of Pool. Beyond the urban districts is a patchwork of brown, yellow and green fields rolling out to the north coast and the towns of St Ives in the west and Portreath to the east. Away from land, the Celtic Sea lays flat on the horizon. James points to the northeast: 'On a clear day you can see the wind turbines on the hill at Carland Cross and the [higher-still] clay tips of mid-Cornwall.'

My car journey to get to Wheal Buller came via these places. Carland Cross is under 20 miles (32 km) away. The clay tips a greater distance.

James prepares us to move on. He turns Jake to make a start on the descent of the west slope. Before Jake puts a hoof down on the downward path, James quickly backtracks to where the rest of us are still at halt, he dismounts and tucks the young horse in the shelter of the rock formation with Jake's quarters facing the footpath: 'Don't dismount, come off the path and keep the horses close together.'

He indicates using his hand to where the horses should stand side-by-side close to the monument. When everyone is in position, he explains his action: 'The red hand glider is coming up the path.'

James's swift preparations pay off. None of the horses flinch as a man in his late thirties goes by dragging a mass of red sailcloth. Even though James hadn't expected Marble, Fergie, and Harvey to do anything they still get a pat for being impeccably behaved. James suspects Jake didn't see the glider nevertheless he too gets a pat for good behaviour. James remounts and restarts the descent when the red hand glider is out of sight.

Initially, the footpath goes through moorland vegetation where the horses have to step carefully over granite rocks. Despite going downhill, the lack of anything tall on this part of the hill allows for a clear view to the fields below and back up the hill on the far side of the valley. One of the properties on the far side will be Wheal Buller Riding School.

James then halts the ride again and dismounts. This dismount is to help me adjust my slipped saddle. I'd been focused on the view and hadn't put enough attention on my seat to maintain an even balance. Marble's humane-girth prompts me to focus my mind on the riding as well as surveying the scenery.

As our course turns to the south, Marble alerts me to something moving up ahead. The point of interest making Marble prick her ears forward and fix her eyes is a watering hole. Possibly the remnants from a long-abandoned quarry. Ferns have taken root on the steep rocky perimeter to obscure the surface of the water. Marble loses interest the moment the cause of the camouflaged movement gets revealed. Two boys have climbed down onto a rock at the edge of the water. They are using fishing rods and have more faith than I have in their ability to catch anything in this hole.

A white sand and stone path succeeds the moorland footpath. Here the horses can only continue in single file due to the path being hemmed in by head height fern-covered hedges. Underneath the ferns and summer foliage, there will be a traditional stone wall. The hedges funnel us down to the base of the hill where we take a right onto a bridleway enclosed by walls covered in grass and bramble-bushes with tiny blackberries in infancy-red. Back in the pastureland, patches of mottle-shade cover the track, cast down from trees rooted to the upper part of hedges. Heat builds in the shelter of the valley's network of country lanes as the sky rapidly clears of white cloud. Here and there, footpaths weave through the rougher zones of the mining past where ruined single-level storage buildings symbolized by crumbling walls and roofless adjoin old engine houses. We ride by some of these abandoned icons on the lower slope. Others stand like sentries on the summits of distant hills. Drenched in sunshine our pace is a walk. Songbirds serenade us in the peace-and-quiet of Sunday afternoon.

With James and Jill talking at the front, I take the opportunity to chat with the young girl riding Harvey. She is a local from the village of Pool. She doesn't have a horse of her own and to compensate goes riding at various places throughout Cornwall. After she describes some of those places, I recall a couple of local rides I recently went on. The first was in the vicinity of the Gannel estuary near Newquay, the second on Bodmin Moor. Hoping to inspire her to venture further afield herself, I summarise my trips to Iceland and Egypt. She is a quiet and polite young lady, who like me demonstrates an independent character and is happy to go off horse riding on her own. Another commonality is our dislike of jumping. We comment on how the riding scene in this country verges on the brink of obsessive about tackling fences, and how anyone who doesn't enjoy jumping gets perceived as rather odd. On this subject I can provide reassurance, 'It's okay not to like jumping. Thankfully, this obsession to jump everything in sight does seem to be solely a British thing and does not reflect the attitude of the rest of the world.'

The return to Wheal Buller Riding School is from the west using a broad and flattish part of The Great Flat Lode trail tacked onto the side of the hill. Had we remained on the trail, it would have taken us around Carn Brea hill and back to this point, essentially full circle. Back down in the valley is Carnkie, a rural village featuring a cluster of white-washed and stone buildings topped by brown or grey-pitched roofs. Behind the village, traversing the lower moorland of Carn Brea hill are derelict engine houses, chimneys, and mining buildings. During the 18th and early 19th centuries, Carnkie would have been a hub of industrial activity. A hundred years later it's a pretty-postcard village tucked away in a sheltered, picturesque and tranquil valley.

Trailside on the right is steep uphill banks covered in grass and an old stone chimney. To the left on a slightly lower gradient is another chimney that sticks up from behind a roofless engine house and a long-single-level ruin decayed to a skeleton of crumbling walls. After we pass the ruins, James scans the trail for other users. Satisfied the coast is clear, he initiates a short canter bringing the ride back to walk ahead of the next corner. As the trail rounds the bend, it dips down through a shady thicket to a gateway cast in shadow. On the other side of the gate is the bottom of the stony track that ascends past the higher cross-country field and up to the stables.

Back on the main yard, we halt close to the tack room and dismount. There is a lot of action again amid Ruth and Linda removing saddles and carrying them back to the tack room. The young girls who had been in the yard earlier are receiving their tutelage. Under Ruth's guidance and supervision, they're to fetch the Exmoor pony and piebald horse from their respective stables. The worked horses are to be turned out in a field adjacent to The Great Flat Lode.

In single file, we lead our horses between the chalet and the wooden stables where we had found Marble and Fergie before the ride. As we pass through, each horse in order gets a hose down on their saddle area and legs. There is no need to dry them off for the cloud has reduced to wisps drifting out to the coast leaving a glorious late afternoon of blue sky and warm sunshine. There is a brief halt in the outer yard to wait for Linda and the girls leading the Exmoor pony and piebald to catch up. Then we set off back down to The Great Flat Lode trail. The gate to the turnout field is at the bottom of the stony track straight across the trail. Linda controls the gate as the horses are lead in and turned back to face the fence. Bridles are taken off, and the horses select a spot to have a roll in a paddock of cropped grass and dry-dirt patches. The horses are in a top paddock that provides access via a track to two spacious-grazing fields. The track starts at the paddock's bottom, northwest corner and goes down the valley into a barren plot where wild-shrubs grow beside a watering hole. Past the watering hole is the unobstructed entrance to the grazing fields, which span back up to The Great Flat Lode. As the five horses walk the route, they stop at the watering hole to drink then move on to join the horses already turned out in the fields.

On the way back to the yard, Jill and I plot to immediately depart to the bungalow and get in the hot tub. It's been a long day (more so for Jill than me), and we are ready to relax tired riding muscles. We wash the bits on our bridles at a tap fixed to the corner of the lower stable block then hang them up on the named pegs in the tack room. Before we leave the yard, we join Ruth back in the office: 'What do you want to do this week? The options are, dressage, show jumping, cross-country, day ride, beach ride, swimming with your horse, side saddle and western riding.'

Jill wants lessons, flat, jumping, and cross-country. I request a mixture of flat lessons, hacks, and the beach ride. Jill is keen to go swimming because she did not get the opportunity on her previous visits. I'm not so keen, primarily because of this country's climate and the knowledge of how cold the water will be. I remain uncommitted. I'll make my decision on the chosen day of the swim. At the least, I will welcome the ride out to the swim location. To conclude we all agree Jill and I will be back in the yard at 9:00 am tomorrow morning. I will be going to the beach. Jill will stay at Wheal Buller and have a jump lesson.

Gwithian Beach

Early the next morning the sky is dull and overcast and the chill from last night lingers. In the act of trying to wake myself up, I leisurely prepare and consume a breakfast of porridge, crumpets, and coffee in what would be silence if there wasn't the constant whirl of the conservatory's drinks machines. Jill hasn't emerged from her room yet, so I take the opportunity to reflect on the snippets of information she'd disclosed yesterday evening.

When we'd retired to the bungalow after the Carn Brea hill ride, the remainder of the afternoon had stayed clement. On the sheltered deck, Jill and I had relaxed through two cycles of the hot tub. Partly submerged in 40-degree water, amid the bubbles and gurgles our faces had reddened, and beads of perspiration had peppered our foreheads. As the sun made its slow retreat, Jill had disclosed more details relating to Wheal Buller. Linda, who greeted me yesterday, doesn't teach or lead any rides She schools the younger horses, some of which are for sale. Marble is on loan for the summer. Her owner uses her for hunting in the winter and loans her to Wheal Buller for the summer season to keep her in work and fit. The Exmoor pony is Taz. The piebald is called Poldark. Jill has found out the girls who rode Taz and Poldark are in Cornwall on holiday: 'They are not staying at Wheal Buller. They are being dropped off early every morning and picked up again in the afternoon. Neither of them has any previous riding experience. They are on the full programme that includes horse care and tack cleaning.'

We felt exhausted merely comprehending the girls' schedule, and I had responded: 'They are young and have lots of energy to burn, I suppose.'

The chlorine smell of the hot tub got replaced by the enticing-smell of dinner cooking. Jill and I had sat in the conservatory talking to Terry, Janet the joint owner's husband while he prepared our meal. Terry is an ex-police officer. He is a slight man with dark hair and a northeast England accent. He'd reported on a busy season. Throughout the school summer holidays, Wheal Buller accommodated up to 30 children per week. During this hectic period, meals are either taken in sittings or barbequed. Janet decamps from the house to sleep in the caravan on the yard so she is close to their young guests and can ensure they have settled and are safe at night. In the six weeks of mayhem or it could have been preceding, Janet had prepared many of the vegetarian meals I will eat this week. Dinner last night was a delicious nut roast followed by a slice of chocolate cake.

To close a perfect first day, Cornwall had put on a spectacular light show. A fraction after 8:00 pm, I had stood on the bungalow's granite veranda looking out over the roof of the lower stable block and up to the crest of Carn Brea hill. The hill was in effect black and the monument a silhouette against the purple, pink and yellow wispy clouds in a dusk sky. Twenty-five minutes later the hill and monument were jet black, and momentarily the whole-sky was a blaze of red as if it was on fire. Then the reversion of the pinks and purples were superseded by the orange glow of the sun as it dropped behind the hill.

With the sun gone and a chill in the air, I'd retreated into the seating room where Jill and I sat on opposite brown sofas. Using her iPhone, Jill relayed the posts streaming on the Wheal Buller Riding School Facebook page. The laptop she packed and my tablet are redundant for accessing the internet in the bungalow for the only Wi-Fi spot is in and close to the chalet, which I now know is the education room. Jill forgot to ask for the key to the education room and would have had to have sat on the bench the children had occupied earlier at lunchtime. The evening chill had ruled out this course of action.

My attention comes back to the present morning as Jill enters the conservatory. I obligingly flick the switch of the kettle, and the drone of the electronic element joins the subdued early morning conversation and the whirl of the drinks machines.

Not wanting to exert ourselves too much on holiday, Jill and I arrive in the yard at 8:45 am. Although the blanket of white-cloud remains intact, it has risen and is thinning. The girls on holiday had arrived earlier and have been busy helping the staff, who have already brought the horses back from the fields and tacked some of them up ready for a morning ride. The back ramp of the horse lorry is down even though Emma and Karen had finished loading.

Emma has a yellow bucket full of soapy water and is sponging away a blotch of dirt from the upper part of the ramp. The girls on holiday stand watching.

Jill and I sit down on the concrete mounting block. Jill figures there are four horses in the lorry despite only being able to see the small dark bay pony loaded last. Jill thinks the pony is called Trilby. She tries to deduce which other horses are in the lorry based on the riders going and the fact only certain horses go to the beach – many horses and ponies don't cope with the boundless-space and become uncontrollable, and a danger to themselves, their rider and other beachgoers. With no evidence, Jill concludes there are two horses and two ponies loaded. I will ride one of the horses, and the girls will share a pony. The remaining horse and pony will be for a mother and daughter who are yet to arrive. Emma finishes her unscheduled cleaning, and while we wait for the absent riders, she confirms the girls will accompany her in the horse lorry, and I'm to follow in my car. Soon after a middle-aged woman and young girl wearing jogging bottoms and fleece jumpers enter the yard from the direction of the carpark. They are promptly fitted with riding hats and briefed to follow behind the lorry. Less than five minutes later, I'm in my car at the back of the procession trundling over the cattle grid and taking a left onto Buller Hill. In front are the mother and daughter travelling in a dark-saloon car and the slow-moving horse lorry.

Gwithian beach is more or less 10 miles (16 km) away from Wheal Buller Riding School. The first part of the road trip is along quiet country lanes meandering through villages and the brown, green and yellow patchwork fields situated to the south and west of Carn Brea Hill. When the hill is behind us, the route bears north through the urban village of Pool where the road skims a business district populated by warehouse-size stores and office blocks. Traffic is heavy, and there are a few traffic lights to go through. In spite of this, there are no delays for the carriageway is straight and has many lanes to aid the flow of vehicles. Not before long, we go by the campus of Cornwall College on the right, and then the westbound slip road comes up on the left to take us onto the A30 dual carriageway. Remaining together is easy, particularly for the duration the vehicles are linear using the inside lane of the A30. Here traffic is neither heavy nor light and users travel unobstructed at or close to the national speed limit. Soon after, our convoy exits the A30 and takes a right at the top of the slip road to cross a bridge over the dual carriageway. The rest of the journey is along country lanes going north and then west through a landscape of patchwork fields, hamlets and clusters of farm buildings. Approximately 20 minutes on from leaving Wheal Buller Riding School, we arrive at Godrevy Beach located at the northeast-end of St Ives Bay.

The lorry and cars are parked beachside in a limited unofficial carpark. I stand alongside the two girls and the mother and daughter while Emma unloads the horses' one by one and hands their reins over to the allocated rider. We're instructed to let the horses graze at the edge of the track while Emma secures the lorry. In turn, the horses walk calmly down the ramp. Trilby is first and then Taz the Exmoor pony. A small grey horse called Storm comes after. Last to unload is Poldark, who I will ride. The mother and daughter will be riding Storm and Trilby respectively, and the two girls will share Taz. There is a flurry of mounting, tack checks, stirrup, and girth adjustments and finally, everyone is ready to go. Holding onto Trilby's rein, Emma leads the way. Storm is next in the line, then Taz, and Poldark at the rear.

Our way to the beach starts back on the road. Blown from the adjoining dunes is a light covering of sand on the tarmac. It is a common sight on beach roads along this coast. Roughly 200 meters further on is an entrance onto the dunes where a trail winds through a setting of spiky-marram grass and sand mounds. On the right is a pool of water the size of a modest boating lake. I recognize the pool and the two-storey white building on the far bank. The building is the Sandsifter, a beach bar, and bistro and the venue of a friend's fortieth birthday party a couple of years ago. Back then it was a cold Saturday night at the beginning of May. The theme 1970s retro. Loud music, laughter, and dancing went on into the early hours. Right now the Sandsifter is closed, and there is no sign of life. I am sure it will come to life later on, maybe at lunchtime. Though the children have gone back to school, there are still plenty of tourists in the county taking advantage of the quieter closing weeks of this year's holiday season.

Out of the shelter of the dunes at the point of descent, the whoosh of waves fills the air as they roll onto the beach below. Gwithian (or Gwithian Towans) is a magnificent beach boasting a spectacular view. Set in St Ives Bay, Gwithian beach starts at Godrevy and ends at the Hayle estuary. At the northeast end, just out to sea is the whitewashed Godrevy lighthouse. At 300 m (984 ft.) tall the lighthouse stands alone on an island of rock. Looking westwards from the lighthouse out to the far side of the bay is the town of St Ives. St Ives is well known for being the home of the Tate St Ives gallery, and a mecca for artists, who flock to capture the vivid-natural light. I'm sure the prettiness of the town and its setting contributes towards its popularity too.

Onshore winds blown in of the Atlantic Ocean sculpt the high dunes that back the beach. At the foot of the dunes is the dry-white sand. This powdery stuff is cut across to reach the expansive playground of wet sand freshly exposed by the ebb of the receding tide. Beneath the overcast sky, the sea is a cold grey-blue, and the surf messy as the waves crash in to break on the beach.

The red-and-yellow lifeguard flags flutter to the east and thus confirm an onshore breeze. When lifeguards are present, there is nearly always a pair of red and yellow stripe flags used by the lifeguards to keep people in the safest place in the water to swim. For safety reasons, it is imperative for swimmers and boogie-boarders to always remain between these flags. The lifeguards too will station themselves central to these markers, but onshore so they can keep an eye on what everyone is doing. At all times, they are ready to spring into action at the first sign of anyone getting into difficulty in the strong ocean currents.

Despite it not being cold, the temperature is lower than it has been over recent weeks. The temperature reflects the number of people swimming: just a pair of brave teenage girls determined to make the most of their beach holiday. Past the safe-swimming section is the participants of a surf school, recognizable by the school's yellow rash vests put over the black full-length wetsuits worn by all the pupils. They're lying on broad red and blue foam surfboards practicing paddling out while remaining on the beach. Much further up the shore are three kite-surfers making equipment preparations on the sand and another kite-surfer out on the water, flitting between airborne, and surfing the waves. I'm sure last week this beach would have been packed full of windbreaks and beach tents on the account it was August bank holiday and the weather fine and settled. Today there is just a smattering of dog walkers and joggers using the uncrowded expanse.

Cornwall is a county with 300 miles (482 km) of coastline adorned by over 400 beaches and where every piece of land is less than 20 miles (32 km) from the coast. The beach as a collective has been a familiar recreational ground for me throughout my life. There had been family days out comprised of picnics, beach cricket, buckets and spades, rock climbs, boogie boards, inflatable dinghies and inner-tubes, and fishing nets. In the years following my childhood beach activities shifted to walking my dog, swimming, surf lessons, beach parties, and barbeques. Of cause, here and now, the strongest memories are of the many Saturday mornings I spent as a child cantering on a local beach at low tide 4 miles (6 km) from where I live. The noise of shod hooves thumping wet sand and the continual whoosh of the rolling tide. My favourite pony from childhood, Star, loved the sea. She used to splash the surface using a foreleg and get me soaking wet. Decades had passed since I'd ridden on a beach in Cornwall and as I look across the long stretch of sand and breath in the familiar fresh-salty smell of the sea, it feels good to be back.

Considering she has a trio of young beginner riders and a lady who has not ridden for some time, Emma is going to walk up the beach and back escorting Trilby, Storm, and Taz. She tells me, I can go off on my own so I can enjoy a trot and canter. This is, of cause, okay with me. However, as Emma and the others walk out to the shore and advance up the beach, my partner airs his displeasure in being asked to remain closer to the dunes and cliff and blaze a trail by becoming fretful and neighing. So, for half an hour or so, I establish a compromise. To start, I take advantage of the natural arena and perform lots of walk-trot transitions on circles and through figures of eight to get Poldark listening to me. Whenever I have Poldark's complete attention, I ask for canter using the width of the beach in zig-zags, so he is always in the vicinity of the slower-moving horses as they remain on a course pointing towards Hayle. For me, Poldark isn't easy to ride on the beach. He is too anxious about being away from his fellow equines, and it is hard to get him to respond to my aids and voice. I do get a response if I use my whip more assertively than I usually do. I'm not surprised Poldark doesn't want to leave his friends and go off on his own in the company of a complete stranger. Nor am I surprised at his reluctance to go in the sea when an attempt is made to go in for a quick splash. Under the blanket of cloud, it looks cold and uninviting to me too.

As I'm not overly keen on using the whip to the extent I have to, I decide to quit exerting myself when I see, Emma turn the ride around. Instead of fighting a reluctant mount I'll admire the stunning seascape instead. To Poldark's delight, I ask him to re-join the procession of horses to make the return leg back down the beach in the direction of the Godrevy lighthouse.

There has been a minor drama while I was elsewhere. A young female jogger, listening to music and oblivious to everything around her ran up behind Storm and startled the mare who unseated her rider. Everyone is in good spirit, and the blame for the incident is solely on the jogger. Still, the mother is unnerved, and Emma keeps a reassuring hand on Storm's reins so the mother can enjoy the rest of her ride. I jog twice a week, and I'm stunned how a fellow jogger, having the range this beach offers, thought it would be a good idea to jog up behind the horses. Not only was her action inconsiderate it was stupid, and she was lucky she didn't get a kick from Storm. Worse still, she didn't even stop. She just jogged on.

I become aware of my complete state of relaxation on the walk back, a feeling I hadn't felt in ages. A beach ride is a fabulous activity to enjoy on a Monday morning. I chat with the two girls, one on foot the other riding Taz. They are from Norwich and are staying at Hendra Holiday Park on the outskirts of Newquay; a 35-minute drive from Wheal Buller at a push.

'That's quite far for you to come every morning. What time do you get up?'

In unison, 'Very early.'

'Have you been to the indoor fun pool yet?'

The girl on foot, 'We went on the first day but were too tired yesterday.'

'I've been there once when my nieces were children. They loved the flumes and rapid-ride.'

Considering their first day of horse care and riding, I am not surprised they were too tired.

We're not far from the dunes we'd cut across to get to the beach when we encounter an obstacle, a man is preparing his kite buggy for racing up and down the sand. On this part of the beach, there is an outcrop of rocks jutting out from the cliff. Ideal for climbing, for any other activity you need to go around. The kite surfer's four-wheel buggy is stationary close to the water's edge. However, the long rope that secures the kite is stretched out taut across the sand, leaving a narrow gap between the outcrop and kite canopy for the horses to go through. The main concern is the wind will catch the kite canopy and make it flap as the horses pass. Thankfully, the canopy stays down and motionless.

Back on the dunes, I recall another visit to this beach five years ago. It was a hot and cloudless day in August. A friend and I arrived mid-afternoon at high tide and joined a gathering of friends who had congregated on the crowded dry-powder sand. The rest of the day was spent chatting and watching people surf or swim in the aqua sea. The sounds made by people talking, laughing and shouting on a packed beach accumulates in an echo that drifts on the salty-seaweed scented air. Gwithian beach and St Ives Bay was an awesome-sight against a backdrop of blue sky and radiant-sunlight. This morning the sun did not come out nevertheless the beach ride was fantastic, and hopefully, I won't leave it quite so long to ride on a Cornish beach again.

I go straight into lunch when I arrive back at Wheal Buller from the beach. The earlier cloud cover has dispersed, and the sun's rays fill the conservatory as Jill and I exchange details of our morning rides while devouring vegetable soup, quiche, and salad. Jill has had a flat lesson, a jump lesson, and an hour hack. The conversation moves on to this afternoon's itinerary: a lunge lesson, poles-and-jumps, and a flat lesson. It has been a busy morning for both of us, and I'm relieved Jill's lunge lesson is first at 1:00 pm and mine scheduled for 1:30 pm. I won't take it easy in the bungalow for an extra half hour though as I'm going to watch Jill's lesson.

Shortly after, I'm in the front row of the gallery next to the entrance of the indoor arena between the letters C and M. The arena is warm, and sunlight spills through the skylights to cast rectangle patterns on the wood-chip surface. At the centre of the arena, Jill is on Max, a hefty weight-bearing chestnut with a flaxen mane and tail, white socks and a blaze. At roughly 16.3 hh (1.70 m), Max is a proper warhorse. I can imagine him going into battle carrying a knight in armour wielding a shield and sword. Max circles Emma, who is walking the centre of the arena holding a taut lunge line and whip. Jill has quit and crossed her stirrups over the saddle and Emma is running through various exercises to correct and improve Jill's riding position. For the second time today, I'm catapulted back to another period in my life as I recall memories of my life 17 years ago when I was a student studying equestrian and business studies at the Berkshire College of Agriculture. There, I'd watched fellow students receive their lunge lessons and learned the techniques to lunge a horse myself. Fatefully, I hadn't lunged a horse since.

The same amount of years had passed by since I'd ridden a horse the size of Max, so directly after Jill and I swap places 20 minutes later, I find myself feeling quite high up – the mare I regularly ride at home is about 15.2 hh (1.57 m). As Emma commands Max to walk away from her out onto an outer circle, I discover Max's bulk and height produces a comfortable stride to ride, especially without stirrups. An advantage for a lunge lesson as it means I can concentrate on correcting my bad habits pointed out by Emma's expert eyes: legs going forward, elbows sticking out, etc. After I've dismounted, Emma remains in charge of Max. A group is due imminently for a hack, and Max is to be the mount for an adult man. Jill and I are sent off to go in search of our horses and prepare them for our pole and jump lesson.

Not long after, I find myself on Ollie, a bay thoroughbred, riding out of the yard past the house and carpark and into the outdoor arena, entered at the A end. In this perfect setting, the sun shines down on the 20 m x 40 m (65 x 131 ft.) sand arena, the perimeter post-and-rail fence, and the six brightly-painted show jumps set out as a course of mostly low cross poles. As the ride walks the outside track between K and H, there is a superb view of the valley and Carn Brea hill. In such a perfect setting it is a shame, I'm transformed into an anxious rider by the presence of jumps.

There are four riders in the arena. Emma is taking the lesson. Jill is on Bella, an Appaloosa (spotty horse). Karen's daughter, Georgina, who at a guess is eight or nine-years-old, is riding a black mare called Jess. Chloe, who if she isn't a teenager soon will be, is riding Marble. As Emma warms us up by getting us to trot in turn to the back of the ride my nervousness escalates because of Ollie, rushing in the trot. A typical thoroughbred. He is a keen jumper and gets excited in the arena. Emma lightens the mood by pointing out the transformation from a confident rider who was happy to go off on her own for a canter on the beach this morning to a nervous wreck in the jumping arena. After discussing my old jumping accident, we settle on a goal of re-establishing my jump position on the flat and over trotting poles. We practice our jump position while trotting as a ride on the outside track and then each rider, in turn, trots over three poles placed on the ground between a set of blue-and-white jump wings inside the letters E, X, H, G square. For all his keenness, Ollie trots over the poles nicely. The other riders then move on to jump a cross-pole fence to complete the lesson. The cross pole is a step too far for me today, and Ollie is sidelined to watch and wait. Feeling my confidence raise slightly, I consent to a cross pole attempt. The main reason for this decision is there may be an occasion where I will need to jump a log or other obstruction out on a trail ride. For me to accomplish this challenge, I will ride Fergie, the chestnut mare Jill rode to Carn Brea yesterday. Emma and Jill reassure she is the perfect horse for an unconfident rider because she approaches at a steady pace, has a big stride and over low jumps, you hardly feel her leave the ground.

Just after 3:00 pm Jill and I re-enter the warm-indoor arena. I have changed horse and now ride Bella the Appaloosa. Bella is in the region of 15.1 hh (1.55 m). She has a single black marking that partially covers her head and a few spots on her forehead. An abundance of spots covers her neck, shoulders, and forelegs and then reduce in numbers on her back, hindquarters and hind legs. Emma gets us to obediently, if not accurately, ride several exercises: walk, trot and canter transitions, and five-meter shallow loops on the quarter line. Bella magnifies my weaknesses, she falls in and leaves her hind legs behind on corners thus making me focus on keeping my inside leg on and in the correct position. She runs into a canter, so I have to establish and maintain a rhythmic trot to prevent her from rushing. Throughout the lesson, I remind myself to sit up tall. During the transition work, Emma reminds us to use halt to trot transitions for lazy horses and walk to trot transitions for fizzy horses. I have to confess the horse I ride at home is very experienced and responds to light aids; therefore, to ride a less experienced horse is a challenge. All the same, Bella is lovely to ride. She is forward going and willing. I like her a lot.

Carn Marth Lake

Yesterday, after the flat lesson on Bella had finished, Jill and I hosed our horses and put them out in the field. Feeling hot from the afternoon's lesson in the indoor arena, I'd found myself picking out a pair of old pink trainers, a rucksack and a life jacket from the blue-plastic storage container kept outside on the bungalow's veranda. It was easy to find a pair of trainers to fit me as any unclaimed trainers left behind by the children after the school holidays get put in the storage container for subsequent guests to use. The balmy weather had convinced me to brave the cold water and go for a swim.

That was late afternoon yesterday when there was the warmth from the sun in a cloudless sky. This morning, wearing my bikini underneath my riding clothes, I emerge from the bungalow to a yard engulfed by thick fog and sea mist. I don't go back inside and change as Cornwall is a county that often starts under a blanket of grey first thing in the morning. The departure to Carn Marth Lake is an hour away, so there is plenty of time for the forecasted warm and sunny day to get underway. Jill has been monitoring the weather for the scheduled swim on her iPhone. The forecast had indicated this to be the best day of the week with no wind, warmth and continuous sunshine.

Having collected a grooming kit from the tack room, I go in search of Marble. She is in the same stable I found her in on Sunday afternoon, alongside the hose down area. Apart from brushing the mud from Gjáska's coat in Iceland last October, I had not groomed a horse for 17 years. Luckily in the period preceding the 17-year drought, I had groomed over a 100 horses and ponies, plus a couple of donkeys, so it only takes the action of picking up a body brush and curry comb to remember what I need to do. With plenty of time to spare, Marble gets a thorough brush. She is so relaxed I have to ask her twice to lift up the first hoof for me to pick out. It seems grooming induces an effect on her to what a full body massage does to me.

With Marble brushed and tacked up, I lead her to the main yard. To my relief, the fog and mist have cleared to leave the expected breezeless and clear blue sky. Seven of us will ride to Carn Marth Lake. Four of us will swim. Belinda, a calm, small lady with long blonde hair tied back in a ponytail is our escort. With the tack checked and riders mounted, she asks the swimmers: 'Have you got a life jacket and trainers in your rucksacks?'

Our reply is in unison, 'Yes.'

We get ourselves into a single file to exit the yard and set off down the track riding by the house. Belinda leads, riding a large grey with dapples on his hindquarters. The Norwich girls come after, on Taz the Exmoor and Harvey, the bay from Sunday afternoon's ride. Behind them is another young girl of a similar age wearing green and pink-flower-pattern hunter boots. The small horse she is on has a coat the colour of ash; he is aptly called Sooty. Next is Jill on Bella, then me and Marble and Chloe at the rear on Miss Jeepers, a skewbald who is primarily white with a couple of patches.

Carn Marth Lake is to the north-east of Wheal Buller Riding School. To get there, we ride through a valley that connects the southern part of Redruth to the village of Lanner. The ride is relatively short using a network of sand tracks and country lanes in a landscape of high hedges, grazing fields and rough patches thick with purple heathers, brambles, and plants displaying pink or yellow flowers growing in and around old mine buildings. Songbirds serenade us from inside neat gardens belonging to isolated cottages and farms. Belinda's grey isn't impressed by the chorus of songs, and he spooks whenever the tiny birds flutter away too close to him. Riding is hot work as there is no breeze and for this reason and Chloe's disappointment, Belinda, Jill and I concur to ride to the lake in walk – Chloe is at the age when all she wants to do is a canter.

On a hillside of bracken and gorse, a gradually-rising sand track takes us to a grassy lookout point where Belinda halts the ride. We have arrived at our destination. The far-ranging panoramic view from here is incredible: a lookout over pastureland, thickets, hamlets and rolling hills. Carn Brea hill and its monument are in the west. I can make out the north coast, even though it is difficult to discern the horizon as the sky and sea are virtually an identical blue in the strong sunlight. Faraway on the north and south coasts are high whips of white cloud. The remnants of the early cloud system retreating out to sea.

We dismount at the side of a free-standing stone wall conveniently placed to leave rucksacks beside. Chloe takes charge of Belinda's grey in addition to Miss Jeepers. Belinda holds the swimmers' horses; releasing Jill, the Norwich girls and me in turn so riding clothes can be removed and life jackets fitted. Not all the horses are used for swimming, and today it will be Marble and Harvey taking a dip. I remove Marble's saddle and breastplate, taking care to position it on the cropped grass so the underneath of her numnah can dry in the sun.

Chloe remains at the stone wall holding her charges while the rest of us lead our horses to the entrance of the lake on the opposite side of the sand track. Though labelled a lake, Carn Marth is actually a disused granite quarry. By its nature, the water in the quarry is in most part deep with a rim of steep-rocky cliffs overgrown with bracken, brambles and a purple-flower plant I can't name. Ordinarily, the advice for this type of watering hole is never to enter and many quarries throughout the county display, 'Danger, do not swim' signs. What makes this quarry atypical is the entrance has a mini-beach slanting down from the track that is bounded by sandbanks littered with stones, grass, pink-flower bushes and long stems topped with yellow. The dry sand gives way to wet pools and subsequent shallower water. In the shallows, close to the water edge is a line of grey boulders positioned at intervals. This unique topology makes it easy for a horse to enter and exit in a walk. Another safety requirement, shared by Terry as he prepared our dinner last night, is Janet, the joint owner of Wheal Buller Riding School, and her friends dive here to clear away any debris beneath the water that is likely to cause damage to a horse's legs.

There is a set circuit to take in the lake. Belinda informs me of where to go after I use a rock to get back on Marble. The Norwich girl, who is going first, is helped onto the bareback of Harvey. Her instruction is to stay close behind Marble, so Harvey stays on the right course. The final preparation is to wrap our legs against our horse's body and hold onto the mane. Many years had passed since I'd ridden a horse bareback. It would have been in the summer break that separated the two years I'd studied at the Berkshire College of Agriculture. I had spent the summer in Cornwall and worked at my childhood riding stables. That summer the days had been scorching allowing for plenty of canters on the beach and hours of shaded woodland treks. Being a cob type, Marble has a well-covered back and ribs, and she is warm and comfortable to sit on bareback. Bella, Taz, and Sooty graze on the sandbanks as their riders hold their reins and spectate. Belinda stands at the water's edge giving step-by-step guidance. When we're ready to go, Belinda sets us off: 'Walk Marble on and give her lots of encouragement.'

With Harvey, right behind, Marble splashes into the shallow water entering the lake through the gap in the boulders. Belinda's instructions are to stay close to the north cliff until I reach an outcrop of rock jutting out into the lake. The icy water quickly deepens to submerge my trainers and rise up my legs. In a higher pitch than usual, I call out: 'It's cold.'

I don't dwell on the sensation. I'm focused on Marble, and Belinda's instructions, in a calmer tone I award Marble lots of encouragement: 'Walk on Marble. Good girl.'

Marble looks down at the water as she carefully moves forward. To traverse the lake to the south side, I make the turn in front of the outcrop. The water is halfway up my thigh and up to Marble's nose. Using her lips, she plays with the water producing a froth of white bubbles. Then the surface beneath her hooves goes, and I feel her legs going backward and forwards through the water. I gasp in response to the chilly water engulfing my stomach. Though, this unpleasant sensation is replaced swiftly by the most incredible feeling of you and your horse being as light as a feather and floating through the air. Carn Marth is a confined quarry, and therefore there is a limited distance from the north cliff to the south cliff and the horses quickly find ground for their hooves. Marble and Harvey are not asked to swim for long. Instead, they are pointed into shallow water to circle close by to where Belinda stands. When the water level is at the horses' hocks, water-side close to the boulders, Marble along with Harvey is asked to circle again for a second and third lap. This circuit makes the swimming less tiring for the horses as they are mostly on a solid surface where they can walk. Having been immersed, I don't get such an icy greeting from the water on the second lap; nevertheless, the sensation is still quite bracing.

At the end of the third loop, I exit the lake, Harvey follows close behind. I suspect he may have got away with not swimming on a loop considering he decreased the arc in front of the outcrop to remain in the shallower water. Amid lots of smiles and happiness, Jill and I swap reins, and I take charge of Bella. To watch, I lead Bella to the top of the bank on the south side of the entrance. Bella munches contently on the cropped grass making it easy for me to take photos of Jill as she and the second Norwich girl make their three loops. I'm grateful for the gloriously warm and breezeless day as I stand drip drying. On completing her swim, Jill joins me on the bank after we both decline a second go. My decline is because standing in the warm sun, I am practically dry, and I don't relish the idea of another plunge into cold lake water. Now past 11:00 am with the sun high in the sky, it's pleasant in the warm air watching the Norwich girls vocally encouraging their mounts as they complete a few more loops.

Back at the stone wall, Chloe is sat holding the reins of the patiently-standing grey and Miss Jeepers. Reversing the actions of the swim preparations, swimmers take it, in turn, to hold horses and change back into riding clothes. Marble's white and brown patched coat is spotless from her swim and shines in the sunlight. She and Harvey dry super quick allowing for their saddles to be put back on after everyone has changed. Most of us remount using the stone close to the entrance of the lake. Because I'm first up, I get the opportunity to take a look at the incredible view while Belinda helps everyone else to mount.

The county of Cornwall offers many high points to look down from and span its spectacular countryside. There are inland hills such as Brown Willy (the highest point in Cornwall at 420 m (1377 ft.) located 40 or so miles (64 km) away from here on Bodmin Moor) to the steep ascents and descents of the extensive coast path recognised to be the longest stretch of coastline throughout all the counties of Great Britain. In my opinion, though, these high points are exclusively beaten by an aerial viewpoint.

If you're lucky enough to get a clear day for a flight from Newquay Airport on the mainland to St Mary's, the main island of the Isles of Scilly archipelago, as I did a number of summers back on my journey to visit a friend, you are treated to a marvellous view of the Cornish coastline. First, there are the stretches of golden-sand and high-rugged cliffs on the north coast. Breakers continually roll in onto the wide-stretches of sand at Watergate Bay and Fistral Beach. Between these two beaches is the town of Newquay where headland hotels perch on the brows of the cliffs to offer prime views over the harbour and the collection of smaller beaches that adjoin the streets: Newquay is known to be a surfer's paradise. Southwest of Fistral beach around the headland is the Gannel Estuary and Crantock Beach. Further on are the beach and dunes of Holywell Bay primarily flanked by mostly uninhabited headlands. Beyond Holywell Bay is the 3 miles (4.8 km) expanse of golden sand comprising of firstly Penhale Sands and then Perranporth Beach. On the other side of Perranporth, the wide stretches of sand get replaced by the town beaches of St Agnes and Portreath. Here high cliffs provide partial shelter from the force of the Celtic Sea. From Newquay, the landmass of Cornwall tapers, decreasing between north and south coasts. As the distances reduce the land becomes almost a modest island, and you catch sight of the south coast. There are glimpses of the Fal estuary, and the town of Falmouth; a haven where sails replace surfboards. As this is the first week of September, there will still be plenty of yachts moored on the calm-twinkling water of the Fal Estuary and secluded creeks. Back on the north coast, the plane reaches St Ives Bay, the location of Gwithian Beach, the estuary at Hayle and the town of St Ives set beside its town beach and crystal-clear blue water. Before leaving the mainland behind and flying out over Lands End, and on to St Mary's there is a little more of the south coast to view. The medieval castle on an island of rock infamously known to be St Michaels Mount. It looks to be set adrift out on its own in Mounts Bay. And the historical fishing towns of Penzance and Newlyn. To conclude the aerial sightseeing, the plane turns onto a flight path set for St Mary's cruising above 37 nautical miles of open sea.

Our return to Wheal Buller uses the same route as the outbound ride but now and much to Chloe's delight, Jill, and I agree to a canter on a level section of multi-purpose trail. Still, most of the ride is at a walk for midday is almost upon us and in the shelter of the valley, the temperature has risen considerably. I'm completely relaxed and content when the horses clip-clop back onto the main yard. It's been a delightful morning aided by the fantastic weather.

After being in the hot and airless indoor arena, it is refreshing to get back outside onto the yard. We've just finished a flat lesson where we'd practiced turn on the forehand and leg-yielding. For the lesson, I rode Bella. Jill rode Toby a chestnut about 15.3 hh (1.60 m) marked by a white star and stripe and a pink splodge on his nose. Toby is a schoolmaster, who knows everything and holds the temperament expected of this accolade. Jill and I had been joined at lunch by Kay, a petite middle-aged woman with long curly hair, who lives in Bideford in Devon and is a dog groomer by profession. Kay is on her second riding holiday at Wheal Buller as she stayed for the same week last year.

Introductions took place over lunch. As part of her short break, Kay has opted to work towards the Royal British Riding Schools (RBRS) Level 6 certificate in saddle and horse care. Working to gain an equestrian qualification is an offer on Wheal Buller's short break programme. Kay's test for the Level 6 certificate will be on Friday afternoon. Kay also hopes to complete a riding test on Friday to gain an RBRS Level 5 riding certificate; however, she isn't confident in her ability to achieve this. Jill and I acknowledged, Kay's riding aim would bring focus to our lessons, and we'd be happy to work alongside her and practice the relevant exercises in her preparation for the Level 5 test. Now the flat lesson has ended, I must face my challenge of the week: jumping. I hand Bella's reins to Jill and go off to collect the sensible and reliable-to-jump, Fergie.

My apprehension returns on entering the arena and riding the outside track close to the show jumps. The Norwich girls, on Taz and Poldark, and Chloe join me, Jill and Kay for the jumping lesson. Gina a small young lady, with an encouragingly-loud and clear voice is our instructor for the lesson. It was Gina who had us riding without stirrups, practicing turns on the forehand and leg yielding in the indoor arena during the flat lesson. Gina is bubbly and attentive, always checking to ensure you are doing what you want to do. Like Emma yesterday, she understands why I feel apprehensive about jumping after I recount my jumping accident to her, and she agrees Fergie is the right choice for my attempt at a jump today.

The lesson complies to the same drill as yesterday's jumping lesson: a trot and then a canter in turn to the back of the ride to warm up. The girls from Norwich mainly trot with just one of them achieving a couple of strides of canter. So far so good, a trot and a canter on the outside track is firmly in my comfort zone. My apprehension from being amongst show jumps is soothed to a degree by Fergie and her obedient and calm responses to my aides. Next, we practice our jumping position on the flat by trotting as a ride. The ride halts at the C end of the school to end the exercise. Gina then prepares for trotting over poles by adjusting the cross poles of a yellow-and-black double placed with the first set of wings close to the track beside the letter B and the second set just before M. The cross poles are removed altogether from the latter set of wings, and the trotting poles are set up in front of the first set by B. In order, we trot over the poles in our jumping position. Still safely in my comfort zone, I get a feel for Fergie and her fast approaching jump. Her smooth-comfortable stride and sensible-steady manner reassure me. She is quite a big horse for me to ride and I need to use strong aides to keep her going forward: which is good, as it means there is no chance of us rushing at anything solid and heavy.

Butterflies fill my stomach as I watch Jill and then Kay trot from E, take an inside line after A and jump the cross pole that Gina has put up where the trotting poles were. Despite the butterflies, I do feel I can do this, and that is down to Fergie's temperament and how she's behaved so far. Under Gina's guidance, I start trotting on the outside track. Coming up to K, I look for the inside line down the school to the middle of the cross pole. As I make the turn, Gina encourages me to keep my leg on to keep Fergie moving forward. Using strong leg aids, I focus on the arena's boundary fence on the far side of the jump. Holding a chunk of mane, I rise into my jumping position. Fergie pops over the jump. Her movement is very smooth, and I hardly feel us take off and land. A triumphant smile replaces my serious-concentration face as I re-join the outside track between M and C and come to a halt at the back of the ride at H. My sense of achievement is inflated further when Gina and Jill confirm I had executed a perfect jumping position.

After everyone has completed the exercise again, Gina moves everybody else onto jumping the double. I'm not sure of the number of strides between the jumps for I will be sitting this exercise out. I've achieved my goal for today by jumping the cross pole twice. The worst thing I can do is try to do too much in one go. I'm feeling good about the whole experience, and it is essential I finish on a high. When Bella runs out at the second jump I know I've made the right decision. The lesson comes to an end after Jill and Kay complete a course of four jumps.

Our final riding session of the day is drill/formation riding. Georgina, Karen's daughter, joins the rest of us back in the indoor arena. As a result of the continuing breezeless and perfect sunny day, the indoor arena is now hotter than it was during the after-lunch flat lesson. I'm riding Toby, the schoolmaster who is an absolute joy to ride. Gina patiently guides us through a set of on-the-spot-chorography and despite seven horses and riders descending into organized chaos in places it all goes relatively well. The plan is to split into two rides and criss-cross in front of one another either across the school or on the long diagonal. At the split, Jill leads half of the troop, and the other half follow me. For most of the session, we do a pretty good job, and all the chaos happens behind us as the ponies cut a corner or take a shortcut to catch up. Regardless of the younger girls being a little disorderly the activity is a lot of fun and Gina's experience ensures the ride is systematic and light-hearted.

We spend the remainder of the late afternoon lazing on the sun-drenched deck at the back of the bungalow. Jill, Kay and I sit at a garden table while Kay consults her RBRS guide to identify the exercises she needs to practice. I'm again transported back to when I studied at the Berkshire College of

Agriculture, and I'm glad I don't have to concern myself with a test later in the week. These days, I'm happy to stick to riding for leisure. Plus, I've challenged my jumping phobia, and for me, that is more than enough for one week.

Another soak in the hot tub to relax aching riding muscles concludes the perfect day. In a tranquil garden and part submerged in the water, we discuss tomorrows activities. Behind the garden wall, a host of sparrows' twitter on an overhead wire supported by wooden telegraph poles. The small brown birds are watching swallows traversing the late-summer meadow as the swifter birds' dart from tree to tree.

Carn Brea Castle

It's day four, and I've just completed the quickest horse change since my arrival. I must confess up to this point, I've been the last to be ready for a ride, always finding everyone else waiting patiently either on or off their horses as I arrived on the main yard or entered the indoor arena. Just now, I had led Bella out of the indoor arena and down the passageway onto the main yard into a flurry of lots of horses, ponies, and riders getting prepared for a two-hour hack and they were more or less ready to go. Belinda had emerged from the middle of the preparations leading a tacked-up Marble. We'd swapped horses and Ruth, who'd taken the flat lesson in the indoor arena where I'd ridden Bella, checked my girth. The change of horse took less than a minute, and I was soon in the penultimate position at the back of the hack ride.

Marble is enthusiastic to be going out on a hack, she strides forward out of the main yard, and around the corner at the hay-storage area. She is keen this morning, and so am I. Having already had a lesson on Bella my mind and body is awake and alert, my 'slow starter' in the morning persona thawed for another day.

The lesson this morning produced mixed fortunes. Ruth started Jill, Kay and me off by asking us to warm up in open order. I cannot remember when I last shared an arena riding in open order. After many years of not riding, I decided to take private lessons and have the luxury of an arena to myself every week. Thankfully, I did not discredit myself and successfully rode Bella through several halts, walk and trot transitions, 20-metre circles, and changes of rein across the school or on a long diagonal. Stood in the corner by the entrance gate between the letters C and M, Ruth reminded us of arena etiquette. Riding left-to-left: The rider on the right-rein needs to go past the rider on the left rein using an inside track, and the rider on the faster gait has priority on the outside track. As she watched, Ruth flicked through the pages of Kay's RBRS guide. Being her nominated mentor, Ruth is helping Kay prepare for her test. To prepare Kay, she'd picked out the required exercises for a Stage 5 riding test and asked Kay what she needs to practice. Which, instigated the exercise of cantering out of a corner onto a 20-metre circle. I mostly stuck to trot as Bella rarely arrived at the corner with the correct bend for canter. It took most of my go, to get her trotting in a nice rhythm on the outside track. Even though the canter was unsuccessful, the trot improved, so I am happy.

It looks like Marble isn't the only horse pleased to be going out this morning. Gina is riding a dark bay horse called Folly at the front and at the point of joining the stony-track going down to The Great Flat Lobe trail from the outer stable yard, Folly leaps into the air using all four legs to mimic a spring lamb. His frolic is a mere-moderate leap, and within a blink of an eye, he is walking forward again. Next in line, behind Folly are the Norwich girls riding Poldark followed by Taz then two teenage sisters, who are holidaying in Cornwall with their mother. Directly at the back of Taz is the younger sister, a petite 15-year-old revealing cropped-blonde hair just visible beneath her riding hat. She is riding Storm, the grey horse used on my beach ride. Separating Storm from Marble is Ollie the thoroughbred who has the older sister riding him. She is a slim 17-year-old with cropped mousy hair. At the rear of the ride, behind me, is their mother on Harvey. The mother is for sure the rider in the family. She is wearing brown jodhpurs, riding boots, and her own-riding hat. Whereas, her daughters wear coloured jeans and the jockey skull caps supplied by Wheal Buller (identified by a 'WB' in white lettering blazed on the bare surface of the black skull caps).

Today, the weather has changed to overcast where the sun can only hint at breaking through the cloud-laden sky. A cool-wind makes me notice I'm the only rider not wearing a warm hoodie. The colourations of the foliage and grasses in the valley are dull and bland underneath the cover of white cloud. It is a dramatic change in comparison to how the valley looked yesterday evening.

Determined to make the most of the perfect day, Jill, Kay and I strolled down to The Great Flat Lode after dinner last night. The valley was full of vivid colours: green grasses, purple heathers, and white-sand trails all complimented by an unbroken blue sky. The horses grazed in the fields. Birds sang in the hedgerows. Long shadows grew from the west. Locals went by also taking advantage of the remainder of the fine-day: An old man escorted by an equally-old black and tan crossbreed; A man in his twenties walking his white-and-tan bull terrier; A child riding a bike in the company of his marginally-older sibling and their mum and dad walking behind pushing a baby in a buggy. At the time it felt yesterday was summer's swan song and this morning my intuition is proved right.

Our hack destination is the castle on Carn Brea hill. To reach the hill a similar route to the one James had used to the monument on Sunday afternoon is taken: riding on off-road trails and footpaths at walk intermingled by bursts of trot. Where there is some suitable terrain for a canter it is my job to hold Marble back and give Gina enough time to open up a gap by leading the four inexperienced riders on Poldark, Taz, Storm, and Ollie further up the trail. The instant they are out of sight, I ask Marble to trot and then canter to catch up. Not wanting to be left behind, Harvey canters on her heels. Marble's canter is rhythmic and steady. She always listens to my aides and comes back to walk ready to re-join the back of the ride. I've adapted to her humane-girth and no longer have any problems keeping her saddle in place.

Storm drops behind Ollie as she sneaks a bite of herbage from a conveniently placed hedgerow. The action makes her nervous young rider panic somewhat. To dilute the situation, I calmly encourage: 'Squeeze using your legs and at the same time use an authoritative voice and tell Storm to walk on.'

When she is back in line, I reassure: 'Storm's not going to do anything apart from keep behind the horse in front of her.'

I only think, and sneak a snack whenever she gets the chance.

She reveals her nervousness is because of a riding accident she had a few years ago. I get the impression this is the first time she's ridden since. I don't catch the entire story due to being a safe riding distance behind and there being a slight headwind; though a fractured-bone gets mentioned. She seems to relax a little after I mention Storm gets used for the beach ride and only calm and sensible horses get to go to the beach.

The ascent up the north side of Carn Brea hill is via a single-vehicle sand track that meanders through a section of hillside teeming with dense bracken. Nearing the crest of the hill the track forks. Pointing westwards to the monument and away from the direction of travel is a footpath. Our course stays on the track as it curves to the northeast towards Carn Brea Castle. Past the fork, the hill flattens, and the seascape of the Godrevy-Portreath heritage coastline is in the distance; though, stubborn cloud lingers out over the grey sea to hide the horizon. The whiter clouds above Carn Brea have risen and broken in places to reveal patches of blue. Pink flowers are plentiful on the hill and stand out in the thick cover of bracken. In the shorter grass at the edge of the track buttercups have taken root and here pink and yellow intermingle. On our nearside, beyond an ample area of bracken, the grey-stone cross of the monument touches the sky. At the point of turning our backs to the monument, the castle is still a short distance away hidden behind a substantial outcrop. As we advance, turrets, undersize-rectangular windows and the arched windows of the upper part of the castle materialize. A scattering of boulders edges the expanse of pink heathers, greenery, and buttercups. The pigmentation of the plants looks intense against the grey stone. The outcrop transpires to be on the opposite side of the track to the castle. As we go by the lee side, I estimate the outcrop to be a formation of at least ten massive granite rocks.

At the foot of the castle, the track merges into a roughly-circular and empty carpark. Gina halts the ride in a semicircle on the outer edge where the horses can nibble on the verge in the shelter of a circumference hedge grown from shrubs and a couple of young spruce trees. The castle commands a lofty vantage point within a formation of outcrops running northeast to southwest on this side of Carn Brea hill. A thin sand pathway crosses a bank of wild plants and grass and ends at the entrance door to a two-storey granite building designed to imitate a medieval castle including turrets, parapet, and slim-glazed windows.

Records suggest a building has been here since the 14th century; though the original structure is listed to have been a chapel. Later in the 18th-century modifications where made by the Basset family who renovated the chapel into a hunting lodge designed to look like a medieval folly castle. Back in the 1980s, the castle became a Middle Eastern cuisine restaurant, and it has been this incarnation ever since Its current use explains why the carpark is empty and the castle shut at 11:15 am – back down the track we'd passed a wooden sign informing passers-by that the restaurant is open every evening from 6:30 pm.

The castle is the summit of the hack, and from here the return leg begins. Our return trail to Buller hill will weave through hamlets, go alongside patchwork fields and pass some of the engine houses scattered across the valley.

Over lunch in the conservatory, Jill, Kay and I exchange details of the riding we'd done since we split up after our early-morning flat lesson. I recap the hack up to Carn Brea Castle, and they recount the highs and lows of their shared jump lessons. The first took place in the outdoor arena and the second in a field on the lower, west side of The Great Flat Lode where a course of show jumps is set-up.

After lunch, we're back in the indoor arena in the company of Ruth. Determined to improve our partnership, I'm again on Bella. As we warm up in open order, Ruth's expert eye picks up on my usual bad habits. The main exercise for the lesson is to practice canter transitions as this is Kay's weakest exercise, and it may let her down during her Stage 5 riding test on Friday. Using a figure-of-eight we are to canter at either the A or C end, then come back to a trot through X to change reins. Each rider will practice the drill while the other riders halt out of the way at either G or D. For the most part, Bella and I complete the exercise in trot. Our canter work still comprises of her rushing, and an incorrect bend whenever I ask her to canter out of the corner. Her trot work has improved. She is always forward going, but now the gait is rhythmic and steady. She's a lovely little horse in character and to ride. Ruth thinks so too. Bella is for sale, and Ruth is trying her hardest to resist buying her.

There's no time to spare after the flat lesson. As soon as I untack Bella in a stable on the main yard, I go in search of Marble to get her ready for an hour hack. I find Karen and a lady with a blond bob tacking Marble up in a stable on the outer yard. Karen introduces the lady by name and informs me she is Marble's owner. Marble's owner has a friendly-forthcoming nature, and straightaway tells me how Marble never wants to leave Wheal Buller at the end of the summer. I'm not surprised. Marble is schooled, jumped, hacked and she swims. She is turned out in the company of a herd of horses, and the children who regularly ride here adore her. The level of exercise, stimulation, and attention she gets at Wheal Buller is impossible to mirror by a single person. What does surprise me is when Marble's owner tells me Marble is six-years-old. I'm amazed at how young she is, 'Really? Wow, you've done a good job. She is such a pleasure to ride.'

For the next hour, Gina takes me, Jill, the Norwich girls, Georgina and two experienced riders on holiday for a whistle-stop tour of the local valley using country lanes and converted tramways. I say whistle-stop for the majority of the ride is in trot except for in a few places where the trail narrows, and we have to walk, or widens enough for a canter. Marble and I again get enlisted to hold the ride back for the canters, so Gina riding a large-grey called Delmar can trot off into the distance leading the Norwich girls on Poldark and Taz.

My role is to wait and lead the remainder of the ride on a catch-up canter: Jill on Max, the holidaymakers on Folly and Harvey respectively and Georgina at the back on Crystal, a small chestnut horse marked by a white star. In the act of Gina putting us through our paces, the scenery rushes by, and my single observation is mist drawing in to cover the distant fields. I hope it stays there.

We arrive back into a hive of activity on the main yard. Tomorrow is an extraordinary day for Wheal Buller Riding School because a BBC film crew is scheduled to arrive here first thing in the morning. Wheal Buller and Gwithian Beach are going to be used to produce an episode of the CBeebies television programme: *Something Special*. The programme is aimed at toddlers, pre-school and special needs children and incorporates early years' sign-language and symbols in its educational format. The main characters are Justin and Mr. Tumble. It is Justin who will be here tomorrow accompanied by a child helper to film the scenes for the episode: *'Something Special – We're All Friends – Horse Riding by the Sea.'*

Karen temporarily leaves the preparations of trimming Trilby, tack or lorry cleaning to assist the dismounting ride. She takes Max from Jill. Max has completed his day's work and is next in line to have a shower and shampoo. Karen doesn't know the height and weight of either Justin or the child actor, so she's preparing two horses and three ponies. The hosing-down area is occupied by a skewbald mare named Stella, who is the preferred choice for Justin to ride because she is always impeccably behaved on the beach. Stella has been brought back to the yard after having a few days off grazing on land away from the riding school. She is a nice-looking horse with a white and cream patched coat. Max is being prepared just in case Justin is too heavy for Stella. Trilby, Taz, and Dotty are the potential mounts for the child actor. Dotty has a flea-bitten flecked coat and iron-grey legs and is the littlest of the three ponies. Taz will have his shampoo after the final ride of the day, another session of drill/formation riding.

An outcome of having completed five hours of riding previously to leading Toby into the indoor arena is I'm flagging a bit. So, I'm grateful that the drill/formation session is just a bit of fun at the end of the day, and I'm riding the 'I know what I am doing' schoolmaster.' Gina does a fantastic job again of keeping us moving in the right order amidst a lot of laughter and a rider veering off course once or twice. Jill is on Max, who is the horse equivalent of a light-aircraft carrier in ships. Because of his bulk, he takes a fraction longer to manoeuvre around a bend than Toby and in the act of pairing up, say down the centreline, Jill and I need to ensure she starts her turn ahead of me. As she concocts the routine, Gina notes the sequence of movements on a piece of paper. She suggests a song is chosen this evening so the routine can be ridden to music tomorrow. The girls from Norwich and Georgina are keen on this idea, and Georgina agrees to source a CD as nobody had packed any music. When I'm back on the ground leading Toby, Gina hands me the piece of paper the routine is scribbled on just as I exit the indoor arena. Back out on the main yard, I hand the paper swiftly on to the Norwich girls, who plan to practice the routine on foot at Hendra Holiday Park this evening.

Back at the bungalow, Jill and I find Kay sat on the deck steps drinking a cup of tea while reading her RBRS Level 6 notes. Throughout the time spent out on the energetic hack and the subsequent drill/formation ride, Kay was with Ruth. They had been in the tack room where Ruth had shown Kay, a collection of less commonly used tack and an assortment of bits, rugs, and martingales. Ruth had carefully selected and explained the purpose of each item based on the questions Kay might get asked in her test.

Jill and I leave Kay to her study and retire to the hot tub for two cycles. As our tired muscles get soothed in the 40°C bubbles, Georgina is spotted rapidly approaching from the direction of the conservatory and onto the deck. She excitedly tells us she has chosen a Jessie-J track for tomorrow's drill/formation ride. Care is taken not to curb her enthusiasm as I report Jill and I won't be on the drill/formation ride. After turning Toby and Max out in the field, we'd returned to the bungalow to find tomorrows riding schedule on the coffee table, and there is no mention of drill/formation riding. To ensure Georgina's excitement isn't crushed, I let her know I'd handed the piece of paper with the routine to the Norwich girls so they can practice this evening. I add, I'm sure they will be keen to do the drill/formation ride, and she should let the girls know what music she picked when they arrive in the morning.

Something Special

The crew and stars of the CBeebies television programme *Something Special* had already arrived at the time, Jill, Kay and I peer out the bungalow windows onto the main yard. The day is grey, there is a chill in the air and an early morning mist conceals the crest of Carn Brea hill. The child star is crying his sobs are coming from the vicinity of the education room and hay storage area. Speculating we'll get in the way of the preparations, we concur not to go out on the yard until a few minutes before the first lesson. The staff of Wheal Buller started even earlier than usual this morning. The horses are in the stables, the yard is spotless, and everything is ready for the long day ahead.

Just after 9:00 am, I collect Bella from a bottom stable on the main yard. She is in the stable next door to Folly, who is getting attention from an oval-faced young-middle-aged man of medium build wearing a pink-fleece jumper. The man is Justin, the presenter of the TV programme. After we exchange hellos, he says Folly is a nice horse. He adds he hasn't been introduced to his horse yet. I don't mention it will probably be Stella.

Gina's five minutes of fame will have to wait for another day because she had drawn the short straw and is in charge of entertaining us while the filming goes on elsewhere. The first ride is a flat lesson in the indoor arena. As Kay's test is tomorrow, we warm up by trotting without stirrups and then move on to practicing canter transitions, figures of eight and trotting 20-metre circles in preparation for going large in a canter. My perseverance is starting to pay off as I'm having more success getting Bella to bend correctly ready for a transition into a canter. I feel a real sense of achievement as I canter out of the corner between A and K and down the long side to C.

Nearing the close of the lesson, Ruth pops up in the entrance to ask Gina to keep her voice down because the television crew's sound equipment is picking it up. The crew is filming Justin and the child star grooming their horses alongside the fence in the outer yard. Gina spends the remainder of the lesson stood at the entrance between letters C and M, the furthest away point of the school away from the filming. She gives us brief guidance as our horse goes by. To hear longer-instructions, we halt at G. Whenever the volume of her voice starts to increase, we direct a joshing 'shush' at our muffled instructor.

I had opted out of the next lesson as it is cross-country jumping. Walking on foot beside Gina, I'm relaxed knowing I'm not making a sound; whereas, Jill, Kay and the Norwich girls horses make clip-clops as they exit the main yard on the way to the outdoor arena. I tease the guilty parties reminding them not to make a noise by holding my finger to my lips as they ride past the hosing arena: the closest point to where the television crew is filming.

Sitting on the grass bank beside the entrance, I watch Gina start the ride off by getting them to practice their jumping position in preparation for jumping a low-set show jump close to the letter E. Jill is on the reliable and steady Fergie. Jill had told me she only gets the opportunity to jump cross-country while on holiday and although she is keen to participate, a lack of practice makes her a little nervous. Kay is on Jess, the dark bay horse with a white star who Georgina rode a couple of days ago. Jess is a well-covered robust mare boasting a lovely thick black mane and tail. The Norwich girls are on Poldark and Taz. Their riding and confidence have improved rapidly since their arrival, aided by the fearlessness of the young.

With the warm-up completed, Gina leads the way to the cross-country jumps. Wheal Buller's course makes use of the two long fields split by The Great Flat Lode trail. Today's lesson will be on a section of the course where there are a few jumps close together. On exiting the arena, the ride diverts away from the yard onto a lower sand track that briefly runs parallel to the higher-track going to Buller Hill. Here a gate opens into a downward-sloping field where we pass a couple of cross-country jumps on the way to a gate at the lower end. We enter and cut across the width of one of the long cross-country-jump fields stopping in the bottom corner close to the post-and-rail fence bordering The Great Flat Lode. The terrain is ideal for a cross-country course: a mix of rolling hills and stretches of moderately-level lush green grass. The mist has cleared to unveil ominous darker rain-bearing clouds in a mainly pale-grey sky. Again, the scattering of engine houses throughout the valley and the monument and castle on Carn Brea hill provide an impressive backdrop.

The first jump to be attempted is a log with an uphill approach on a line looking back towards the stables. Jill is to go first, leaving the others to await their go by walking a circle in the north corner of the field. I stand to the right of the log beside Gina, who continually switches effortlessly between calling out instructions and chatting to me. Jill approaches the fence in a steady canter. Her leg is on to maintain Fergie's momentum going forward, and they clear the jump with ease. In the time, it takes for Jill to re-join the ride, Gina and I discuss if her voice is carrying back up the hill to the vicinity of the yard. She shrugs, 'Oh well. I have to shout teaching cross country.'

Next to jump is Kay. Jess is more forward going than Fergie, and Kay has to apply half halts to check her rushing, they too jump cleanly. The girls on Taz and Poldark are instructed to go together in single file. There is lots of encouragement from Gina as they trot uphill. The girls will, their ponies on with verbal encouragement and their sticks to back-up their leg aids. At a slow and steady pace, Poldark and Taz respectively, obediently go over the jump. Gina lauds like a proud parent as she watches the ponies and their inexperienced riders go back down to the corner: 'I can't believe how good those ponies are.'

Poldark and Taz get given to absolute beginners to ride for a reason. These two equines take care of their riders and know what to do in inexperienced hands. They are the best partners to learn how to ride on even though the girls may consider them to be a bit hard to get going. The Norwich girls will jump the log again, individually. Poldark's more confident rider arrives at the jump in a canter. Whereas, Taz tackles the log in an active working trot.

The next obstacle is a jump made from plywood. There are two sections joined together to allow for a choice of either a high or low obstacle. The higher section is painted to depict a whitewashed two-storey mansion featuring sash windows and a balcony above a central doorway. The lower section is painted to be the mansion's adjoining stable block, and four of Wheal Buller's horses were chosen to model a head looking out over the stable doors. Pitched roofs top the mansion and stable block. The jump is on almost-level turf, and its approach is from the north to the south. Standing close to Gina, I watch all the riders successfully jump the lower stable block section.

The third and final jump to tackle is a horizontal log fixed to posts and filled in by tyres cut into arched half-moons. It is the fence that comes after the mansion-and-stables on the cross-country course. In the same order and amid guidance and lots of encouragement from Gina everyone clears the fence without any problems, their confidence boosted by the successes over the previous fences.

On the way, back to the yard, Gina and I chat at the head of a single file procession of horses and riders. She speaks of the years she attended agricultural college where she trained to become a riding instructor. Simultaneously and alongside her equestrian qualifications, she had completed a business studies course. We agree that had been a sensible choice as the diversification means there are other options available to her should she decide to move away from teaching. I too made the same decision, and it proved to be an important one I left agricultural college having gained a business Level 2 qualification, and it is this element of the course that I have made use of in my working life subsequently obtaining a Level 5 with distinction.

At the gateway, onto the lower track, the ride is brought to a halt to wait for a mini-convoy to drive by. The television crew has finished the grooming piece and have packed themselves and their equipment into a pair of four-wheel-drive land cruisers ready to pull out of the carpark. The crew is waiting for Karen, Emma, and Ruth, who are in the cab of the horse lorry. Stella and Dotty, the chosen mounts for the television stars are loaded and ready to go. A subsequent scene will be Justin and the child actor riding on Gwithian beach. Waves are exchanged as the lorry, driven by Emma, trundles by tailed by the TV crew in their land cruisers.

Our voices are reinstated to normal volume as we enter the main yard, and the riders' dismount. On Gina's instruction, I take Fergie's reins and Jill and I continue on into the indoor arena. Inside, I halt Fergie on the centre line. Jill takes a seat in the gallery and looks at her iPhone. So far, the rain has held off, but there is a drop-in temperature because of the inclement weather. Indoors it is sheltered, calm and warm with an abundance of natural light spilling in through the skylights. Gina, having made a detour to the tack room to collect a lunge cavesson, lunge line, and lunge reins arrives and prepares me, and Fergie for a lunge lesson. Satisfied everything is how it should be she fetches the lunge whip from the hidden shelf behind the letter M and attaches the lunge line to the lunging cavesson. I always appreciate a lunge lesson particularly on a comfortable and steady long-striding horse like Fergie. With Gina in control of the horse, I can focus on correcting the bad riding habits being expertly picked out: 'Tuck your bottom underneath you. Relax and stretch your leg. Sit back and tall.'

The Norwich girls arrive in the company of Kay shortly after the lesson starts and join Jill in the gallery. When Fergie is brought back to a halt to change the rein, Gina asks the Norwich girls to find Belinda and ask her to get Taz ready for lunging. Many years had passed since I lunged a horse so I'd requested a lesson to regain this lost skill.

Taz is equipped for lunging when Belinda leads him into the arena. Gina takes charge of Taz and Belinda leads Fergie out of the arena. As previously mentioned, Taz is an Exmoor pony, a breed native to the British Isles. The description of the breed on the Exmoor Pony Society website (exmoorponysociety.org.uk) is 'Definite 'pony' character; hard and strong; vigorous alert and symmetrical in presence; mealy muzzle; prominent hooded toad eye.' The society goes on to say a stallion or gelding should be: 'No more than 12.3 hh (129.5 cm)'. I size up Taz to be 12.3 hh. The native Exmoor pony is the resident wild pony of Exmoor national park. An expanse of hilly moorland approximately 100 miles (160 km) away from Wheal Buller Riding School, close to the Bristol Channel coastline in the county of Devon. The earliest record of wild ponies roaming the moor is in the 1086 Doomsday Book, a survey of the land commissioned during the rule of William the Conqueror (William I). Though, it is known wild ponies had roamed the land for thousands of years preceding the composition of this historical record.

I'm first up in the lunge lesson. Gina instructs me to hold the whip under my arm, so it extends behind when not in use. She holds Taz so I can safely prepare the lunge line by creating generous-size loops ready to feed in and out of my hand before clipping it onto the centre ring of the lunging cavesson. There is a lot to do simultaneously. Under the guidance of Gina, I get myself into the correct position and Taz out onto a circular track by pointing the whip at his shoulder to push him out while ensuring the line feeds out twist free. A triangle is formed with me at the point and central to the saddle on Taz's back. The sides of the triangle get formed by the taut lunge line connecting my hand to the cavesson and the long lunge whip pointing at his hocks or down at the floor.

Taz certainly holds the traits of his breed. He's kind, caring, hardworking and cheeky. Gina reminds me of the importance of voice aids when lunging. Slow-pitch to go down a gait, 'W.a.l.k.'

High-pitch to go up a gait, 'Trot on.'

Being a cheeky pony, Taz isn't going to do anything unless you use a clear voice and the appropriate tone. Gina teaches to use the whip above his hock and ask him to move forward: 'Use one slightly harder whip; do not 'fly fish. It will just tickle the horse, and he will not respond.'

Overall, my lesson is a success. Taz has responded well to my actions and voice. Satisfied by my achievement, I join Jill in the viewing gallery and watch the Norwich girls have their lunge lessons.

No sooner had the lunch plates and cutlery been cleared away another guest arrives at the bungalow: Sylvia, a matter-of-fact, tall middle-aged lady who is distinguished by large features to match her size. Like Jill and Kay, she is staying at Wheal Buller up to noon on Saturday. The first ride of the afternoon and together is a flat lesson in the indoor arena. I ride Bella again, Jill is on a large dapple grey called Jasper, and Sylvia is on Harvey. Kay is riding Sooty, who is kitted out in a blue-blinker hood. Gina schools us through trotting without stirrups and canter transitions. When the rest of the ride moves on to cantering without stirrups, I decide to leave this one-step-further out and concentrate on maintaining a decent canter transition with stirrups.

After the flat lesson, Kay joins Ruth for a stable management lesson on the main yard. Jill, Sylvia and I decline the offer of joining them and retire to the brown-leather sofas in the bungalow's lounge for a chat. Soon into the conversation, Jill and Sylvia discover they ride in the same district of Southeast London. In spite of never previously meeting, they know many of the same people, stables and horses.

We're all back in the indoor arena at 3:00 pm including the Norwich girls on Poldark and Taz. I'm riding the beautiful Fergie. Jill is on Bella. This lesson primarily focuses on the trot and using poles to extend the horses strides. The adults complete the exercise without stirrups.

It is close to 4:00 pm when we emerge onto the main yard and prepare for a hack. I swap Fergie for Marble. Georgina joins us having returned from her first day back at school. Escorted by Gina at the head of the ride our troop sets of towards The Great Flat Lode. The threat of rain has hung in the air since sunrise, and this outlook comes into fruition as misty rain engulfs the countryside cascading down from the hilltops into the valley.

The first part of the hack retraces the route we'd used on Sunday afternoon. Mostly sticking to the multi-purpose off-road trails going northwards to close in on the presently shrouded in mist Carn Brea hill. There is temporary shelter on the incline through the tunnel of thicket trees to meet the lane going into Church Town. Instead of going right towards the church, the ride takes a left, southwards down a country lane. Further down the lane, there is another off-road trail winding through an old mining area, which is now scrubland. Encircled in mist and amid the patter of steadily increasing rain the surroundings take on the ambiance of spectral moorland. It is the type of weather that encourages the re-telling of local fables and tales passed down the generations. Stories of the eras when smugglers, wreckers, and ghosts prevailed. It is easy to grasp how the setting and weather can bring atmosphere to these types of stories, and this is particularly prevalent in reaching the ruin of Wheal Basset Stamps.

In single file, we enter the ruin at the engine-house end and keep to a central pathway covering its length, east to west. There is no roof, leaving the ruin's interior exposed to the elements. Rocks, stones, and long-tufts of or foot-trodden grass cover the ground. Bramble bushes group against the crumbling granite walls. The north-facing wall incorporates 13 arches, which on a clear day would frame 13 vistas of the valley, Carn Brea hill, and the coast. Today there are no views as the mist allows for nothing but the interior to be visible. The air is hushed. Nothing stirs. Just the hooves of the horses hitting the hard earth break the silence. This situation is spooky enough to be the set of a Cornish ghost story.

Wheal Basset Stamps is close to Wheal Buller, and on returning, we find the horse lorry is back from the beach. Although most of the day involved standing around waiting, it was still long for the equine stars, Stella and Dotty. Both of whom have been turned out in the field for a well-earnt roll and graze. In the act of changing horses for the final lesson of the day, we learn that Emma and Ruth will appear on the television show for it was impossible for them not to get filmed as they held or led Stella and Dotty. When asked, the film crew would not give a specific date of broadcast committing only to: '...sometime in February.'

Apart from riding hats and half chaps none of us were wearing anything remotely waterproof on the venture out into the rain and mist. Luckily, the shirt I'm wearing is a quick-dry hiking shirt, which dries in the time it takes us to warm up for our flat lesson in the indoor arena. Back on Fergie, I'm soon practicing leg yielding and riding trot in a straight line. Ruth's experienced eyes pick up my riding errors, and her advice is to move my weight onto my outside seat, ensure my leg is on and apply a half halt.

The Last Morning

After breakfast, I stand at the bungalow window looking towards the horizon at the town of St Ives settled on the edge of St Ives Bay. Overhead is a strip of blue sky where the sun has broken through the remnants of yesterday's rain clouds. Sunrays beam down onto the town like a giant spotlight. The spectacular illumination produced demonstrates why St Ives is a haven for artists who seek the best natural light for their canvasses.

My attention is brought back to the yard by loose horses arriving. Each horse finds an open doorway to an empty stable where they enter and help themselves to the food already scooped out in the feed troughs. The horses' escort is Belinda, who closes the stables doors behind them. Wheal Buller retains the luxury of being an off-road site where field gates are safely away from roads. Because there are a lot of horses it has been established the quickest method to get them in from the fields in the morning is to fill the feed troughs with food and leave the stable doors secured open. Before the field gates get opened, members of staff position themselves in specific places along the way. The horses then walk free up to the stables where they know food awaits. Jill mentioned the morning ritual a few days ago, but I had not seen it play out. The whole process works like clockwork. Only Folly gets ushered on after Belinda catches him with his head over the closed door of the stable already taken by Jasper, helping himself to the grey's breakfast.

Today is my ultimate day. Between now and my departure after lunch, I will participate in three rides: two flat lessons riding Bella split by an hour hack on Marble. With an hour to go until the first lesson, Kay is sat on the lounge sofa, cup of tea in hand, cramming in stable management revision in preparation for her test this afternoon. To leave her in peace, I remove myself from peering out of the window and go back to my room to pack.

I find Bella lying down on a thick bed of clean straw in a wooden stable on the outer yard. I wonder if she's had a restless night out in the field in the unsettled weather. Also, being a favourite of mine and Jill's, she's had a busy week entertaining us. The first flat lesson focuses on the exercises Kay hasn't consistently accomplished yet and will be required to ride in her test. Consulting the test guide in her hand, Ruth directs, Jill, Kay, Sylvia and me to warm up in open order then moves us on to trotting without stirrups, riding 20-metre circles and changing the rein through the letter X. Bella and I have come on well together, and I'm getting a nice canter when I ask. Because she is tired today, I am reminded to squeeze her using my legs on each rise to retain the trot.

At the end of the lesson, I put Bella back in the stable on the outer yard. Marble is close by in an adjoining stable. As I tack her up for the hack out, I lavish Marble with lots of fuss and attention. Emma leads the ride with the Norwich girls riding Poldark and Taz immediately after. I'm behind the girls, next is Sylvia riding Stella and then Jill, who brings up the rear on Fergie. We as good as keep to the same route we'd ridden yesterday but now we get to enjoy the view of the valley and Carn Brea hill. The sun is warm, and the sky blue with high white clouds. For now, the darker heavy-rain-bearing clouds forecasted to arrive later remain on the horizon out at sea. Because the ground is dry, there are a few places to canter before we ride through Wheal Basset Stamps again. Free of mist and drenched in sunlight the ruin isn't spooky today, merely a crumbling old ruin exhibiting 13 arches framing 13 pictures of variform vistas. There is a vibrant carpet of green and yellow flora, glossy ivy covers the exit wall, and sky blue replaces the once-upon-a-time roof.

Back in the indoor arena, Emma takes the lesson. For the second time today, I find myself having to ride Bella on as opposed to repressing her rushing. After the hack, I'd found Bella lying down in the stable and she wasn't too keen on the idea of getting up. Like Marble, she too had received a lot of fuss and attention while I tacked up. My final lesson is also Kay's last chance to practice canter transitions in advance of her test. The main advice for me in the transition out of the corner is to keep my inside leg on the girth and use my outside leg to support, look where I'm going and move my weight to the outside if Bella falls in. To compensate for a tired horse, I need to use a lot of inside-leg and use my stick to back up the leg aid if there is no response. Whenever she starts to rush into the transition from trot, I apply half halts backed up by my leg to retain the forward movement.

After I dismount, I reflect on the progress I've made with Bella through the week. Considering my level of riding skill, she is not the easiest horse for me to ride. Nevertheless, she is a lovely mare who is willing to do what you ask her, and I've relished the little victories when they arose. It is a joy to lead her back to a snug stable where food waits for her. After removing her tack and lavishing pats, I say goodbye and leave her to her lunch. I'm sure after she's eaten she will lay down again for another well-earnt rest.

With lunch finished and the car packed, I exchange goodbyes with Jill, Kay, and Sylvia and leave the bungalow. On the way out, I pop my head around the door of the education building where inside Ruth, Emma, Gina, and Belinda sit eating their packed lunches. I thank them for their delightful lessons and hacks, and they ask if I will come back. I'm not sure when I will visit again. I plan to ride in India next year and in subsequent years' other faraway destinations. Be that as it may, Wheal Buller is close to where I live, and therefore it would be unthinkable to assume this is the first and last visit.

Driving down the track and out onto Buller Hill, I reminisce on the last five days. Although I grew up in Cornwall, I had never holidayed here. There were visits to see my parents, during the 10-years, I'd lived in the South East of England, but never an actual holiday. For my first and maybe last Cornish holiday, I am glad I chose Wheal Buller Riding School.

Part 4

A Mediterranean Retreat

Son Menut

It's close to 6:00 pm as the eight-seater white minibus branded by the Son Menut logo of green text and a cantering horse emblazon on its side door rolls to a halt outside a Spanish villa. I'm in the company of another guest, Brigot an athletic German lady in her thirties with doe eyes and brown hair pulled back in a tidy ponytail. We've just completed a 30 miles (48 km) transfer through the countryside from Palma de Mallorca Airport. Our driver and host, Toni Barceló, is a stocky fair-haired native Mallorcan and the owner *(el propietario)* of Son Menut.

Son Menut is a rural estate *(finca)* sited 3 miles (4.8 km) from the westside fringe of the town of Felanitx in the southeast of Mallorca, the largest of the four Spanish Balearic Islands located in the Mediterranean Sea. The journey from Palma de Mallorca Airport takes you from the west side of the island to the east side using roads in good repair. However, this discontinued on the final approach down to Son Menut's main gate when, through an area of ploughed-fields, the minibus had bounced along a stony lane full of shallow potholes.

Grand sandstone-block pillars capped by slabs of taupe-grey stone and a vanilla ornamental sphere flank a gateway wide enough for a sizeable lorry to drive through. The pillars are at the ends of traditional croft sandstone walls; an apparent common feature of the Mallorca countryside considering I'd seen many of the same on the journey from the airport. On the near side of the gateway is a metal-sculpted sign. This sign is a piece of roadside art with vertical and horizontal tubular poles framing a painting and a rusty-welding of the word 'Restaurant' and a cartoonish fish skeleton on a plate. The painting has weathered better than the welding. At the centre are a grey horse and a chestnut horse with a star and strip. The grey is in nearside profile. The chestnut has its head looking over the grey's neck and its quarters pointed at the 45-minute angle on a clock face. They stand in a green meadow against a backdrop of alpine-trees. Forming an arch around the horses are the words: 'SON MENUT ESCOLA D'EQUITACIO' (Son Menut School of Riding).

Inside the gateway, the minibus turned left in front of a tangled hedgerow formed by a hot-climate shrub and two enormous trees that conceal everything behind from view. The largest tree has thick boughs full of green and brown leaves. Luscious dark green leaves and pink flowers cover its slighter neighbour's branches. Summer clings to the island in early October. Unlike the autumnal United Kingdom, I departed from several hours ago. From here to home there is a distance of ten-degrees north on the latitude line and for the next few weeks a difference of a season.

A capacious-sand surface driveway lined by overhanging trees casting shade onto six or so parked vehicles tapers in to end at the familiar sight of the main accommodation building. Familiar for I had seen it on the Son Menut website. Painted in the tones of apricot and salmon the villa is classic Spanish, two-storey topped by a pitched roof with a three-arch balcony characterized by black-wrought-iron railings. Wooden-shutters painted leaf-green adorn the windows and doors. At opposite ends of the building at the point where the ground and first-floor meet are lantern-style exterior lights protruding out and upwards. In the back, northeast corner on the ground floor are the archways of a loggia. At the base of the building is a row of terracotta pots containing succulents or native-leaf plants broken in line only by a wooden bench and a doorway with its outer green-shutter door secured back against the wall.

The minibus trundles past the parked vehicles, grey MPVs, a white passenger van, and a sporty black SEAT. And here we are outside the green-shutter door. I step out of the minibus's side door into the peacefulness of the Felanitx countryside. A horse whinnies and another reciprocates; an indication the stables are nearby. Momentarily, a dinky black-and-tan terrier pops up yapping-intently until it sees it is Toni and the minibus that has arrived. Then it goes back to wherever it had been before.

'El Perro.'

Toni and Brigot reward me by flashing broad smiles in response to this demonstration of my limited Spanish vocabulary.

Earlier, coming out of the airport terminal, we were greeted by a heavy shower. Thankfully the wet weather cleared quickly to reveal blue sky and white clouds. Now the dark rain-bearing clouds drift above distant hills. The temperature for sure feels the 26°C (78°F) that was displayed on an electronic billboard someplace on route from the airport. Our suitcases get unloaded from the back of the minibus, and Brigot and I say 'Gracias. Adiós' to Toni as he jumps back into the driver seat and pulls away.

During our journey, Brigot had brushed off the cobwebs of her excellent English and revealed who Toni is and explained he doesn't speak any English. Although Brigot has enough Spanish vocabulary to form basic sentences, most of the conversation during the transfer was between us, the guests. In the course of the journey, I found out this is Brigot's second visit to Son Menut. Her previous trip was back in July, and she enjoyed the week so much she decided to come back. Brigot shows the way by passing underneath an oval dark-wood plaque displaying the word Reception hanging from a black-metal bracket above the green-shutter doorway.

We enter a box-shaped room where a high desk splits the room in half. There are framed-photographs of Pure Spanish Horses *(Pura Raza Española (PRE)* covering the walls: mainly muscular iron-grey stallions parading long manes and tails as they stand or move in a convex outline. A tall, slim lady distinguished by long and thick dyed-blond hair greets us by introducing herself as Maria Antonia. In limited English, she tells me in addition to her native language she is fluent in German only. Brigot is tired from many hours of travelling and struggles to recall her English on the account she hasn't used it for a few months. Cooperatively they manage to get me checked in and issued with a key to my room and safe. The check-in concludes with the reassurance Catalina, who speaks fluent English, will be on reception in the morning from 9:00 am to answer any detailed questions or queries I may have. Maria Antonia opens the desk hatch and walks through indicating we're to follow her.

Back outside we pass underneath another oval sign, displaying the cream-colour words Bar and Restaurant, to reach the loggia. All the decoration and designs reflect rural Spain. At the end of the loggia's archways are potted succulents placed on the floor. Hung on the white-washed west wall is an engraved picture in the style of ancient Rome or Greece. It depicts five semi-naked dancers, four young women and a young man at the centre blowing into a pan-flute. At the loggia's centre is a traditional barrel decorated in a cream mosaic applied to depict horses and horseshoes. Above the barrel is a green-glass lantern that dangles down from a ceiling covered in curved terracotta tiles. An arched wood-frame window with a windowsill ornamented by a row of cactus and succulents individually growing in more terracotta pots dominates the white-washed south wall of the loggia. A glance through the restaurant window is into a lifeless interior that is narrow and long. There is a window matching the window I look through on the back wall. To the side of this window is a set of double doors that reveal through the panes the trees out back.

The loggia's back-right corner is taken up by the closed solid-wood door of the restaurant. Maria Antonia double backs outside the restaurant door to lead us up a cream-tiled outdoor staircase enclosed by black handrails and whitewashed walls. The staircase turns at a right-angle halfway up, thereon another 10 or so steps deposit us at the beginning of an open-fronted passageway. On the left is another whitewashed wall. On the right are the stone arches and black railings previously observed on arrival. Since this is not Brigot's first visit she advises Maria Antonia, she can find her room from here and peels off into the depth of the upper floor. Maria Antonia and I continue for the length of the balcony aiming for a red-wood door at the end. From the balcony, you can see the driveway splits, north and east. On the north split, a white-stone pillar marks the entrance to the stables where tangerine outbuildings with corrugated pitched roofs border the continuing track. I conclude it is the stables from the intermittent-whinnying and more authoritarian neigh of a stallion, which are coming from this direction. On reaching the door, at the far end it is revealed there are two more doors in an alcove. Beside each door is a charmingly decorated pale-yellow tile cemented into the wall in a diamond shape. The tile outside my room has tulip heads painted at the points on an indigo border. In the centre is the number 2 and what looks to be the text: *Es Gallovel* or *Es Gazzovez*. Inside the threshold, Maria Antonia quickly points out the obvious-fixtures plus a red card folder on the top of a chest of draws. She then makes her apologies explaining she needs to get back to the temporally unattended reception desk.

Directly above reception, my room looks out to the front of the building. The theme remains equal to the outside, white walls and terracotta tiles. Square in shape it features a double wood-framed window and a high ceiling to give the space a cool-and-roomy ambiance. At the centre is a single bed made up using white sheets and a sun-faded-green over-blanket. There is a suite of double wardrobe, chest, dressing table and bedside cabinet. Just as described on the Son Menut website, the room has a small flat-screen television, telephone, safe, and fridge. I never travel without earplugs, and I'm thankful for this detail because the fridge isn't discretely out of sight and hearing in an enclosed unit. It is freestanding in the back-corner buzzing and humming away. Despite this, the room is more home than a hotel and I know I'm going to be comfortable here.

On the opposite side of the room to the entrance is the en-suite bathroom where the white-tiled walls are pointed to create a diamond pattern, a faint indigo flower head decorates each point. The bath is deep yet short in length. Not a problem for me as I'm a shower person. At the centre is a mirror fixed to the wall above a sink unit dressed up with a curtain drawn across the bottom. Overreacting somewhat, I decide not to move the curtain for in my mind behind it is a haunt for spiders and minuscule bitey things. Plus, there's enough space on the blue-tiled surface skirting the sink for me to leave my things. Mosquitos love my blood, and because of this, I carry out regular checks in my room. I go back into the bedroom to where my suitcase is and dig out my insect repellent.

After unpacking, there is still an hour to spare before dinner. I know I should go outside and explore, but as a consequence of a long day of travel, I'm exhausted. Since leaving home before 6:00 am this morning, I'd embarked on two flights and a wait at London Gatwick Airport and Palma Airport. I reason it will be more beneficial if I stay put and rest. So, I sit on the bed and read the contents of the red-card folder. Inside there are details of meal times, a list of staff and the *Naturals Parc trails* programme for the week. When I've finished, I connect my tablet to Son Menut's free Wi-Fi and look at the Felanitx weather forecast. Outside the stillness of the late afternoon is disturbed by the intermittent-whinny of a horse, no doubt a stallion. Already my mind and body are fully tuned in to the relaxation and contentment offered by this peaceful environment.

At 7:30 pm, I go down to the *Restaurant Cuina Mediterrània*. The solid-wood door is secured back against the wall to reveal a glass-panel double door. This secondary door opens into an L-shape room that maintains the same terracotta square-tile floor and whitewashed walls as outside. A screen of wrought-iron and taut white-linen cloth partitions the horizontal part of the L-shape from the door. Light pours in through the windows and double doors that provide access to a terrace. Solid-wood chairs are placed around red-wood tables running the length of the vertical part of the L shape close to the wall. The tables stop just short of the bar and the doorway to the kitchen behind. This section of the restaurant presents a homely-look using pictures of various breeds of Spanish horse, an old upright piano and a bookshelf and dresser pushed up against the wall between the entrance door and bar.

A young fair-haired family, who look to be Scandinavian occupy a set-table in the back-corner close to the double doors. The parents are entertaining a boy of about eight-years-old while his sister, perhaps twelve-years-old, sits at a desk behind the wrought iron screen. She focuses contently at an old desktop PC provided for guests to use. Table one, nearest to the bar, is un-set. Table two and three are set using white-cloth over a red-cloth and arranged to accommodate eight diners apiece. Maria Antonia, now in the role of the waitress *(camarera)*, delivers a warm greeting and directs me to table two. She informs me this is the table where the guests on the *Naturals Parc trails* programme will dine. Table three is where the guests on the dressage programme will sit.

I'm not the first riding programme guest to arrive. Both tables are already in use, each seating a couple sipping pre-dinner drinks. As the dressage programme table is closest to the door, I briefly stop here first. A late middle-aged couple from Sweden stands to introduce themselves. I ascertain the wife is on the dressage programme and the husband, Anton, a non-horse rider and keen cyclist is here to explore Mallorca on his bike. Throughout the introduction jets of cold air blow out of an old air-conditioning unit fixed to the wall close to their table; its toil provides a comfortable temperature for dining.

I join the couple at my table and sit beside a woman in her early thirties blessed by a smooth-youthful complexion and natural short-blonde hair. More introductions commence, and there is an unexpected surprised, they too are from England. The young woman is Hayley. She is with her partner Chris, a thickset man in his forties with dark hair. They are from Southampton, a city located on the south coast of the UK. Brigot arrives and joins us sitting opposite Hayley and me, beside Chris. There is a pause in conversation to allow Maria Antonia to take our drinks order and then we share brief overviews of lives back home.

Chris is a security manager at an oil refinery. Hayley manages the pub they jointly own in Hythe, Hampshire called The Glens. The pub was called the Glen Eagles. However, as a result of numerous calls from people wanting the infamous golf course in Scotland, 470 miles (756 km) to the north, they decided to change the name. Though, the name change hasn't eliminated all of the erroneous-calls. The pub's garden backs onto the edge of the New Forest National Park, an area of countryside spanning approximately 219 sq. miles (352 sq. km) that primarily consists of woodland, heathland, and grassland. The New Forest National Park's most famous resident is the New Forest pony. Measuring up to 14.2 hh (1.47 m) the New Forest pony is the largest of the British Isles moorland and mountain native breeds. Hayley owns seven New Forest ponies; though, not all of them are turned out onto the New Forest to roam. Two are kept at and used by a local riding stable. Hayley is particularly proud of her riding-school kept pony, Charlie. For Charlie was certified as a class 11 sports pony recently. We ascertain this is a good achievement despite none of us knowing what it means. The ponies were all purchased at the New Forest horse sales held on specific dates throughout the year. In jest it is suggested, Hayley stays away from future horse sales seeing as she already owns seven.

Brigot works for a car rental firm. She recalls stories of cars not being returned at the end of a hire or coming back with parts swapped out. Suspicion levels are raised by a potential customer asking for a car with a specific specification. A couple of years ago, at the back of 15 years of ownership, she lost her horse to old age. She won't be looking to buy another horse any time soon because of work and other commitments. When she was here in July, the guests then were mostly English. She doesn't mind talking in English. Though, it would be nice to speak German, to give her a break from having to formulate the words and sentences in her head before speaking.

Whenever a guest on the dressage programme arrives, they briefly introduce themselves to our table then take their seat on their own. For the next couple of hours, Brigot, with knowledge from her previous visit, outlines the week ahead while we dine on a delicious meal. My choice is tomato soup followed by baked-aubergines, rice, and potato fritters; all complemented by a couple of glasses of white wine. Due to late flight arrival times, it is after 9:00 pm when the rest of our group arrives from the airport – just after a tasty slice of chocolate gateau is finished off. The new arrivals sit down and their evening meal is served swiftly amid introductions. Sebastian is a polite thirtysomething from Switzerland. He is tall and slim, wears glasses and has no hair. Having no previous riding experience, he is booked on the beginner programme and is staying at Son Menut until Thursday. Brigot is pleased to discover Sebastian is fluent in German as well as English. Travelling together is Sofia and Tyra from Sweden. Sofia is middle-aged, petite with fine-features and grey-shoulder-length hair. Tyra is Sofia's daughter. She is an attractive young woman in her twenties favoured by a clear complexion and natural long-blonde hair. Tyra lives in the city of Manchester in the Northwest of England and having resided there for many years she speaks with a British-Mancunian accent. She does most of the talking for her and Sofia.

Maravillosso

First light penetrates the unlined cream curtain when I get woken by my alarm set for 7:15 am. Outside a cockerel crows'. He keeps up his cock-a-doodle-doos while I shower, dress and head to the restaurant at 8:00 am. In the exclusive company of the people on the riding programmes and Anton, breakfast is a more subdued affair than last night. Bleary-eyed guests select from the ample buffet laid out on the dresser and a catering trolley. Chris and Hayley had the least restful night. They'd opted to take a bottle of wine up to their room after the bar closed and thus stayed up much later than everyone else. In the early hours, Chris was woken by the vocal cockerel, whose cock-a-doodle-doos started a lot earlier than when I heard him after removing my earplugs in response to my alarm.

As I'm finishing breakfast in the habit of savouring a black coffee (amazing Sebastian for he cannot recall meeting an English person who doesn't partake in a customary morning cup of tea) a lively middle-aged man in jodhpurs, shirt, and a wide-brimmed hat comes through the interior doorway at the end of the bar and introduces himself to our table. Animated by a strong-clear German-accented voice and a twinkle in his eye he announces he is called Joe and he is our guide *(guia)* for the week. When he's satisfied, everyone knows where to assemble ready to prepare their horse for a riding assessment, he departs as quickly, as he arrived.

At 9:00 am I traverse the main-drive and take the north fork between the white-stone pillar and a mature palm tree, which mark the entrance to the stables. The track runs alongside rustic tangerine farm buildings where green or brown doors have a frame of white paint, and modest wooden benches are pushed back against the walls. On my left is a shaded area spaciously planted with tall bushy trees. At the back of this space is another tangerine building enclosed by a metal-rail fence. Fixed to the high vertical beam that forms the top of the gateway is a wooden sign with the word PONIES on it. To the right is a circular horse-walker with the capacity to exercise up to four horses and a neighbouring and closer to the track, high-concrete walled circular pen painted pistachio-green. A double metal-rail heightens the pen wall more so the fortification is raised to exceed the alert head of the powerful iron-grey Spanish Horse currently occupying it. As I go by, the iron-grey playfully makes a partial pivot and springs upwards of the sand-covered ground.

Behind the circular-pen is an indoor stable block where the stallions and other dressage horses are stabled. Here, I reach the corner of the farm buildings where the track bends to the east into a stable yard. Tethered on rings fixed to a tangerine-stone outer wall is a chestnut Arab stallion and a muscular dapple-grey Spanish stallion. A safe gap separates the stallions as their riders on the dressage programme give them a brush in the shade cast by branches overhanging the wall.

Further up on the north side of the stable yard, Tyra and Sofia are busy grooming the horses they've been allocated in a long stone building of open-front stalls painted part whitewash and part shamrock-green. There are five stalls each with a horse standing tethered to the back wall. The larger end stall accommodates twin horse showers fitted using green hose pipes threaded through grey-plastic tubes that hang down from the ceiling.

On the south side of the yard are four adjoining stables designed to conform with the tangerine farm buildings. The stables flat corrugated roofs step up to equal the rise of the white-stone path curving around the corner from where I have just come to match the yard's west to east incline. At the top of the yard is a gateway flanked by grey-stone-block gate posts and more of the same tangerine-stone walls. The adjoining stables stop at an attached building where Joe and Brigot stand in conversation outside an open doorway in the middle of a windowless wall. They conclude their conversation when Brigot gets allocated a horse. Joe then greets me, asks for my name and enquires about my riding experience. He swiftly considers the latter, and in response, he tells me: 'You can ride Ginger.'

We cross the breadth of the yard to the stalls where Joe indicates to a patiently standing grey individualized by a dark mane and tail and dapple hindquarters. 'First, you need to brush your horse and tack him up.'

He points back to the doorway where he was stood talking to Brigot. Taking my leave, I go inside and find myself in the tack room. It is a rectangular room featuring a high-beam ceiling, olive-green walls and a floor of square terracotta tiles. To the right of the door are the bridles and saddles that either hang from or are placed on red-wood racks fixed to the north, west and south walls. Either beside or beneath the racks are the horses' names written in white text on indigo plaques. If there isn't a plaque the name of the horse has been written on the wall using white chalk. On the east wall beneath a generous-sized open window are a wooden seat and an aluminium container full of riding crops. Against the back wall at the window end is a metal cage on wheels and a free-standing wooden-shelf unit, both are stacked full of spare saddle cloths and girths. Close to the door on the nearside are shelf units where spare riding hats and grooming kits are neatly stacked. I select a hoof pick, body brush, and curry comb and go back outside to where Ginger waits.

As I get to work on removing caked-on shavings from Ginger, Hayley and Chris arrive. On hearing about Hayley's riding experience, Joe changes his mind on the horse I will ride and reallocates Ginger to her. He moves me on to Sultan. I find Sultan a couple of stalls down and in a cleaner state than Ginger. He is a grey Spanish-crossbreed marked with black-flecks throughout his coat. Despite getting a bit long in the coat, Sultan is a handsome horse. He appreciates the attention as I brush and then pick out his hooves just moving periodically to pull his ears back at his smaller black-flecked grey neighbour.

As soon as I swap brushes for tack, Joe conveniently comes over to help me. Sultan has an English-style leather saddle, a breast-plate, and a curb chain and D-ring bit on a cavesson noseband bridle. After the tack is fitted and checked, I lead Sultan out of the stall, and Joe helps me get on with the aid of a well-used blue-plastic bottle crate. Sultan looks to be 15.2 hh (1.57 m), much the same height as the black mare I ride at home. Though, I feel higher up on him because of his more refined breeding and her broader frame. Brigot is already on her horse, a dainty-grey. At halt close together, we watch as Joe assists everyone else onto their mounts. Sofia gets on an Arab-face flea-bitten grey. Tyra is on a small dark bay marked by a star and stripe and white socks on all legs except for the right hind. Hayley is on Ginger and Chris on a compact and sturdy black.

After everyone is mounted and Joe has completed his tack checks, he leads us in single file back out of the stable yard, down the drive passing the restaurant, accommodation, and reception and onwards through the carpark to the entrance gate. Coming up on the main gate our procession takes a left curve around the tangled hedgerow of shrubs and trees and continues on passing by the short end of a 20 x 40 m (65 x 131 ft.) outdoor arena to reach the entrance of a 50 x 70 m (164 x 229 ft.) arena.

We enter the larger arena from the north corner where there is a gap in the natural boundary of conifer hedges, palms, and broad-green-leaf trees. The arena's sand surface is divided into thirds using evenly-spaced jump poles laid on the ground. Joe takes the shortest line, outside track on the right rein, to get to the school area marked out at the west-facing short end.

The schooling area my ride has to go through is already in use by two of the riders on the dressage programme, who are schooling stallions: a chestnut Arab and a grey Spanish. Parallel to this school in the southeast corner is another grey Spanish stallion working around four sets of faded-paint-show-jump wings and poles placed off the outside track. More of the same faded-paint poles lay on the ground to mark the central divide between the dressage-programme schooling areas along with a pair of yellow-and-green upright oil drums linked by a jump pole on the ground. Sat in a white plastic garden chair beside the oil drums is the dressage programme riding instructor *(prof. de equitación)*, a tall and tanned athletic young German woman revealing sun-bleached hair tied up underneath a white baseball cap. She delivers her instructions in a clear and loud voice. Her persona is a calm presence with the reassurance of a professional who knows the horses and this environment well.

Already the day is warm, and I'm thankful for the overcast sky. Hayley leads the ride I'm at the back. Straightaway, I can feel Sultan wants to rush and remain attached to the tail of the grey horse Brigot is riding. I compensate for this by applying lots of half halts, and whenever Brigot cuts the corner to close up the gap behind the stocky black horse Chris is riding, I stay on the outside track allowing Sultan to use his forward and active walk. We trot as a ride, first rising and then sitting on both reins. Continuing as a ride the rein is changed in a walk by either turning across the school or on a long diagonal. Followed by walking a three-loop serpentine and then taking it in turn to canter on both reins. I need to apply half halts to ensure Sultan doesn't take off on the tail of Brigot's grey at the start of her trot to canter transition. I successfully canter on both reins using the right lead leg but fall in off the outside track. Like the mare I ride at home, Sultan possesses lovely swinging gaits and is comfortable to ride. He is well behaved, despite pulling his ears back at the grey stallion schooling in the same part of the arena as the chestnut Arab whenever their inverse tracks go side by side.

As well as directing the assessment, Joe speaks about the trail riding routes and the scheduled breaks. On Wednesday if the conditions are right, there is the opportunity to swim with our horse. He then takes and notes down our drink orders for the rides. When riding out, he requests we use both legs in trot and canter to conserve the horses' balance and ensure they don't get one-sided. His final piece of advice is to make sure we carry and apply plenty of sunblock. Joe assigns a horse to a rider by giving us the horse's name. My horse has a Spanish name I can't pronounce. There are two failed attempts at repeating it back to Joe thereupon he adds the English translation: Mister Marvellous. Then at the moment the assessment concludes, the cloud breaks up to allow the sun and blue sky to dominate the rest of the day.

Back at the stables, I lead Sultan back into the stall and untack, swapping the bridle for his head collar. Joe is on hand in the tack room to demonstrate how to put Sultan's saddle backward on the rack so the cloth can dry. He then points me towards the outdoor tap, a shallow stone basin placed on circular pillars situated behind the east-facing wall of the tack room. The basin is decorative, displaying diamond-shape white tiles with pattern borders placed to protect the wall behind. A selection of old toothbrushes is supplied to scrub off hard to remove stains. After I return the bridle to its hook, I collect Sultan from the stall and take him for a hose down. In the shower stall, he stands with his nose almost touching the back wall on a floor made from lots of cream bricks assembled as a ridge to prevent wet hooves from slipping. As I bring the hose to wash behind his point of elbow and girth, he swings his head around and takes the hose in his mouth and uses it like a drinking straw. Me, Tyra, Sofia, Hayley, and Chris find this very amusing.

After his hose down, I lead Sultan to his box, which I find in another yard of stables behind the tack room and the adjoining-front stables. Access is via the window-end of the tack room, past the outdoor tap and taking a right onto a concrete surface with a covered gutter running down the centre. There are approximately 16 stables, eight on each side, manufactured from mahogany-wood slats and metal rims and fixtures, including an anti-weave top door grid fixed to the central bottom door. It is the type of stables that would be inside a sizeable barn in colder and damper climates. Outside every door is a head-collar and lead-rope hook and the horse's name written on the wood in white chalk. Most of the occupied stables contain a grey Spanish horse or Spanish crossbred. A pitched roof extends to overhang the stables to shelter any heads looking out over doors. At the far end is part of the east facing back wall of the farm building past on the way into the stable area. An undersized-doorway, near to alignment with the yard's central gutter, is positioned beside equally-undersized rectangle windows beneath a steeply-slanted pitched roof.

When I find the stable with Sultan chalked on the slats, I unlatch the door and lead him in. A bed of clean shavings covers the floor. There is a self-fill water trough in the back corner and a feeding trough at the front. Sultan remains still as I remove his head collar and leave the loose box closing and securing the door behind me. Disregarding the food in his trough, he puts his head over the door, so after hanging his head collar on its hook, I pat his neck. Tyra, Sofia, and Birgot have already identified the horses they will be riding in the neighbouring loose boxes. A couple of boxes down from Sultan, I find Maravillosso chalked on a door. Because I struggle to pronounce his name, I ask Birgot to confirm this is the right stable. An interested, pretty and refined grey with a dark forelock and a pink snip on his nose has his head over the door. I say 'Hello' and pat him.

Brigot wants to show me some rare breed horses kept close by so we leave Sultan and Maravillosso's yard, passing the outdoor tap and exit the main yard using the stone-block gateway in the east wall. On the other side of the gateway are four high-wall runs with equally high green-metal gates. The runs contain an open-front shelter at the back where the resider can rest on a bed of straw or shelter from the rain. The horse runs on the left side of the track are square, to the right they are rectangular and long. A sturdy iron-grey wearing a pale-green head collar occupies the first square pen. Because this pen is adjacent to the main yard, I'd seen part of the iron-grey while preparing Sultan. By lifting his head, the iron-grey can poke his nose over the east wall and watch what is going on in the main yard, and it is for this action I've nicknamed him, 'The Nose.' It is nice to see the nose belongs to a sweet horse. In the neighbouring pen is an iron-grey Spanish horse standing-quietly as it peers between the gate rails. This iron-grey is stunning, beautified by a thick and long mane and tail. The greys are interested and friendly, yet we don't linger as these aren't the horses Brigot wants me to see. After taking a right at the end of the rectangular horse runs our brief quest ends.

Close to the gate in the first run is a chestnut approximately 15 hh (1.52 m) with a white stripe and pink snip. The chestnut retains a distinctive short mane and tail; no more than tufts. Its barely-there summer coat has the appearance of silk in the sunlight. Brigot explains this horse is a Curly. The Curly breed is suitable for people who are allergic to ordinary horse hair as they have a special-coat, which can shed to virtually bald in the summer. In the neighbouring pen, there is another Curly, a white-faced palomino. The palomino is slightly different from the first Curly as he possesses a thick and long white mane and tail. He is in the shelter at the back of the pen and is too busy escorting a scanty black-and-tan chicken that is rummaging in his bed of straw to show any interest in the humans at the gate. Considering the climbing temperature and feeling hot from our ride, we come to the same decision: To leave the horses for now and spend the rest of the pre-lunchtime period in the company of the outdoor swimming pool.

After I'd swapped riding clothes for swimming attire back in my room, I wander around to the extensive back terrace where diners can eat alfresco. The white-stone slab terrace extends behind the full length of the restaurant and kitchen and ends at an ornamental wall of terracotta-and-cream stone that partitions the swimming pool area. The terrace is shaded in part by a couple of sizeable trees. There is an assortment of palms, succulents and red blooms potted in a variety of planters placed beneath the open-shuttered windows of the restaurant and in rows at the base of the outer, black-metal railings. The outlook is of a lime and orange orchard in the foreground and over the hedgerows and fields of the Felanitx countryside to distant hills. Guests can select from an arrangement of black-metal garden chairs and tables in either full sun or shaded by the trees and a pair of broad cream umbrellas. Still, in their riding clothes and drinking beers, Hayley and Chris are sitting at a table shaded by an umbrella.

In the partitioned pool area is a 5 x 11 m (16 x 36 ft.) swimming pool decorated in white and indigo pattern tiles. The black railings continue with partial views of the arenas. At the far end is a plot of a dozen olive trees. Clusters of cappuccino sun loungers are on the white flag-stones surrounding the pool. I find Sofia, Tyra, and Brigot sunbathing on the sun loungers nearest to the dining area. Overhead is a clear-blue sky, and the sun is at its zenith. Because I want to use my tablet, I select a sun lounger in the cluster at the far end of the pool and take advantage of the mottle-shade thrown down by an ample-tree full of vibrant-green leaves and an abundance of pink blossom.

A dressage lesson had already begun in the large arena when I decide to take a swim. Stood up, I can see it is the young and attractive Scandinavian couple on the dressage programme who are riding. They wear matching white t-shirts, black hats, jodhpurs, and long leather-riding boots. She is riding the dapple-grey stallion I'd seen her grooming. He is on a grey stallion. They're receiving their tuition from the German instructor who stands on the centre line of the closest schooling area. My attention shifts back to my dip and I use the pool steps to submerge into the lukewarm water: a refreshing sensation in the heat.

Suddenly there's excitement on the terrace, and everyone stands up and moves to the railings. I jump out of the pool and join the other spectators who are looking in the direction of the large arena. The young Scandinavian woman has been unseated by the dapple-grey stallion, who is running loose in the arena below. Her partner is instructed to bring his stallion to a halt in the middle of the school and dismount. The German instructor assists the unseated rider and gets her to also stand in the centre. She then attempts to calm the loose horse using her voice while he canters and trots close to the outside track. As the stallions' neigh to one another, it becomes apparent the loose horse's goal is to get back to the stables. He dashes to the entrance in the hedge where his escape is closed off by a couple of ladies on the dressage programme who have been standing there watching the lesson. They quickly create a barrier by raising and outstretching their arms to shoulder height, so their fingertips meet. The stallion spins around and aims for another exit in the back, southeast corner. In the moments preceding the attempt on fleeing through the main entrance, a dark bay horse had been led past by a young twentysomething Spanish man accompanied by a girl, who looks to be about 10-years-old. This mini procession is on a path that curves around the east end of the arena alongside the orchard. Because there is no human barrier to block his escape in the southeast corner the stallion leaves the arena and takes a left to put himself on a collision course for the dark bay. The young Spanish man halts the dark bay, and the trio waits calmly for their encounter. Seeing his way is blocked again, the stallion backtracks to trot past the southeast-corner entrance. His new route to the stables takes him the long way around the arena's perimeter. The stallion's freedom culminates when his familiar trainer 'cuts him off at the pass.' The German instructor has walked out of the arena's entrance and at the point where he is almost full circle she stands to block his way. Using her full height and outstretched arms she makes an authoritative: 'Ssh.' He stops, makes a semi-turn and then thinks better of it, stops again and lets her walk up to him and take hold of his reins. He calmly walks back with her to collect his rider looking as if nothing had happened.

With the excitement concluded everyone goes back to their sun-loungers. The rest of the morning goes by lazing on the terrace. There are hushed conversations, occasional splashes as a guest enters the pool, bird songs, cockerel crows, a delivery truck crunching the gravel on the drive, a bark from a dog of a distant neighbour, a light aircraft flying overhead, children departing in a car following their pony rides and the clutters of lunch being prepared in the restaurant kitchen.

We regroup on the terrace for a late three-course lunch where paella gets served as the main dish. Two tables have been pushed together and shaded by the free-standing umbrellas set down at each end. The table tops are laid with a white cloth over a red-cloth and set using white plates, cutlery, and wine glasses. Orange cushions are tied to the backs and seats of the black metal garden chairs to make them more comfortable. I sit facing the accommodation building with my back to the orchard. A perfect spot for watching a gecko, after Chris points it out, scuttling vertically up the wall from a first-floor balcony to the roof.

After a long and un-hurried lunch conversing with my fellow programme members a cloud system arrives to periodically interrupt the sun and persuade me to take an exploratory walk in the grounds of Son Menut. Starting at the loggia, I go by the east wall of the restaurant where there is a grassy patch colonized by four or five species of trees growing close together. One tree has multiple trunks and long spiky leaves. The tallest has leafy branches that surpass the roof of the accommodation building. In the shade of this copse is a black metal-frame bench positioned to overlook the orchard.

Instead of going back onto the terrace, I set off down a stony track to brush the citrus orchard's east and south facing boundary. At the start, facing the orchard, are four compact dark-wood-plank chalets, all with a concrete veranda furnished with yellow garden chairs and a modest table. Several of Son Menut's guests are staying in the chalets (I believe Sofia and Tyra share the first one. On the other side of the chalets is a massive sculpture resembling an electric pylon. At its highest point is a huge-yellow windmill that looks like a sunflower. This sculpture is a wind pump.

The stony-track alongside the orchard's southern boundary has long-grass and bushy-weeds growing down the middle. Rocks and a sparse wire fence edge the orchard. On my left, behind a line of trees and shrubs is a ploughed field. As I progress, there are glimpses of the accommodation building and the terrace through the gaps in the orchard's tree branches. In the places where saplings have replaced established citruses, it is clear to see the orchard trees are in neat rows and there is an uninterrupted sightline of the raised terrace, its trees, and umbrellas. Built underneath the terrace is the glass-frontage of the Son Menut spa. I'd learned from Brigot that the spa has been closed down for some time. Only massages are available on specific days when a local masseur is onsite. After breakfast, I had gone to reception and enquired about a massage. Unfortunately, the masseur's availability had clashed with my riding itinerary.

With nothing but the coo of a dove and the occasional rustle of leaves whenever the wind briefly picks up to accompany my stroll, I feel deeply relaxed without the aid of a massage. At the point where the orchard ends the track forks. Here, I can either keep to the track and go behind the length of the large arena, or walk by the west side of the orchard towards the swimming pool. I'm in the place where the dapple-grey stallion made his escape earlier. Unlike the other corners of the arena, there is no natural hedge, and the gap in the perimeter is marked out by horizontal blocks. An easy-obstacle for a horse to step over.

I choose to continue westwards for the length of the empty arena. At the far end, the path forks again. Now the choice is to either take the right fork northwards and use the stallion's escape path or go away from the arena using the left fork through a spinney of olive-green trees casting shadows northwards I choose the latter. The spinney ends near to where it begins at a staggered crossroads in the southeast corner of a substantial-square field. The level surface of the field is made up of soil, stones, and grass tufts and a row of telegraph poles breaks the sightline out to distant hills.

Directly in front is a green-metal-post-and-rail horse run split into three sections, which covers the length of the field. The nearest section is primarily under roof, sheltered by corrugated sheets suspended on eight green-metal supports. In the shelter are three grey mares, individualized by the varied-amounts of flecks in their coats, and a light-bay mare. The mares supervise two foals, an iron-grey marked by a white star and a paler-grey marked by a white blaze. I don't stand by the railings for long due to the number of flies buzzing about making the horses swish their tails and stamp their feet. Just long enough to observe the foal with the blaze is shy and clings to its mother. Whereas, the foal with the star is bold and friendly and wants my attention. Whenever he tries to get to me, the mares shoo him away to the back. He must need to be kept in line.

On my retreat from the flies, I count another eight grey mares and four iron-grey foals. They stand by a circular feeding station in the middle section of the run. Further back, close to the fence that divides the middle and far sections is another light-bay mare on her own. From this angle, it looks as if the gate to the middle section is open to enable the mares and foals to interact. There is a whinny from a horse; however, it's not coming from any of the mares. Sweet bird songs float out from distant hedgerows joined intermittently by a cock-a-doodle-doo.

I return to the front of the finca via a straight ornamental roadway of concrete and white stones, which brings to mind an ancient Roman road. The roadway runs parallel to the track used by the stallion on his quest to return to stables after unseating his rider; though, the arenas are hidden from view by a row of densely-packed and tall conifer trees. To the west and northwest, there is a prospect out to where dark clouds threaten the tops of faraway hills. Here, the air is serene, and it remains dry with the sun intermittently popping out from behind the lighter clouds overhead. Close to where the 'Roman road' ends there is a second entrance gate situated up the lane from the gate Toni used on our arrival from the airport yesterday. This gate is similar to the main gate with the same sandstone-pillars and croft walls. A long-arched metal gate has been slid back behind the west wall. Using the gateway, I cross over the boundary of the *finca* out into the lane where the westbound byway drops out of sight amid palm trees and scrub-hedges. All around are ploughed-fields, bordered by trees, stone walls, and wire fences.

Back inside the gateway, I've just about come full circle. To complete the circuit, I use a track running parallel to the lane back to the main entrance. A tall box hedge encloses the track and hides everything behind except for the odd glimpse of the small arena, the cream umbrellas on the terrace and the sunflower wind pump. The dinky black-and-tan terrier encountered on arrival yesterday materializes from somewhere and trots past. With its tail held high, the terrier is clearly on a mission, to do what I don't know. It completely ignores me as it disappears as swiftly as it appeared. Quite soon after, the terrier is back. Still, on its mission, I'm ignored again. I've made it to where a white horse lorry and a couple of trailers are parked when it runs by, passing the entrance gate and onwards to the accommodation building and reception. My passage is at a slower pace for I linger to admire the main entrance gate. This gate to is pulled back behind the west wall. Made from metal weathered to rust-red, the gate is in the form of a massive tulip head at the centre, and upside-down horseshoes curve around the bottom and line the panels.

It's late afternoon when I re-cross the drive from the accommodation building to the stables. On entry, there is the usual neigh from somewhere. The circular-pen by the stallions' stables and the horse-walker is in use. Inside are a female instructor and her charges: a trio of cute-young children riding equally cute ponies. The horse walker revolves as it exercises a pair of black horses, a bay and a grey. Joe is on hand again and is busy flitting backward and forwards from the tack room to the stalls, ensuring everyone knows where to find their horse and running through the drill of grooming and tacking-up. Except for Hayley, who continues to ride Ginger, there is an air of first date nerves for the rest of us as this is to be the first ride on the horses we will use for the week.

Maravillosso waits patiently in the stall adjoining the showers. I say Hello, pat him and offer him my hand to sniff. He wears the same green and yellow head collar as Sultan. He looks to be 15.2 hh (1.52 m). His summer coat is clean and relatively quick to brush. However, his tail is thick and long and takes an age to comb out using a body brush. For the duration, he stands calm and patient. He is a sweet horse. Maravillosso has a brown leather bridle with a cavesson noseband and a D-ring snaffle bit. Joe demonstrates how to fit his breastplate and English-style saddle. Triplicate D-rings behind the seat of the saddle lead me to assume the design is for long distance riding. There are dual saddle cloths. A navy-blue-padded numnah goes over an orange-felt saddle-cloth.

With everyone mounted, Joe riding a black horse differentiated by a white star leads us out of the yard. Hayley is immediately behind on Ginger followed by Chris on the tallest horse, a solid bay mare. Brigot is behind the English couple riding a black horse called Nobel. A late-middle-aged lady expat rides behind her. I'm between the lady expat and a local older gentleman. The three of us are riding greys. Bringing up the rear is Tyra on the smallest horse in the ride, a freckled-grey called Aswan and Sofia on a purebred Andalusian grey mare flourishing a long iron-grey mane and tail.

An hour is spent riding on unmarked country lanes with worn surfaces. Using lanes edged by grasses, plants in yellow flower and squat-wooden telegraph poles, we ride through a landscape of brown and green patchwork fields and orchards of orange trees matured on patches of unkept soil. Stone croft walls or spindly wire fences border the smaller fields and orchards. Trees and hedges form the perimeters of the large-scale fields.

Near to Son Menut is a hamlet of farm buildings and homes built using stone and finished with green-painted shutters and doors. At the centre of the hamlet where the lane curves, is an old *finca*. Its adjoining buildings forge an upside-down L-shape filled in by a courtyard laid using mismatched flagstones. Two massive palm trees of different varieties grow in a courtyard. One palm is tall and thin and rises above everything. The other is low and sprawling. Red clothes are pegged out on a clothesline suspended between the stumper palm tree and an old barn where steep and crumbling stone steps ascend to a pane-less window on the first floor. On the hamlet's northern approach is walled coppice of hefty succulent plants bearing pudgy leaves the size of paddle heads.

We ride by the gates of grandiose country villas situated at the end of long tree-lined drives and characterized by tall-shutter windows. All, have gardens bordered by fields. The villas are a mixture of newly constructed or renovations. The rural byways encompassing Son Menut are long and relatively straight. In the places with a low hedge, there are views over the countryside to the faraway hills. Apart from a brief encounter with a couple of cars travelling in opposite directions, there is no traffic.

Maravillosso is forward going and responsive to my leg. His trot is lively and comfortable. His walk is slow. He is energetic and needs to be ridden using a light hand and half halts when required. Everything goes well until the local man behind me decides to pay more attention to picking pods of the many roadside carob trees and less on riding his horse. Then, whenever the horses are asked to trot his grey comes right up behind and makes Maravillosso toss his head. The horses are just playing. However, because this is my first ride and this action is repeated a couple of times and concluded by Maravillosso producing a buck, I am a little unnerved. On observing the antics, Sofia and Tyra suggest I change places and ride behind the man. This change in order calms the horses.

Close to the entrance gate of a lavish *finca*, Joe turns of the lane onto a footpath. Initially, the footpath follows a high natural hedge and a crumbling croft wall raised by the use of a mesh fence. Loose stones have tumbled down from the wall onto the dirt path. Branches overhang above our heads. Occasionally white butterflies flutter nearby. The footpath temporarily widens to open up a vista over a soil paddock, then narrows again to go through a roofless tunnel of deep croft walls and tall trees. At the end of the footpath, a sizeable orchard emerges where the trees have been spaciously set apart on the soil. The trail is mostly free of stone as the ride goes through a gap in a wall and a subsequent open gateway, which opens into an ample-size field sectioned into horse runs with metal post-and-rail fences that conform to the mare and foal run – including shelters and circular feed stations.

Our course uses the south to north perimeter track going past the gateways of the runs at the shelter ends. The first holds a pair of beautiful-palomino Haflinger horses, the far end run, a herd of chocolate-brown donkeys. Past the donkeys is another sizeable orchard. On our offside is a row of trees going up to more horse runs similar to the runs occupied by the Curly horses back at the main yard: high stone walls topped with a rail. Most contain two or three Pure Spanish Horse yearlings. As the ride goes by, moving west to east, the inquisitive youngsters put their heads over the wall, prick their ears forward and whiny.

Crumbling gate posts mark the northeast corner of the horse runs field. I know where we are now as we've arrived at the mare and foal run. I'd missed the gateway on my previous visit to this spot because I was too busy looking at the mares and foals. The introductory ride out concludes using the same route I'd walked earlier back to the stables.

When I go for dinner, the restaurant is a hub of speculation as both groups of riders' compare experiences of their hacks out. When we'd arrived back at the yard at the end of the late afternoon ride most of us had handed the reins of our horse to a person on the dressage programme, for they too were scheduled to partake in an hour hack. I'd handed Maravillosso to a Swedish lady, who is always immaculately dressed for dinner in a crease-free brilliant-white shirt and has equally neat-grey-cropped hair. The horses were spirited for the dressage riders too, and Maravillosso had kept up his play with his equine friend. I know I can't cope with a horse playing all week and for the first time since taking up riding again, I may need to request a change of horse. I decide to discuss this with Joe in the morning. Tyra, the least confident rider on the programme relates an earlier conversation she had with Joe when she had an attack of pre-ride nerves. She'd asked for a horse that wouldn't do anything to which, Joe in his matter-of-fact manner replied: 'You cannot ride dead horses.'

We chuckle at Joe's dry humour.

When everyone's settled at their respective table, I have another decision to make: Do I succumb to the temptation of the house red? My hesitation is because I'm on a course of antibiotics to clear an ear infection and have a day's dosage left to take. But, I find the red wine is too irresistible. Made from the grapes grown at Son Menut, the wine is bottled offsite where the Son Menut yellow label with black horse design is stuck on the bottles. The instant I taste the wine, I'm glad I succumbed. It is very nice. While I savour a couple of glasses over dinner (for me, bread and olives, potatoes and grilled aubergines finished off with a dessert of nougat ice-cream flat cake), Hayley educates us on the New Forest drifts.

The purpose of the drift is to round-up all the ponies that roam free in the New Forest National Park and muster them together at the pound for veterinary checks, worming, and replacement collars. If a rider completes six drifts during the year, he or she can enter the annual Boxing Day (26th December) point-to-point race where the agisters (rangers) race each other. There's no set course for the point-to-point. Competitors get informed of where the finish line is in advance yet will not get told the whereabouts of the start line until the day before so no one can practice their course. A blanket of heather covers much of the New Forest, and there are many hidden ditches and holes. Therefore, drifts need a horse that can take care of its feet if it trips and doesn't rely on the rider. A horse or pony nimbler and faster than a New Forest pony is also an advantage. Hayley's first and only attempt at a drift got thwarted when she became unseated by a low-hanging branch at an early stage.

Consolació Monastery

It has gone 9:00 am when I go to the yard in search of Joe. A beautiful iron-grey Spanish stallion wearing a red headcollar stands at the back of the circular run. His ears are pricked forward as he looks to the east where the sun is rising and casting a shaft of light right through the otherwise blackened run. The air is unstirred and the sky blue, it's going to be a warm and sunny day. I find Joe prepared for the heat, dressed in brown jodhpurs, a yellow shirt, and a wide-brim cream hat. He's already moved the trek horses out of their stables and into the stalls where they wait patiently for their riders.

Joe's reaction is of surprise when I describe Maravillosso's playful behaviour yesterday, especially on hearing Maravillosso had bucked. He tells me this is uncharacteristic behaviour. If Sofia and Tyra had not witnessed the out-of-character behaviour, I would at this moment doubt it myself. Joe reassures me that the reason for his playfulness was probably due to his day off on Sunday as Maravillosso wouldn't have come out of his box except for a stint in the horse walker. He sticks to his choice of horse. Joe reminds me to use a light hand when I'm dispatched to prepare Maravillosso for the day's trek.

I find Maravillosso with Ginger in the shower stalls. Much the same as yesterday he behaves impeccably while I get him ready. He is a sweet horse. Because of his nature, my apprehension reduces further. Joe attends at the right moment to show me how to secure Maravillosso's head-collar and lead-rope as the equipment will get used on the lunch break. The head-collar goes over the bridle's noseband and headpiece, and behind the cheek-pieces and throat-lash. The lead-rope is loose round Maravillosso's neck and tied using a secure knot to prevent it from hanging and moving too much.

Today's destination is Consolació Monastery situated 8 miles (12.8 km) southeast of Son Menut close to the town of S'Alqueria Blanca. The ride will take us through the rural countryside of the municipality of Felanitx.

Isabelle, a slim and tanned German with a black bob is joining us today. She works for Lufthansa in the role of cabin crew and is on a stopover in Mallorca. She is riding Cleo, a pink-skin grey mare who is a similar height to Maravillosso. Brigot and Isabelle chat enthusiastically upon discovering they are fellow nationals. Their conversation is cluttered by Isabelle responding with multiple 'Ja' in response to whatever Brigot says. Brigot jokes she had put in an order for a fellow German when she booked the holiday.

With the ride order established our troop rides out of Son Menut using the main gate. In single file behind Joe, who is riding the black horse with a star, is Hayley on Ginger, Chris on the big bay mare, Brigot on Nobel, Isabelle on Cleo, me on Maravillosso, Tyra on Aswan and Sofia at the rear on the Andalusian grey mare.

To start, we ride through an area of open countryside. A network of single-lane byways takes us by vineyards with long rows of vine trees and unfenced arable fields. Isolated white clouds drift on the horizon in an otherwise clear blue sky. Sandstone-croft walls edge fields with exposed soil – perhaps a consequence of a plough or overgrazing. There are mulberry tree orchards and fields scattered with mature native oaks. Behind one rustic gate is a herd of eight chunky brown pigs and 12 adorable piglets. Their snouts are down snuffling in dry soil in the shade of an oak tree. It is always delightful to see free-range pigs.

Shortly after leaving Son Menut, I discover that the five horses in front of me are long-striding quick walkers. So, whenever a gap opens up, Tyra, Sofia and I need to trot to catch up. Which means we're already limbered-up when Joe calls back and gives the signal for the first official trot of the day.

Yesterday's apprehension gets expelled during the first canter. The change of gait is up a long-sloping sand track bound by stone walls and shaded in places by the branches of the bordering oaks and other trees. Maravillosso holds a steady canter and obediently comes back to trot and then walk at an appropriate distance behind Cleo. Not long thereafter, Joe takes the opportunity to survey his riders at the back as we turn a corner. He produces a satisfied grin when he sees me and Maravillosso relaxed. I hold a long-loose rein with my left hand. My camera is in my right-hand snapping photos.

Though there are no huge-industrial farms every piece of land is either lived on or farmed in rural Mallorca. The land is tended in the traditional methods as most of the properties are quaint family farms and smallholdings verged by croft walls or natural boundaries of shrubs and trees. No doubt many of the plots are passed down from generation to generation. The broader fields yield neat rows of grape vines for the production of wine or brandy. Herds of sheep are kept in scrubby woodland or in fields where they pick at weeds or vacuum up dropped leaves. The adults are rangy and long-legged. They have a white face, a pink nose, and pink ears. Their tinged wool makes them look as if they've had a dip in an orange rinse. The lambs are long-legged, white and fluffy. Several of the adults carry a Swizz bell on their collar that produces sporadic clangs as the sheep move.

A prominent feature of an old-fashioned farm is a circular silo built using sandstone and crowned by a flat roof. It stands at the side of a one-level outbuilding characterized by wooden doors and a slanting-tiled roof. Conforming with many of the properties in this area there are chickens and roosters clucking and scratching the earth. The birds are not cooped-up together enclosed by mesh. They roam free popping up from behind walls or retreating into the foliage of a scant hedge.

Another neighbouring farm is set back a field width from the track behind a high-mesh fence. The two-storey building features undersize windows and a sloping-ridge roof. The property and fore field are un-kept. The grass is a sun-scorch brown and settled by opportunist scrub bushes in yellow flower. The windows look paneless. I conclude the property is currently uninhabited and waits for a new owner. Someone who possesses lots of money and renovation ambitions.

Because animals occupy the adjacent fields, there is always some activity at a property. Like a horse grazing in the company of a flock of sheep, or a young woman wearing denim jeans and a red t-shirt pegging out her laundry. For most of the ride though, we're in the company of ourselves, and the occasional farmer sat on an old-fangled tractor chugging along as a billow of smoke rises out of its chimney.

After two-and-a-half hours, Joe halts at the roadside on a sandy plot verged by bushes, trees, and decaying stone walls. He points to where we need to tether our horses, so they are kept a short distance apart and then busies himself with removing water bottles from the leather saddlebags Sofia and Chris's horses are carrying behind their saddles. After dismounting, I take

Maravillosso's reins over his head and roll up my stirrups. At the same time, he enthusiastically tucks into the long-yellow grass growing between the branches of the closest bush. Joe hands me a 500-millilitre water bottle with 'R' written on it in black marker pen. Because of the relaxing and pleasant ride thus far, I thank Joe for making me stick with Maravillosso. I beam as I declare: 'I love him.'

Joe's response is, 'Yes, Mister Maravillosso is a sweet horse.'

There is another hour of riding to reach Consolació Monastery and lunch. The trail continues through farmland using the same dust and stone single-vehicle tracks sandwiched by old stone walls. Fields, vineyards and almond orchards are predominant, and the prospect ends at distant farms, villages, and hills. There is another occurrence of the opulent villas ringed by neat gardens and accessed via long palm-tree-lined paved drives. The majority of the properties are modern renovations of traditional-bygone farms. The abundance of vines must be because the slope of the land has an ideal orientation for capturing the sun to grow the grapes. A particularly extensive vineyard has an impressive three-storey château at the base of a long vine-covered slope. The château is in good repair with gleaming white painted walls, and an apricot pitched roof. Cotton-wool clouds meander across the deep-blue to temporally block out the sun's rays and cast silhouettes on the farmland. As it is close to midday, these patches of shade provide a pleasant temperature to ride in.

As the morning ride draws to its conclusion, the countryside becomes more dramatic for we've arrived in hill-country with the higher slopes reaching up to 200 m (656 ft.). A tarmac road winds through the lower slopes where affluent cream villas featuring archway-verandas reside on spacious-plots. Swimming pools and white parasols enhance gardens full of native plants. Expensive cars are parked-up on the palm-lined driveways. The villas and the neighbouring patches of brown-fields are sheltered by the steep and rocky upper slopes, which are either capped by either a level or rounded peak abundant in scrub and green-leaf trees.

Our final ascent is on a footpath that cuts through a briar of green-leaf trees and shrubs on the north side of the monastery's hill. Close to the summit the footpath curves to the west and ends at the road going up to the monastery Before, a hoof steps onto the tarmac, Joe halts to let a dark MPV go by and disappear around a bend further down the hill.

On the hilltop, the road morphs into a gravel carpark laid at the foot of the Monastery's fortress-high bell tower and walls. The structures dominate the skyline and are only beaten in height by a couple of widespread-boughed trees. These trees semi-hide a staircase of worn stone steps that go through a raised rock garden to end mid-way up the fortifications. Built in the 16th century the monastery's name comes from the hill it is sited-on: 'Consolació.' A hill with an elevation of 205 m (672 ft.).

For Joe and the horses, there is a familiar sight. On the opposite side of the gravel to the monastery, parked in the dapple umbrage beneath a pair of large mature trees is the Son Menut white minibus with a four-wheel trailer in the shape of a mini horse box attached. The trailer is in the same green livery as the minibus: Side profile of a cantering horse above the text 'SON MENUT' emblazoned on the side. It was driven here by Fernando, a local Spanish man with a slight paunch and black stubble on his face.

Our arrival triggers a flurry of activity. Riders dismount and lead their horse to where Joe directs. Lead ropes get secured to branches in various shady spots around the carpark perimeter. Bridles and saddles come off. Head-collars stay on. I tie Maravillosso to the branch of a scrubby tree growing out of a wall close to the monastery's northeast corner. His nearest nearside neighbours are Aswan, tethered at the base of previously hidden steps, and the black horse with the star, Joe is riding, tied to a bush growing at the side of the stone staircase. Noble, the black mare Brigot is riding, is to the right of Maravillosso. Her lead rope is attached to a bush at the end of the carpark close to a long rustic tie-rail that wouldn't look out of place outside a saloon in a Spaghetti Western. The tie-rail is where Joe tells us to put the saddles and bridles ensuing the underside of the saddle cloths face the sun so they can dry out.

Fernando has placed green-plastic buckets on the ground that are being filled by a hose siphoning off water from one of two white-plastic containers installed at the back of the trailer. We wait in turn to take a full bucket of water back to our charge to drink. Unlike most of the horses who drink the whole contents of the bucket, Maravillosso takes meagre-sips and loses interest. When I offer the bucket to Joe's black horse, it finishes the water off, so I go back to the trailer to collect more for the black to drink. While the horses quench their thirst, Joe clutching a drinking bottle walks up to them and washes their saddle and girth area.

Fernando removes black-rubber feed buckets from the trailer and Joe assigns which bucket to take to a named horse. Joe then sets about assembling a circular fold-away table and eight chairs that he's unloaded from the trailer. Plastic containers full of food get unpacked from steel-blue cool-boxes. The table gets set with orange and white plastic plates. This process is so well-rehearsed it is not long before eight riders are sat at the table eating a picnic of pasta dishes, salad, meat, bread, and olives accompanied by a selection of condiments. The drinks, ordered at the end of the assessment yesterday, get handed to the relevant person.

With my back to the monastery, I sit beside Joe. Brigot and Isabelle are opposite. Behind the Germans, is a low wall and a view traversing a lowland of villages, farms, and trees to culminate at Mallorca's southeast coastline and the Mediterranean Sea. Sat by the back doors of the trailer, separating Brigot and Joe, are Chris and Hayley. Sofia is to the left of Isabelle and Tyra sits between Sofia and me. Behind Sofia and Tyra is a rope hanging between the boughs of two trees. The closest tree has a thin trunk and is a dwarf in comparison to the thick trunk and widespread canopy of its neighbour. The latter supplies most of the shade to the horses tethered to the rope. Ginger, Cleo and the bay mare Chris rides stand quiet and relaxed occasionally swishing their tails if an insect comes too close. Hayley observes, 'It's a horse washing line.'

In reaction to the water applied by Joe, pale-grey patches have materialized on Cleo's coat. Joe's explanation is she must have pinto in her bloodline.

When lunch is over, Joe encourages us to go off and explore. He directs us to an archway with a heavy wooden door built into the monastery's outside wall close to the broader tree supporting the horse washing line. Six white-stone steps ascend to a gate within a gate; the inner gate is secured back to invite visitors to enter. Inside is a pleasant courtyard enriched by white-stone paving and ornamental walls. Palms and succulents in terracotta pots edge the steps to draw the eye to a quaint white-washed two-storey house with undersize windows and wooden shutters and doors. An outside staircase goes up the side of the house from the ground floor door to a door on the upper storey. A frontal thick-stone column provides essential support to the ridged-roof of the loggia that shelters the house and the staircase. To strengthen the roof, a thick bough spans the length to anchor wooden roof beams.

The white house is attached to the bell tower building, at the north end of the courtyard, and another two-storey house constructed from sandy-brown stone with more undersize wood-framed windows. This second house forms the southern end of the row of houses with its south and east walls overlooking the courtyard. Protruding from the sandy-brown house's southeast corner is a hexagon well, shaped by stone-block pillars and a slab lintel fitted with a simple pulley suspending an aluminium bucket. A thick rope cascades down from the pulley. At the other end, the rope is coiled haphazardly on the ground. Set into the wall of the house near the well are 15 white tiles decorated by a black mural edged by a triangular pattern. At the centre is a cross and the date, '1677'. Beneath the cross is the inscription:

'L'Arxiduc va treure la mostra d'aquestres rajoles que està en rellen mig menjat al coll de la cister-na. La nostra pedra no vol esser trepitja-da ni malmenada per cadenes de ferro.
Any del Senyor 1971, el da la plantada de pins… Deu les aferri.
Crux fidelis inter omnes arbor una nobilis.'

Succulents and leafy plants flourish in terracotta pots edging the courtyard's outer walls. These terracotta-pot lines are interrupted by the occasional bushy conifer or neat silver-trunk tree. At the centre of the courtyard growing out of holes in the paving is a spiky-leaf tree and a huge palm matured to roof height. In the bottom corner of the courtyard is the monastery's public toilets, a converted ground-level outbuilding forming part of the west wall. To me, this pretty courtyard is the best part of the monastery. Though, for the local congregation and the volunteers who come every morning and evening to open and subsequently close the doors, I expect the monastery's church is their main draw.

Facing the bell tower, I re-cross the courtyard and go up the staircase, adjacent to the white house. The steps stop at an archway where a solid-wood double door has been left open. Over the threshold is an unpretentious well-maintained chapel featuring whitewashed walls, alcoves, and a vaulted ceiling. Rows of long wooden benches mostly cover the width of the polished mustard-tile floor. The alcove on the facing wall contains a floor-to-ceiling wood carving. At the centre of the carving is a full-length statue with a portrait on either side. I presume this is the web-advertised: '18th-century statue of the Madonna of Consolation'. The benches face a white-painted modern alter graced by plinths of flowers and backed by a wall constructed using many pieces of stone – not dissimilar to the chimney stacks found in old country cottages back home. High up on this wall is a statue of Jesus on the crucifix illuminated by an abundance of natural daylight spilling in from somewhere.

Back outside, I re-cross the courtyard again and leave through a narrow ungated archway in the monastery's outer east wall; by the public toilets. I find myself at the back of the monastery where fortified walls rise-up from a terraced hillside garden full of trees, palms, sprawling-succulents, conifers, bushes, and ornamental walls. A light wind rustles the branches of a tree where an old metal-frame swing hangs from the lowest bough. Gravel crunches beneath my feet, and I'm serenaded by birdsong as I progress along a route of winding pathways and tiered steps. The widest-route includes descending steps going away from the monastery to deposit you at a low-walled circular look-out point. To the northwest, the view is abrupt, blocked by a higher, tree-covered, hill. The remaining outlook is a panorama across a plane of cultivated fields and sporadic settlements. The land fans out from the close by football pitch sited on the outskirts of the town of S'Aqueria Blanca to the fishing village of Portopetro on the coast and onwards pointing south through the unspoiled Parc Natural Mondragó and back inland to the out of sight town of Santanyi.

It is mid-afternoon when the ride departs from the monastery. In preparation for our departure, the horses have been offered more water, brushed and tacked up and this time, to my relief, Maravillosso had a good drink. With everything packed into the trailer, Joe and Fernando helped us remount and checked tack. Mounted, we waved Fernando off as he drove the minibus out of the carpark. Although a more direct course will be taken back to Son Menut the distance is still the equivalent of two hours riding. Not a problem for the horses. As a result of the break and with the knowledge they are going home all the horses are lively and keen to get on.

The return leg takes us back through a network of quiet country lanes and farm tracks. Maravillosso is livelier than he was this morning and there is a momentarily lapse in communication between us during a trot on a levelled tarmac road. The gap from Maravillosso to Cleo had expanded to a distance that he felt should be closed by a canter to catch up with the mare. Half-halts are applied, but he is adamant in his canter. I call frontwards and get the long striders to come back to walk so he can catch up at a sensible pace. It also allows for Sofia and Tyra to catch up too as they had dropped back even further than I had.

Unique to the rest of the day's ride, there is a small town to transverse. I believe it is the town of Cas Concos Des Cavaller. Late afternoon has fallen as the horses enter the clean streets of terraced stone houses. Many of the houses are whitewashed. Most display blue, brown or green shutter doors and windows. Some have a flat roof and a satellite dish. Here and there the rows of houses end at high-walled courtyards full of stunted trees or shrubs. The street, Joe selects to ride down is quiet with just a few parked cars to negotiate. I hear moving traffic in the background and assume it is travelling on the street that runs parallel to this street. We're almost out of the town, on a street where the doors of the houses open onto a barely-there pavement of white paving slabs when a late middle-aged lady with long-greying hair and an equally long skirt comes out of a briskly-opened doorway. She was alerted by the clip-clop of hooves on the tarmac, and she is not happy. In an unfriendly-manner, she exchanges words with Joe then goes back into her house. Joe lets us know she had complained of horses going by her door and dropping manure outside. He's not fazed by the encounter, shrugging it off in his carefree manner.

Back in the neighbourhood of Son Menut, there is the perception of every villa or *finca* garden passed containing a black Labrador-type dog. Most of the dogs are secured by a chain that they pull taut in the act of protectively barking. The breed is a Mallorcan Shepherd dog used to guard sheep and property. Despite their similarity to a Labrador their temperament and demeanour are austere. I can understand why they are a popular choice of the wealthy locals whose nearest neighbour can be at least half-a-mile away.

Another sign of us getting closer to Son Menut is the presence of the roadside carob trees. These are a particular favourite of Ginger, who is a carob-pod addict. Whenever he senses Hayley isn't fully concentrating on what he is doing, he puts his head down and scoops up a few pods. The surplus gets stored in his cheeks, and as he walks along, he eats the pods one-by-one.

With Maravillosso untacked and hosed down, I lead him to his stable and a trough full of grain before helping Tyra hose Aswan. On arrival at Son Menut, Sofia got whisked away in a taxi to visit a dentist in Felanitx. She's been suffering from a toothache since her flight from Sweden on Sunday, and the staff at Son Menut had arranged an appointment. Because Aswan is twitchy during grooming and hosing and Tyra is a less confident handler, Sofia had told her not to tend to him alone. As I'm scraping the excess water from Aswan, Joe walks by and teases Tyra: 'Ah, you have a different groom today.'

I'm happy to help Tyra as Joe is busy seeing to his horse and Sofia's. We're asked to put Aswan in the third stable down from the tack room. I hold the door as Tyra leads Aswan into a roomy-stable with a thick bed of straw and a long feed trough full of grain down the right side. Aswan has a noisy neighbour. The most vocal stallion on the yard is in the adjoining stable. I deem the stallion to be iron-grey, yet it's difficult to confirm his colour because if anyone gets too close to his stable, he kicks the door. Joe reminds us to steer well clear.

North Mallorca

I admit up to this point of my holiday I've not been able to pronounce Maravillosso's name. No matter how many times either Joe or Brigot said it, I couldn't repeat it back correctly. My inability to say Maravillosso's name had come to be a topic of humour for me, and Brigot. Determined not to spend the week referring to Maravillosso as 'My horse' or 'Mister Marvellous,' I took direct action yesterday evening to resolve this issue. When I put Maravillosso back in his box, I'd noticed his name is written in chalk on his stable in a way that breaks up the syllables using four of the wood slats 'Ma ravi llos so.' 'Ma' and 'ravi' are pronounced the same as in English; however, 'llos so' is pronounced, 'yo sso' with stress on the 'sso'. So, the pronunciation is, 'Maraviyosso.' The power of the written word soon has me rolling it off my tongue. Aided by a photo of the chalked slats, I had practiced speaking his name in my room before dinner and can now confidently refer to Maravillosso by his correct name.

After another substantial breakfast, we pack into the minibus with the trailer in tow and begin the hour drive up to Santa Margalida, a municipality in the north of the island. The journey takes us through Manacor, a residential town with a population in the region of 25,000 and the hometown of the world-famous tennis player Rafael Nadal. Rows of houses and apartment blocks featuring long-vertical windows and either a flat or pitched roof grace Manacor's clean boulevards. There is a brief and unscheduled stop at a chemist so Chris and Sofia can purchase painkillers. Sofia's evening dentist appointment revealed an infected tooth, and Chris pulled a back muscle in the night. They both look a lot happier as they exit the dispensary clutching white-paper drug bags.

It's close to 10:30 am when the minibus reaches the outskirts of C'an Picafort. Situated on the coastline of the Bay of Alcudia, C'an Picafort was formerly a fishing village that has morphed into a holiday resort over the last 50 years. Driving the slower horse lorry, Joe had departed ahead of us. We find him un-loading the horses from the lorry he's parked-up in a lay-by at the side of a plot of undeveloped scrubland on the corner of a suburban boulevard. On the other side of the road are four well-maintained tennis courts and a football pitch. The minibus pulls off the street onto the scrubland close to where a couple of thick ropes hang from trees to create another horse washing line. The horse washing line is where Joe is tying most of the horses: the black with the star, Maravillosso, Cleo, Aswan, the big bay mare and Ginger. Nobel gets tethered to a tree close to the lorry and Sofia's Andalusian mare, the last horse to unload, is secured to the front bumper of the now parked-up minibus.

Today the trailer is fully stocked. The tack is neatly-placed on saddle racks fixed to the sides of the interior. Hoof picks and brushes get unloaded as Joe directs us to swiftly-prepare our horses for the day's ride. Although the sun is out, there are darker clouds above the coastline prompting Joe to encourage us to pack our rain clothes in the saddlebags. I don't feel it is going to rain, so I risk it and leave my coat in the trailer. When everyone is ready, and the lorry secured the ride sets off.

The tennis courts and scrubland are on the corners of a T-junction where the boulevard we'd driven down meets another long-boulevard. At the T-junction, the ride goes straight across to join a hard-packed sand trail going north to south and then west to east through a rough expanse of dry-brown grasses and intermittent-patches of stunted trees and bushes. Joe picks a suitable place for a canter bringing the ride back to walk when the ground turns to soft sand, and the trail reaches a dense thicket of pine trees. The tree line gets temporally uprooted by the dry riverbed of the Torrent Son Bauló, which we have to ford before ascending a steep pine-covered bank into the forest of Sa Canova Natural Parc. In the process of crossing the Torrent Son Bauló, Joe announces, 'There are no rivers in Mallorca, just riverbeds.'

Veering to the north, we use a sandy path parallel to the Torrent Son Bauló where pines give way to hardy green-and-purple bushes as the trail emerges from the shelter of the forest and out onto dunes. These essential bushes grow densely packed together to protect the fragile dune eco-system. A brisk inshore wind carries the smell of salt and seaweed and waves roll in and crash on the beach or onto rocks. An overcast sky bears a fraction of dark clouds containing enough moisture to drop rain.

At the mouth of the Torrent Son Bauló is a cove-size beach. With C'an Picafort at our backs, the ride picks up the coast path: a thin seam that separates the beaches and rocks on the coastline from the extensive-dune-system and forest. The topography is relatively even; though, in some sections, the coast path narrows and winds through rocks close to the grey sea. In other places, the path straightens to cross flat-top dunes or wide-grassy areas. It is on the latter terrain where we get to enjoy a fast canter whenever the path is clear of walkers. There are a few visitors to the *natural parc,* extended families and couples out walking or clambering over the rocks. The numbers of pedestrians reflect the day of the week and season: Tuesday morning in the first week of October. Mallorca's tourist season is in its winding-up phase.

Initially, our route hugs the coastline where there is a panoramic view out to the rugged headlands in the Bay of Alcudia. At the most northerly point of the bay, the headland curves out from the town of Port d'Alucida, east to north. At the most westerly point is the headland of Cap Farrurx.

Maravillosso is lively this morning. Though not as lively as Nobel, who feels she should be cantering fast whenever we reach a suitable section of the coast path. Brigot spends most of the early stage of the ride at a jog while the rest of us take heed of Joe's first-day instruction of keeping the horses in single file close behind one another. The result of this action is when Nobel falls out of line the rest of the horses remain well behaved and relaxed in a walk. To compensate, Joe picks places for a trot or canter when Nobel is calm and not anticipating the change of pace.

Close to noon, our course skirts Son Real, a cove-size beach on the east side of the village of Son Serra De' Marina. On the outskirts of the village, Joe points out a house owned by Rafael Nadal. I glance over to where he fixes his sightline but don't register the actual house as I'm too busy ensuring Maravillosso stays close-up behind Cleo and as I won't be popping in to visit soon, I don't consider it to be essential to know the exact property.

Son Serra De' Marina marks the end of the usable-coast path for horses. Walkers can continue through a small marina. Horses must merge alongside the rest of the traffic down long boulevards lined by villas and exclusive holiday apartment blocks set within walled or fenced gardens embellished by a palm tree. The transit through town runs parallel to the coastline, and there is a vista of the sea at every crossroad. Like the coast path, the streets have an empty end of season/Sunday morning feel. Unoccupied vehicles are parked-up at the kerbside. A couple of cars go by at a crawl. Then there is just the clip-clop of horses' hooves echoing down the street to disturb the sleepy ambiance.

Son Serra De' Marina isn't a vast-settlement and aided by a long-trot where a street is clear of parked vehicles we soon arrive at the western edge. Here there are a few busy restaurants. Beneath parasols or under purple awnings, people are seated at tables in wooden booths; relaxed and in conversation, while they dine alfresco. On the other side of the street to the restaurant is a rank of occupied parking spaces delineating the western perimeter of the village and the beginning of Sa Canova beach. A concise bank drops us temporally onto a slightly crowded part of the sand where the essentially-dry river, Torrent de Na Borges, joins the beach splitting the village from the *natural parc*. To progress, we have to use a short section of the beach; all the same, Joe does not linger. To take us from the village streets to another extensive dune system, he uses the most direct line to traverse the deep sand, while at the same time taking care to give the beach users a wide berth.

Long-marram grass is now the dominant plant on the dunes. The marram grass expands out to the west where I can make out dwellings and distant farmland at the foot of a range of steep-sided hills. Not every hill holds a rounded summit I count four peaks. Because of this feature, the Mallorcans refer to the hills as mountains despite the highest measuring no more than 400 m (1312 ft.).

Trails are marked out using posts and low-hanging rope to guide the walker and horse rider to where they should tread. At the point of going away from the beach to angle inland, there is a miniature sand-stone obelisk close to the trail. It looks like a medieval tower in miniature with tiny holes to represent the arrow slits and a thin door. Further back where the dunes rise to a backdrop of outcrops and bushes is a twin obelisk. It marks the entrance into the forest and a network of nature trails. I don't ascertain why the obelisks are here and for what purpose.

Beyond the second obelisk the marram-grass-covered dunes and coastline retreat. The air stills and all you hear are the occasional songs of birds, a click of hooves on stone or hushed conversations between riders. Underfoot there is an abundance of tiny stones. The stunted bushes saw on the coastline prosper here, away from the onslaught of sea breezes and wind most have grown higher and broader, about the size of a wild rhododendron. Squat-scrub plants thrive on the exposed edges of the trail or grow on low-lying rocky banks; the plants' flowers provide a shot of purple in a sea of greens. Throughout the time spent weaving through the forest visual reminders pop up here and there to reveal the trail is close to the coast. Depending on the direction of travel there is either a glimpse of the sea, the pinnacle of an obelisk or the headland of Cap Farrurx.

An hour on from Son Serra De' Marina the ride halts for a water break, high up on the east bank of the Torrent de Na Borges. Tall-spindly pine trees grow out from a surface of sand and shelter horses and riders from the mostly overcast sky. The bank is high and steep, dropping abruptly to the riverbed in the valley below. From this lookout, the green film covered riverbed wends southwards into a backdrop of rolling hills. The dominant scrubby trees in this landscape cover the opposite bank. The trees sizes vary. Determined by the amount of shelter and light where an individual plant grows.

Before the ride re-starts, Joe and Brigot swap horses as Nobel would not stop jogging and pulling in anticipation of the faster paces. Brigot has ridden her well, but her arms are tired. Joe doesn't want her to stay on Nobel his justification is Brigot is on holiday and should be relaxed and enjoying the scenery. He's disappointed because while Nobel had performed like this in the past, recently she's been well behaved. His voice carries concern as he says, 'We thought we got this out of her.'

The consequence of Nobel not behaving is she will no longer be a suitable mount for the trail rides.

After the break, our pace is a meander. Climbs are undemanding. Trails are stony and flanked by steep-tiered banks camouflaged by a variety of plants. The course has swung coastward when Joe halts the ride and dismounts. He's spotted a bush bounteous in glossy-green leaves and a plethora of red-berries on the first tier of a trailside bank. Leading Noble, he clambers up to where the bush grows. After eight of the ripest fruits get harvested, he comes back down to the trail and walks down the ride handing a berry to each rider: 'These are wild strawberries native to Mallorca. They are edible.'

To demonstrate he eats a berry. The fruit is two centimetres in height and width with tough skin covered in rough bumps. The flesh is a fiery-orange. The fruit looks sharp and sower, yet the flavour is sweetish. I'm surprised that it has a pleasant taste, though I shouldn't be considering berries are my favourite fruits. Tyra says she wouldn't want to eat more than a couple. Isabelle loves them, and for the rest of the ride, she tries to pick a berry whenever a wild-strawberry bush is within reach.

There's a temporary emergence out of the network of forest trails where the climb climaxes on the cusp of a hill; here the vegetation grows around hefty-boulders. The hill gifts a look out over a blanket of treetops and across the bay. A portion of the roofs in Son Serra De' Marina come into view and in the distant west is an ample-cluster of roofs in Can Picafort. The grey clouds hanging above the bay cast the faraway western hills and mountains as ghostly silhouettes. On the closer, eastern side of the bay, the mountains and hills are beneath a clearing blue sky. The colours and contours of the rugged slopes are easy to make out in the sunlight. Close to the base of this range are the distant rooftops of the town of Colónia de St Pere, the most easterly settlement in the bay.

Away from the beach, the nature trails are deserted and thus afford many opportunities for a canter. The result of having Noble at the front is a fast pace. I quickly learn to make sure Maravillosso is close behind Cleo at the start of a canter, so he doesn't gallop to catch up. I'm out of my comfort zone on a down-hill trail, and I have to concentrate hard to ensure my head is up and looking forward. My soft seat, practiced a few weeks back in Cornwall, becomes more refined. On the contrary to Maravillosso falling behind in walk or trot, he has no problem maintaining the pace of the long-striders in a canter. He sticks close behind Cleo as clouds of dust billow up as the horses pound the ground.

The presence of the Son Menut trailer, parked-up at the side of a clearing informs us, tourists, we have arrived at the site of today's picnic lunch. I suspect the clearing serves as a beach carpark and if it had been the weekend or summer season, the trailer would be amongst many vehicles parked up around the tree-lined circumference. A surface of beach sand and stones announce the carpark's close-proximity to Sa Canova beach. The constant whoosh of waves rolling in confirms this proximity. Our approach is on a track that gives vehicles access to the carpark. For sure, Fernando successfully drove through the forest to leave the trailer and will come back for it later after Joe makes the call to say we're setting off for Can Picafort.

Right on cue for the picnic the sky clears to blue and basks the carpark in sunlight. The horses get tethered to branches in Joe's selected places around the perimeter where they can opt to be in the shade of a tree. After we un-tack, the horses get watered and fed, and Joe washes their saddle areas down using a bottle of water. In the act of going to and from the trailer and horses, I spy the sea through a gap in the trees where a sand pathway leads down to the beach. Now in the sunlight, the sea is a stunning aqua-blue.

Another plentiful lunch comes out of the trailer and is laid out on the picnic table. Accompanied by olives, bread, and salad today's main dish is a particular favourite of mine, Spanish omelette. As we dine, Joe discloses he's lived in Mallorca for 25 years and has worked at Son Menut for eight years. I comment on how quiet the *parc* is. Chris jokes saying it would be if the women on the ride didn't talk so much. Brigot and Isabelle have been talking enthusiastically to one another and Tyra has been talking to Aswan to calm her nervousness. Chris thought she was talking to Sofia and there is a chuckle as I share my observations: 'When Tyra speaks in English she is talking to Aswan. When she talks to Sofia, it is in Swedish.'

Tyra confesses she had sung to Aswan because singing relaxes her. Sofia has also encouraged her in the canter stints by saying she is doing a great job.

Joe declines our offer of help to pack away the picnic equipment and insists we go and spend time on Sa Canova beach. The atmosphere changes away from the ring of trees protecting the carpark, and grey clouds move swiftly in on the strong inshore breeze to cover the sun. To get to the shoreline, we have to span a dune system. The dunes are intersected by the east-to-west coast path that runs the entire length of the 1.2 miles (2 km) beach. From the carpark, there is a drop down to level terrain where the intersection with the coast path has formed a staggered-crossroad. To protect the fragile dunes, and the bounty of stunted purple and green flora there is a rustic fence of cylinder-shape-wooden posts suspending rope threaded through holes to prevent peoples' feet from straying of designated trails. On the beachside of the staggered crossroads is a raised boardwalk provided so destructive feet keep off the planar dunes. At the end of the boardwalk are nine steps down onto the beach.

Beachside only the soft dry sand is exposed. There is a trio of twentysomething girls sitting or lying on the sand, they are in pullovers and scarves and are trying not to look cold. Having walked ahead of me, Isabelle is sat on the top step of the boardwalk looking at her mobile phone. Sofia, Tyra, and Brigot have rolled their jodhpurs up to below their knees and had taken their boots off. They paddle on the shoreline and take photos of each other. A little way up the beach, facing Son Serra De' Marina, is a couple exercising a sizeable black dog. Further back still two figures walk the shoreline not far from the obelisks. Apart from Hayley and Chris, who are walking down from the carpark, there are no other people in sight.

From the eastern headland, the rugged hills stretch inland to reach the range of Mallorcan mountains and one particular peak stands out. Erosion has cut a bare-rock column on the west face, which juts up from the vegetation-covered lower slopes. In silhouette, the peak resembles a giant nipple. Brigot joins me and divulges the mountain belongs to Toni's brother, an artist who lives in Paris. She goes on to say the beautiful Haflinger horses back at Son Menut were purchased to live and work on the mountain; evidently, they are yet to fulfil this destiny.

It is just after 4:00 pm when the trailer is locked-up, and the ride sets out on the return leg, a two-hour ride back to Can Picafort. To start a circular route takes us to the eastern side of the bay to the furthest point of the ride; it's also the closest we'll get to the sea on horseback today. At lunch, Joe explained horses are not allowed on the beaches, and there is a €200 fine per horse if you get caught. Initially the route curves to the west away from the forest and onto a segment of the coast path balanced on a thin formation of rock where the breakers splash water beside the coast path. Chris's bay mare doesn't like the water. She jogs until we reach the section of the east-to-west coast path detached from the sea by Sa Canova beach.

After this brief detour, the course back to Can Picafort is mainly on the coast path where horses are permitted with a deviation back through the streets of Son Serra De' Marina. Noble is still full of energy and jogs where she feels we should be in a canter. Joe accounts for this by taking greater care especially if there are walkers nearby. For me, a particular canter will forever be in my memory. It is for a short distance on top of a natural seawall of rocks where the topography points you straight towards the sea. Just as you envision you're about to fly off the end into the water below, the ride is brought back to trot and then walk to take a sharp left to remain on the coast path.

A Day Out in Palma

A sunset had greeted us when we arrived back from Can Picafort yesterday. Burning with a ferocity of yellow at its centre encompassed in an orange hue, it looked like a beautiful orb of fire had been dropped onto the horizon. It was nearing 7:30 pm when the horse lorry rolled in slowly past the posts of Son Menut's main gate and pulled up, so the rear ramp faced the accommodation building and stables. Since it was late, Joe instructed us to wash down just the horses' saddle and girth areas before putting them back in their stable where a trough of grain waited.

Later, at dinner, there was much talk about the itineraries for today. The dressage riders were in a flux of nervous anticipation as it is their turn to take the trail horses out. Tired from their lessons and recalling memories of the horses misbehaving on the hour trail, they had built themselves up for a disastrous day. Pre-dinner, Sofia had partially soothed their nerves by reporting on the good behaviour the horses had demonstrated over the subsequent days. I passed on tips to the immaculately-dressed Swedish lady who will again ride Maravillosso.

Today my group has a non-riding day with an optional day trip scheduled to Palma (*Palma de Mallorca*), the largest city and capital of the Balearic Islands. Under normal circumstances, I would be first on the minibus. However, for the reason I'd finished a course of antibiotics 36 hours ago, I considered it better for my health and wellbeing to spend the day relaxing at Son Menut, instead of a long day of five hours in Palma sandwiched between an hour of travel each way. In the wake of a lot of contemplation at dinner, I'd concluded it means I have an excuse to come back to Mallorca for another holiday and visit Palma. Brigot also decided to stay at Son Menut. She wants to use the day to relax, and she'd visited Palma on her previous stay. So, on the back of a late and unhurried breakfast, it was Chris, Hayley, Sofia, and Tyra who boarded the minibus at 11:00 am. Chris and Hayley are going in search of padded cycling shorts for Chris. Sofia and Tyra hope to meet a friend of Tyra's, who works on a cruise ship currently docked in Palma. They will be back for 6:00 pm.

My plan for a relaxing morning is to go on a two-hour cycle ride. It won't be as energetic as it sounds. I'm used to two-hour cycle rides at a leisurely pace, and I don't intend to go far. No more than a quick spin out into the local countryside to take in the sights I'd missed on Sunday because of Maravillosso playfulness. Catalina, a pretty and petite young woman, who Brigot informed me is Toni's daughter, is in reception when I go to ask about hiring a bike. She is sat behind the reception desk holding a phone to her ear using one hand and clasping a long canister of fly spray in her other hand. After ending her conversation, she puts the phone down and aims the canister releasing a burst of spray into the flies circling and buzzing overhead – there are too many flies for such a confined room. Speaking fluent English and in a friendly manner, Catalina comes out from behind the desk, and within moments we're on the opposite side of the carpark in a reasonable-size lockup full of bikes of varying dimensions. I select a silver ladies' mountain bike branded by DECATHLON in white text on the frame. A handy black-mesh basket is attached to the handlebars where I put my water-bottle, sun-protection cream, mobile phone, and camera. Catalina helps me find a suitable cycle helmet and bike lock from the available selection and then hands me a Son Menut business card. She tells me to call the telephone number if I get lost, and someone will come and find me.

On two wheels, instead of four legs, I start on the route taken at the beginning of the hour trail: bearing north and then east on the pothole lane and up a slight hill to the quaint hamlet characterized by flagstones, farm buildings, and a massive palm tree. The humidity is on the rise. Fuelled by sunken cloud in an overcast late-morning sky where only scant patches of blue, break through. The cloud is so low it almost touches the old monastery buildings and landmarks set on the crest of Puig de Sant Salvador, a mountain of 509 m (1669 ft.) raised amongst a band of lower hills (Mallorcan mountains) approximately 4 miles (6 km) away to the east.

The first property I come across boasts a high black-metal-rail gate connected to a low-drystone wall by equally-high twin stone pillars. Inside is a garden of mature palms, firs, and various trees in full leaf that obscures the majority of the house and outbuildings. Brigot had mentioned, she believes this is Toni's house. In the process of going by, a longer peak inside the boundary is unsuccessful. My presence has put a duo of family dogs on alert, who persuade me not to loiter with their loud and continuous barking.

A few more turns of the wheels and I trundle past an apricot two-storey villa converted from an old farmhouse. The walls are smooth and have immaculate paintwork. Casement windows fill the original insufficient slots, and a pair of domed finials adorn the newly-tiled pitched roof. There is another high black-metal-rail gate at the end of a driveway going up through a landscaped garden to the house.

In the act of peddling uphill, there are indications of a change in seasons. While the temperature is like a sultry-summer day, many of the fields are ploughed ready for planting next year's crop. Coming up to the hamlet, I spot a farmer standing beneath a tree in a modest orchard where trees grow in an intermittent pattern on exposed soil. The tree the farmer is tending is at the back of the orchard. He pokes the higher branches using a long thin stick. I assume he is harvesting almonds.

There is no laundry out in the courtyard today. The hamlet is deserted of human life and left to the birds and their sweet songs and tweets. On the other side of the lane from the courtyard, behind a thick hedge, is an old silo partly concealed by the sprawls of palm branches. It is identical to the silo seen on the way to Consolació Monastery, circular featuring a flat-roof and tiny windows. At the T-junction, I take a right away from the road going to the town of Felanitx. Just as I stop to look back at the hamlet a tanned-man in trainers, black shorts and a white t-shirt jogs by, he soon drops out of sight up ahead in the direction I now go in. The hamlet marks the apex of the hill and trundling on where the jogger had already trod, I spot the upper part of the Son Menut wind pump, downslope on the right. Which, puts me on the south side of the *finca*. The sunflower protrudes upwards above the canopies of trees growing in a copse at the bottom of a stepped farm track overgrown with clumps of grass down the centre and enclosed by drystone walls.

I spend an hour cycling by many old *fincas* and modern villas situated within generous gardens or on a plot of agricultural land. Bound by natural hedges, carob trees, and tumbledown walls, the lane is never more than the width of a single vehicle. I catch sight of a slim, older lady wearing a headscarf and patterned dress. She remains up ahead after she steps out from a farmyard and walks briskly to another set of farm buildings a few metres on. A flock of

Mallorcan sheep grazes close to a two-storey salmon-pink villa. Black shutters flank the villa's eight-windows, and the garden's perimeter is protected by a wire fence not dissimilar to a school playground fence back home. The sheep and fluffy-white lambs pick through roots, twigs, and stone or lie in the shelter of a coppice of unkept trees. The clangs of Swizz bells dangling from the neck of a select few accompanies the cock-a-doodle-doo of a rooster. From here villas get larger and more elaborate. Walls and gates are grandeur and ornamental. Adjacent orchards grow in size and exhibit neat and well-tended rows. Every property possesses a dog or two, big and small. Because I'm always escorted past by continuous barks or yaps, I'm grateful the villas are far apart.

I return to Son Menut's main gate from the west having circled back to the front of the *finca*. My progress had been slow owing to many pauses to take in the views. Feeling energetic and knowing I'll spend the rest of the day by the pool, I've decided to quicken up the pace and go again to the hamlet where I will turn left at the T-junction and onwards to the outskirts of the town of Felanitx. It will be a round trip of 9 miles (14 km).

After my ride to Felanitx and back, I return the bike to Catalina and wander over to the arenas where I find Brigot. She is standing outside the small arena watching Sebastian having a lesson. A slim Spanish lady in a pale t-shirt and dark jodhpurs walks the centre track giving instructions to Sebastian while he practices his trot transitions on both reins. I'm pleasantly surprised on recognizing the grey he is riding: 'Sebastian is riding Sultan.'

Brigot nods. She is holding Sebastian's camera and periodically takes a picture or film of him as he goes by. It's Sebastian's ultimate lesson. He will leave Son Menut within the hour for he is due back at work tomorrow. At dinner, every evening he's updated us on his improving riding skills. His favourite horse is Jonny Walker, a solid liver chestnut marked by a white star. Jonny Walker was used for the day treks until he was retired from this work to become part of the lessons and shorter hacks team. Sebastian likes Jonny Walker's character, whenever he uses his legs too much, Jonny Walker swings his head around and attempts to bite him. Sebastian is tall and slim, so when a heavier-man joined one of his hacks, he was not able to ride the weight carrying Jonny Walker. Sebastian had been disappointed because he wanted to ride him. We're all frilled, Sebastian mostly, as his lesson concludes with his first canter transitions. Sultan is an extremely well-schooled horse and obliges politely. As we walk back to the stables, I enquire: 'How was Sultan?'

With eyes wide and spilling enthusiasm, Sebastian replies, 'He is fast.'

Leaving Sebastian and Brigot to carry on to the stalls, I make a brief detour underneath the 'PONIES' sign at the side of the horse-walker. Here, I find a barn in miniature where six stalls, two of which fill up the back corners, had been fitted beneath a slanting roof. The fittings are much the same as in Sultan and Maravillosso's stable yard but decreased in height and width. Pint-sized head-collars hang on hooks fixed beside the doors. Adjoined to the barn is an indoor shelter housing a long-feed station accessible from a back run. Most of the ponies are out of sight in the run. Only a light skewbald with roan patches and a stubby tail is inside. This purpose-built barn is a nice touch. Where I rode as a child, the ponies and horses used the same horse-sized stables.

I re-join Brigot and Sebastian as Sultan begins his trick of using the hose as a drinking straw. While Sebastian scrapes the water off Sultan and takes him back to his box, Brigot and I give 'The Nose' and his iron-grey neighbour a bit of attention. The day remains overcast, warm and humid, and the right conditions for an abundance of flies. Two cockerels walk on the roof of the stalls. One has a fiery plumage of red, orange and yellow; though its tail feathers are black. The other cockerel is entirely white except for its red head. They cluck in the process of chasing a puny white hen. At a moderate pace, they drop from roof to wall and down into 'The Nose's' run. Yesterday, Chris passed on the fact chickens are free to range without boundaries in Mallorca because there are no natural predators on the island. That is why a hen can pop out of a hedge practically anywhere. Great for the birds not so good for collecting eggs.

A late light lunch in the restaurant is followed by a couple of hours reading and lazing on a sun lounger by the pool. The intermittent motor of a faraway strimmer is all that breaks up the lull of the afternoon. Of cause, there is always the high-pitch neigh of a stallion and the intermittent cock-a-doodle-dos from the many free-range cockerels. Though white clouds drift across to block the sun, the temperature is hot enough to sit in and catch the wafts of sweet-smelling blossom and the not so sweet chlorine.

It is close to 4:00 pm when two young women ride into the large arena. They both have blonde hair tied back in pony-tails underneath their riding helmets and wear grey t-shirts and pale jodhpurs. Their equestrian partners are a pretty-grey Arab that begins to school in the area nearest the entrance and a thick-set liver-chestnut flaunting a white blaze and long flaxen mane and tail. The rider on the liver chestnut begins to school in the section of the arena where my assessment took place on Monday. The liver-chestnut is striking and looks to have Haflinger in its breeding. It brings to mind the beautiful Haflingers seen on the first hack, and I decide to go and pay them a visit.

I use the same route I'd walked on Monday afternoon, but on reaching the mare and foal run, I pick up the track we'd ridden on later that same day from the contrary direction. The cloud has dispersed to allow the sun to stream down from an increasing blue sky and develop a patch of welcome shade thrown down by tree branches overhanging the crumbling gate posts in the north corner of the yearlings' area. My arrival at the gateway disturbs a couple of hens, which cluck and flutter wings in hast on their retreat into a bush.

Three beautiful and inquisitive yearlings are in the corner run: A dominant palomino with a white blaze, a grey displaying a long-thick iron grey mane and tail (the friendliest), and a tentative grey marked by a star and stripe with a tufty-mane. In the aftermath of a few failed attempts, I cease trying to get the perfect photo of them as they will not pose majestically together. As I continue none of the horses in the neighbouring runs show any interest in coming forward; perhaps, they are shy or disinterested, or it could just be too hot to make an effort. I disturb a rooster and hen in the west corner of the field. Amid a flutter of wings, they dive into a hedgerow close to a derelict wall and entrance doorway of a bygone-building that has lost its roof and side walls as a consequence of many years of abandonment and decay. What survives forms part of the boundary, and maybe a nesting place for the hens? Closing in on the Haflingers, I move southwards passing the orchard on my left and a high hedge on my right. The hedge is too dense to look through and too high to look over. Behind, horses make their presence known by a stamp of a hoof or a soft whinny.

After, the orchard is the post-and-rail runs. The first run houses the herd of brown donkeys. There is an open-side shelter at the anterior and a feed station full of hay three-quarters of the way down, yet the donkeys huddle together at the back fence. Because the sun is in the west, the bushy-trees growing behind the back-fence project a strip of shade for the donkeys to stand in. I count six, though some may be hidden from view by the feed station. Lying close to the hooves of the adults is a fluffy and adorably-cute foal, alert to my presence with its ears pricked forward. Standing beneath a beating sun amid a mass of buzzing flies, I know I don't stand a chance of getting them to come forward, so I move on. In the neighbouring run, a pair of iron-grey horses shelters beneath the branches of a couple of sparse trees planted towards the rear. I can't ascertain from here if they are yearlings or mares. They have no interest in my presence and continue to graze on the green shoots growing in the shade of a tree.

The Haflinger horses are in the outlying-run that unlike the adjoining runs where you have to stand at the gate end, there is access to the long fence on the south-side. It's here where I find the Haflingers stood together, stamping a hoof and swishing their tails in failed attempts to dispose of a multitude of flies. Like the yearlings, the Haflingers are keen for a bit of attention and immediately walk up to the fence. Native to the Tyrol region in the Austrian Alps, they are thickset-strong horses, dark palomino and have long-thick flaxen manes and tails and four white socks. Their distinguishing-markings and how you tell them apart is one has a white blaze on its face and the other a white stripe. They demonstrate a docile and friendly nature. Despite the constant irritation, they endure the swarm of flies, I suppose, they have no choice. Both lap up my attention, and I reckon they would let me pat, stroke and talk to them for the rest of the day. I leave disappointed-looking Haflinger horses when I retreat away from the irritating buzzes and constant waving away of the flies. I expect these native mountain horses would prefer it on Toni's brother's mountain. Hopefully, they will get there one day.

The yearlings spot me retracing my steps and put their heads over the wall ready for my arrival. Just as I reach them, the serene ambiance of the afternoon is temporally disturbed by the loud calls of children advancing. The yearlings raise their heads, prick up their ears and look in the direction of the unseen clamour. The pose lasts for a few seconds: My camera clicks. Then the children arrive through the gateway and send the yearlings into a hasty flight halfway down the run.

Back on the terrace, I notice another lesson has begun in the large arena. The young woman who had ridden the pretty-grey Arab is back in the schooling area closest to the entrance, only now she is on the ground. She teaches a lady riding a stocky albino horse. A Spanish man wearing a red t-shirt and black jodhpurs schools the dapple-grey stallion who unseated his rider earlier in the week. They make a handsome pair, and I trust the man to be a regular rider of the stallion as he rides him beautifully.

My day concludes by savouring a glass of Son Menut's red wine sat at a table on the terrace watching the sun drop behind the trees at the back of the arenas. The birds sing their dusk chorus while the chef goes to and from the kitchen and outside-oven. Everyone else is either in the restaurant or their room. At nightfall, I move into the restaurant to join my fellow guests.

Over dinner and more Son Menut red wine, I hear about how the horses behaved for the dressage riders on their day out and of a day out in Palma from four exhausted, yet happy tourists. Chris and Hayley didn't manage to find any cycle shorts. After many hours spent combing the shopping streets of Palma, they heard of a cycle shop on the outskirts of the city. Unfortunately, in the hour they'd checked the bus timetable there wasn't enough time to get there and back. At this point, they opted to retreat to a bar where they spent the rest of the day eating and drinking. I didn't mention the bike shop I'd seen in Felanitx as right now it wouldn't provide any comfort. Disappointingly, Sofia and Tyra hadn't met up with Tyra's cruise-ship-working friend since she wasn't scheduled to get off work until later in the day. To compensate they had a walk on the beach that was followed by a long and late lunch at a restaurant where they had spent most of the afternoon.

Cala Mesquida Natural Park

The next morning, we embark on the second trip to the north of Mallorca. Our departure from Son Menut is 9:30 am. The journey is again via Manacor to Capdepera, a small municipality in the northeast of the island. The ride will be on the northeast peninsula in and around the eastern headland of the Bay of Alcudia.

The minibus had driven out of Son Menut without Isabelle. She cannot join us today because at the time of her enquiry the extra space on the ride was already booked. A twentysomething Spanish man had booked and paid for the ride as a gift for his slightly-older-looking girlfriend's birthday. After he'd dropped her off at Son Menut, she'd revealed it had been an incredible surprise. Although she is German, I have an inkling she resides in Mallorca because she wears a gilet over a thin black pullover, an indication of being used to warmer weather. It is cooler today. An overcast sky bears darker clouds, which look like they might drop rain.

Fernando pulls the minibus off the road into a makeshift carpark – a clearing covered by roots and dry soil bound by tall pines. Joe had already arrived and parked the lorry out of the way, semi-hidden in the midst of trees and bushes. There looks to be a garden gate on the back boundary. As the gate is accessible on foot only, our party being here is not an obstruction. The horses get tethered to branches around the edge of the clearing. They wait patiently for their rider to brush and tack them up. During the preparations I notice Joe is wearing a thick-black pullover, he must be feeling colder too. He asks us to pack our rain clothes in the saddlebags, Sofia and Chris's horses will carry. Feeling rain in the air, I pass my raincoat to Sofia.

Our new German companion will ride Cleo. Joe will ride a grey mare. On the drive here, Brigot disclosed, Joe had not brought Noble because there is a steep and rocky section of terrain on the ride and he can't risk her misbehaving. Everyone else is on their usual mount. After our separation, yesterday it's nice to see Maravillosso. He is such a sweetie, and I did miss him.

The first obstacle of the day is a road popular with the lycra-clad cyclist community. A few of them whiz by in the company of the motor-vehicle traffic. Hayley, second in line on Ginger, is asked to lead the ride across and wait on the other side. As soon as the road is clear, Joe halts in the middle where he can watch for and stop any oncoming traffic. After everyone is safely across, Joe re-takes the front of the ride. On this side of the road, there is a trail that curves at the base of a hedge through an area of grassland. As there are no other users, Joe initiates the first canter of the day, and the horses set off at a steady pace.

Soon after, the trail enters the pine forest which sets apart the resorts of Cala Agulla and Cala Mesquida. The forest is managed to let plenty of light seep down through the overhead branches onto even the narrowest of trails. Under hoof, there is either sand or dry soil sporadically exposing roots. Where the trails climb and widen, the surface is stony with an adjacent boulder here and there. In these places, light funnels down from an unconcealed band of sky. Initially, the forest is busy with visitors. Striding with purpose walkers carrying backpacks and walking poles and extended families on a leisurely stroll. We come upon a couple of rides made up of eight horses and riders. One of these holds the exact amount of horses matching the same colours to our own: six greys, a black and a bay. I joke, 'It's like looking in a mirror.'

Chris disagrees, 'No, we are better looking.'

Though the temperature is more clement than it is at home, the thick-low cloud promises rain and makes the sheltered forest a popular destination this morning.

Eventually the pedestrians clear and there is a feeling of being deep in the forest enhanced by an eerie silence. That is until we come upon another ride, a sign we haven't wandered too far off the beaten track.

There is nearly an incident initiated by a mountain biker. Joe abruptly halts the ride at an intersection with a downhill footpath just before an unseen by me biker cuts across his path and vanishes. The horses in front prick their ears forward and take a good look but do little else. Joe lingers momentarily and for a good cause. Seconds later a flash of red goes by on the footpath higher up the bank, it's the first mountain biker's buddy, who races at a pace comparable to the first. Joe is right to remain still. He anticipated cyclists tend to come in pairs. All the horses prick their ears forward and take a good look as he too flies downhill on the same course. Another piece of evidence to identify human activity is a kiln-type structure forged in a semi-circle at the side of the trail. I say type because the decaying stone walls are clean inside without a charred piece of brick in sight. I don't know the purpose of the structure.

As the trails narrow further, the bordering grasses almost obscure the soft-sand ground. I soon discover another situation where I'm out of my comfort zone: In a canter on a trail, I cannot see where there are sticking-out roots. All I can do is tail Cleo and completely trust Maravillosso and Joe. Maravillosso to look after his feet and Joe on his selection of ground. I for sure prefer the faster paces in open countryside. Preference is about what you are used to, and my early experiences of riding the faster gaits were on a beach.

Our semi-isolation is temporary. Amid a build-up of the pedestrian forest users, we approach the sedate resort of Cala Mesquida. Nestled in the hills of the *natural parc*, Cala Mesquida is the most northerly resort in Mallorca. The resort consists of multiple holiday complexes sited up the side of the west hill and down to the beach. The first view of Cala Mesquida is from the east, looking down on its empty beach and the uniform in colour, size and style holiday apartment blocks: Four-storey buildings painted cream and complemented by pale-terracotta roofs and closed balconies set in treed complexes. Many of these complexes boast a circular outdoor pool. Cala Mequida's reputation is of a quiet and isolated holiday destination popular with European retirees. Brigot's parents winter here every year and are currently in residence. They had discussed meeting up then they'd conceded they see enough of each other at home and should cherish their separate vacations.

At the crest of a low-lying hill, the forest transforms into the outskirts of town. Here the trail goes through a property accommodating stables, rustic-buildings, and exercise-runs sheltered by the trees. Ponies poke their noses through gate railings and watch with interest. As we make the descent, trees continue to inhabit the banks all the way down to the bottom where there is a long carpark close to a U-bend connecting two of the resort's streets. Along from the carpark, a wood-framed pictorial tourist noticeboard fixed on vertical poles beneath a pitched roof marks the entrance to the forest.

Trees would have been felled to clear the land used for the carpark and in an attempt to blend it in with the forest behind some trees remain for savvy drivers to park underneath the copious canopies. On the corner of the U-bend, there is a single-level cream and terracotta painted café topped by a flat roof, a couple of satellite dishes and a large red and white Coca-Cola sign. Blackboards listing menu items flank shut wooden concertina doors. A corrugated awning goes over the forefront, perhaps when the café is open, table and chairs are put underneath.

Close to the tourist board is the start of a paved walkway lined by orb street lamps that goes down to the beach. Forest side is a band of scrubland. Resort side, there are walled gardens of cream three-storey apartments with identical railed balconies. As the ride follows the U-bend, going west there are more walls and apartments. This part of Cala Mesquida presents a well-maintained and clean resort designed for the tourist: zebra crossings, pavements, street parking, manicured gardens, and tree-lined streets. Our transit hugs the edge of town where the accommodation blocks command views of the countryside and forest.

There are pedestrians and drivers leisurely going about their business. Quite soon the roadway reaches a roundabout graced by a neat garden of trees and bushes at the centre. Although there are a few cars, Joe expertly manoeuvres the ride to the second exit and onwards past three glass-front shops sharing a red awning. On the near side of the road is an entrance to the *natural parc* situated on the west side of Cala Mesquida. A few cars are pulled off the street onto a level sand surface that is passed on the way to ascend a hill covered in long grasses, wild bushes, and stunted trees.

This *natural parc* differs from the sheltered-forest. Pinewood trails are replaced by rocky footpaths that ascend and descend steeply through a sparse landscape of hardy grasses, stunted bushes, puny trees, and outcrops. The terrain demands no more than a walk, and I appreciate why Joe chose to leave Noble back at Son Menut.

With midday gone, everyone dismounts for a water break. The location is a hilltop clearing with a plethora of rocks and roots underfoot. The blanket of cloud is now white and higher. Maravillosso tucks contently into a tuft of long coarse grass. The sea is close, yet not seen. A break in a series of spindly trees reveals the higher vegetation-covered neighbouring-headland. After remounting and moving on, the footpath takes us close to the cliffs where there are vistas of a grey-blue and uninviting sea. Another land mass sits on the northeast horizon Joe announces: 'That is Menorca.'

Menorca is another inhabited island of the Balearic archipelago.

After a particularly steep descent, the trail drops down onto the soft and deep sand of a beach on the east side of the Torrent de Sa Font des Pí. Unexpectedly and playing out within a matter of seconds, to everyone's surprise, not the least mine, I find myself standing on the sand aside Maravillosso. An unrehearsed circus trick has been performed by Maravillosso bending his legs and imitating a stunt horse going down to play dead in a movie. Because it was played out in slow motion, at the right moment I was able to step off to the side holding the reins in my hand and watch him briskly stand up again. He must have thought better of it, or remembered I was riding him. Joe's concerned and surprised as Maravillosso had never done this previously. Horses will be horses, and I remain in light humour while he helps me to remount. We conclude it was a reaction to a, particularly annoying fly. There have been flies here and there. Whenever they are present they irritate me, and Maravillosso as they have the knack of always being out of swotting reach. Brigot puts forward another theory. As we descended the steep drop, I used my voice to slow Maravillosso down and repeated '*lento*" (slow) in a drawn-out low-tone. She says I relaxed Maravillosso to the extent he wanted to lie down on the beach. In case this is a contributing factor I chuckle: 'I won't be doing that again.'

Continuing westbound, our course enters the lowlands of a sparse forest where the multi-purpose trails are more suitable for moderate cycling and less-adventurous horse riding and walking. Many of the trails are for vehicle access and have empty forest carparks at the side enclosed by rustic-fences and settled by an accumulation of puddles. There is no evidence of any other forest users in the vicinity, just placidity, and isolation. It could be that this vicinity comes alive at the weekends, or maybe because the summer season has ended the forest has already moved into its deserted phase.

Out from the shelter of the trees, the footpath ends at a road used to trackback seawards. We're on a finite headland where scrub grows amongst the rocks and footpath off-shoots. The road ahead rounds a hairpin. Before the bend, there is a makeshift carpark where a Spanish family of four, parents and twentysomething-offspring retreats back to a solitary-car. An onshore breeze gusts onto the exposed cliff and whips up the waves, so they crash noisily onto the rocks below.

At the second bend, the road double backs and tilts downwards to a beach at the bottom of a dip then subtly rises back into the forest. A wood-pole fence separates the roadway from the sharp drop down onto the rocks and beach.

Puddles strewn the rough-concrete surface to suggest here, rain has fallen recently.

It is Cala Mitjana, a deep cove where the beach is tucked in amid the rocky cliffs of headlands and the vegetation-covered hills at the back. Cala Mitjana is the neighbouring-cove to the Torrent de Sa Font des Pí, which we have accessed from the east side after circling behind the cove through the forest. The beach has a band of seaweed and shells on the wet sand at the shoreline and dry-powder sand secured down by a patched-quilt of grass and stunted bushes further back. There's an untidy pile of litter at the base of dual pictorial tourist information signs erected on the beach. Now a shade darker, the blanket of cloud has dropped, and in the dull light, everything looks gloomier and colder than it is.

At the dip, facing a roadside tourist information board is an entrance to a secluded clearing. Set back from the road at the foot of a high bank, a fringe of trees borders a carpet of soft sand, soil, and decaying pine-needles. The ride dismounts in this sheltered spot where even the crashing of the waves gets muffled. Joe soon secures the horses to trees along the outer edge or in a cluster close to the back of the trailer, which has again been purposely abandoned by Fernando. Our orders today are the same as the previous days with the exception saddles are to be kept on and girths loosened. Because of the cooler temperature and threat of rain, I expect Joe has judged without the heat of the horses the saddle cloths will not dry and it would not be comfortable for the horses if the saddle cloths and their backs get wet. Maravillosso is at the end of the clearing close to Cleo. In the role of herd sentry, he takes his position seriously. His ears are pricked-forward, and his eyes are focused as he keeps a lookout through the trees.

As the picnic lunch concludes it gets noticed Aswan, tied to the closest tree, has left a portion of his food. At the same moment Ginger, further up the bank, decides he wants some more. He picks his empty bucket up in his mouth and throws it towards us repeating the action until his fourth throw rolls the bucket out of his reach. Ginger's luck is in, Joe gets up from the table, collects Aswan's bucket and empties it into Ginger's. I suppose if you don't ask, you don't get.

Women being women, Hayley and I fall into a discussion about riding clothes. Neither of us is fond of the English riding attire modelled by the traditional 'horsy set.' Hayley usually rides in jeans and purchased jodhpurs especially for this trip. I do own denim jodhpurs for riding at home, but prefer the riding trousers I save for holidays. For trail riding, I prefer quick-drying hiking shirts made from insect repellent fabric. Hayley had noticed Isabelle's riding outfit, a combination of hiking shirt, hiking trousers, and hiking boots, which she seems to be comfortable wearing. I'm sure the question of what to wear will continue to be a debate in preparation for future trips.

The return leg is more direct, ascending and descending the steep and rocky gradients of the coastal hills and headlands. Fit, serious walkers wearing shorts and sturdy boots and equipped with poles climb briskly up a steep footpath as the horses carefully go down. Joe looks back to check on me as the ride re-crosses the deep sand of the Torrent de Sa Font des Pí. He nods an approving smile. In anticipation, I have my leg on and am telling Maravillosso to: 'Walk on.'

Then it rains. The first shower is heavy enough for us to pull on rain gear. For all the effort, the sprinkle is momentary, and soon we are stripping off again as it's too warm for the extra layer. Not long after the shower, a few isolated drops fall. Sofia declares, 'It's raining!'

I look behind and smile, 'That's not rain!'

Sofia and Tyra laugh loud enough to get the attention of the riders in front of us, who want to know what's so funny. The irony is appreciated as the comments get relayed.

Much the same as earlier the trails get busier on the approach to Cala Mesquida. The sun has finally broken through and when the sun comes out so do the people. There are a lot more pedestrians out on the streets, carrying beach towels going to or from the beach, shopping or taking a late afternoon stroll. The route is now reversed, skirting the resort, ascending the hillside and onwards through the stables. Joe manages to find unused sections layered by soft sand where the ride can partake in a long or short canter. Our afternoon water break is at a junction where a wide-sandy trail meets a narrow reddish-soil trail. High-white clouds hang overhead, visible through the branches of tall pine trees.

The pine forest is nearly as congested as Cala Mesquida. Walkers, families and horse riders intermingle while enjoying the late afternoon sun. The last line of horses and riders we meet is not far from where we'd cantered first thing this morning. Miraculously, the path is clear and the day ends in the way it started: Amid a cloud of dust as the enthusiastic horses' rhythmical canter strides cover the ground.

Fernando is waiting for us back at the lorry. He has retrieved the trailer from Cala Mitjana and is on hand to assist with loading saddles and bridles into the back. After the trailer is secured Fernando lowers the back of the horse lorry. Maravillosso is fourth to load and walks in without hesitation. All the horses load easily; however, Ginger steals the show. Ginger is the last horse to walk up the ramp. Without human assistance, he moves sideways from the ramp into the remaining space at the back. He stands without movement as Fernando presses the button and the ramp slowly draws up. Ginger is a shining example of how a horse should load in a lorry.

The Final Ride

It is the ultimate day of the holiday and today's trek begins at Son Menut. Brigot isn't accompanying us because her flight home is in a few hours. She does join us in the yard as the horses are groomed and tacked up. Early thick cloud is breaking up, and the sun casts long shadows to the west. Because the air is muggy, the flies are out in force. The constant-buzzing and landings annoy Maravillosso and me. On each traverse of the yard, from the stalls to the tack room, I notice that the flies' group more around the horses in the stalls. So, in the interval between the completion of my preparations and the wait for the others to complete theirs, I don't leave Maravillosso in the stalls. To escape the pesky flies, I lead him out and stand beside Brigot at the top of the yard close to 'The Nose.' Joe has leather saddlebags for Maravillosso to carry. Apart from Chris's bay mare, who has a trail saddle fitted with saddlebags, the horses take it in turns to carry a set. Maravillosso had a turn on Thursday when he'd carried the saddlebags on the dressage group's trail ride. After securing the saddlebags behind Maravillosso's saddle, Joe checks my tack and helps me get on.

Brigot is disappointed she is not joining us especially as Isabelle is back. She teases Joe by saying she is going to take the black horse with the star home. I comment, 'I don't think Maravillosso would enjoy living in the UK, to start he will be too cold. He would also endure a boring life stuck in a stable or field for most of the day while I'm at work, instead of roaming the Mallorca countryside in the company of his herd.'

Maravillosso's life at Son Menut is secure Noble's isn't. Joe will be riding her again today. It is Noble's last chance to behave herself in the role of a trail horse; otherwise, she will be sold on to a private home where there is dedicated time for her training. Joe, who is incredibly fond of the horses in his charge doesn't want to lose Noble and hopes she is calm and sensible today.

With a wave goodbye to Brigot, we ride out of Son Menut's gate and set out eastwards to the mountain of Puig de Sant Salvador. Roughly 3 miles (4.8 km) from Son Menut, the mountain is visible from the local country lanes, and I'd seen it in the distance out cycling. The range the mountain is in is a constant presence on the horizon as the horses' clip-clop up the hill to the hamlet, take a left at the T-junction and then give way at the next junction joining the main road to Felanitx.

At the main road junction, to the right (southbound) the road bends, uphill and out of sight. Our course is set northbound where the road is straight and dips before it ascends again and disappears around another corner. In this shallow valley sweeping patchwork fields surround opulent villas. The rolling hillocks are the home of large-scale farming, and the northeast slope contains the biggest flock of sheep I've seen on the island. At the dip's lowest point, inside the gate of a roadside field, is a wood-plank trailer holding four huge rolled hay bales. From my bike ride and the trips in the minibus, I know if you go around the bend on the brow of the next hill you will come across a villa surrounded by neat rows of vines in a substantial vineyard. However, we don't get that far as the use of the main road is brief. At the bottom of the dip, a right turn points us to the southeast along a level-track perfect for a canter.

The first part of the ride spans the plain joining Son Menut to Sant Salvador via a network of dusty country tracks. Going by old-style *fincas*, fields and drystone walls, some of the tracks are as straight as a Roman road; others, curve through the Felanitx countryside. In places, the tracks are either lined by Mallorcan oaks or have an oak coppice alongside. The Mallorcan oak isn't as substantial as the mighty oak trees found in the UK, in relative terms, the oaks here are like an ornamental version. Many of the fields are paddock size and look untended mainly because the boundary walls are decaying, covered in wild plants or reduced to the base layers. Now and then, there are no walls, and clumps of wild grass and scrubby bushes mark the boundaries.

Mallorcan shepherd dogs bark protectively as the horses go by what would be sleepy *fincas*. Joe introduces us to the architectural design of the farmhouses. Old-style *fincas* proffer tiny windows on the upper floor. The design was for practical purposes in the days when Mallorcans lived on the ground floor and used the upstairs for storage. The reason for this is the ground-floor is warmer than the upper floor in the winter and cooler in the summer. Because its use was for storage, another feature of the upper floor is a low-ceiling, so low you have to duck your head. Now, if someone wants to convert an old-style farmhouse to a modern home, the plans need to include raising the roof and putting in bigger windows. Another common feature of the older farm buildings and country houses is an outside oven. Joe selects an easy to see example built into an outside storage wall belonging to a *finca* a stone's throw from the track. The primary purpose of the oven is for baking bread; though, it is made use of for a variety of cooking. It explains the presence of Son Menut's outside oven, which is visible from the terrace. In a hot climate, it makes sense for this source of additional heat to be outside.

With every stride, the landmarks on the mountain become more discernible. On the brow of Puig de Sant Salvador is an old monastery still in use as a place of stay for pilgrims. The monastery building is visible in the distance, situated centrally on the crest. At the furthest points, away from the centre are two structures: A 14m-high (46ft-high) stone cross and a 35m-high (115ft-high) statue of Christ. The cross is on the nearside perched on the highest point of an outcrop, atop a mountainside covered in green vegetation.

Maravillosso is tired today. I need to ride using a stronger leg to prevent him from tripping in trot. I'm tired too, so is Tyra and Aswan. The difference is Maravillosso doesn't have any problem matching the speed of Cleo in a canter; whereas, Aswan falls behind. That said, Maravillosso did need my legs on to keep him balanced in the first canter. As she had a rest day yesterday, Noble is the freshest. Her freshness leads to Joe having to periodically halt and wait, even for the other long-stride walkers.

The ever-present tranquillity is interrupted by crossing a road and a moment of jogging from Aswan. At the road crossing, Joe congregates the ride on a patch of scrubland on the corner, bound by thick bushes with a gap allowing access to the roadway. On the other side is a strip of banked woodland where a steep footpath ascends into the trees. Hayley is assigned to lead on up into the wood and halts only when every horse has crossed. Joe will take up his position in the centre of the road to stop any cars should they emerge. A few cars motor by then the coast is clear. Joe gives the signal to cross.

He retakes his position and leads us along an elevated and winding footpath parallel to the roadway. All through the wood, there is an accompaniment of 'whoosh' from the cars driving by below. There are branches to duck under and sticking-out tree trunks at knee height. Concurrent to dodging the flora, I need to prevent Maravillosso from falling behind. Where I can, I close the gap using a slow-jog trot to resemble a pony-club rider negotiating tight bends and obstacles. Where it isn't safe to trot, I call frontwards and ask Joe to wait. Mainly because of Tyra and Sofia being even further behind than me. Secondly, it forestalls Maravillosso and stops him from rushing whenever the long striders are out of view. Lots of half halts are needed to make him walk; otherwise, he will arrive at the back of Cleo rider-less.

Thankfully, we're not in the wood for long for its purpose is to provide a safe passage away from the traffic. Soon we're back out on the farm tracks continuing east towards the mountain. As we gain ground, the landscape begins to change. Dotted back from the track are modern villas set in the anterior of smallholdings. Joe takes a left at a T-junction where there is a cluster of three villas with outbuildings on the corner. Three children sit on a garden wall and babble excitedly as the horses pass by. Simultaneously, a dog barks at the garden gate and pigs noisily grunt from behind the gate in the field opposite. It startles Aswan, who is passing through the commotion. He jogs quickly to reach the back of Maravillosso and stays tight up behind him until the clamour is left behind.

With tiredness comes a deep relaxation that switches of my mind and I lose my sense of direction. Consequently, as the trail starts to climb up the side of the mountain, I don't know the direction we ride in. Away from the farmland on the lower-wooded slope, the track weaves through a sizeable clearing settled by modern two-storey villas in extensive terraced gardens. Some of the villas are the size of a cottage and white-washed, others are expansive and constructed from orange-hue stone. Most of the gardens are bordered by modern-day versions of the tumble-down drystone walls back down on the plain. Access to the properties is from a dusty stone track from where you can peer in through wire fences at the neat tiers of olive trees that thrive on the dry, rocky and sheltered hillside.

After the villas, on the middle section of the mountainside, the track becomes terraced to form an indirect-line up to the pinnacle. Below, amongst the trees are the roofs of the villas. The ridge of the mountain is hidden from view by the continuation of trees (mostly pine infiltrated by an occasional holly or a silver-leaf). A thick wall made from stone that looks like granite confines the track. During the transition from the sheltered wooded middle slope to the exposed upper elevation, the track narrows and there is a refreshing breeze. Higher up, the trees are sparse, and bushes and grass cover the ground. Down beneath through the gaps in the trees and bushes there are glimpses of the lower slopes, neighbouring hills, and vistas out across the plain to the town of Felanitx and the silhouettes of distant hills.

Closing in on the summit the track joins a steep and stony road winding up through the stone-covered upland. This roadway ends at a three-way split, and it is here where we halt for a water break. A lower band of adjacent hills has five peaks that resemble the ridged-back of a giant sleeping dragon. Out on the horizon, the coast reflects a glistening light. Grey clouds loom above the higher ground, and the crumbling ancient wall of the old monastery raised on an outcrop. The wall is a ruin: uneven-outlines, tufts of scrub and nothing but sky behind four arrow slits at the height of what could have been a tower. When there is a pause in the conversation, there is just the crunch of tiny stones beneath hooves or boots, and Maravillosso munching on grass.

Our water break is at the topmost point of today's climb. Re-mounted, we take the wider-track to descend steeply through the pine-covered upland on the other side of the monastery's ruined wall. Clearings to the side reveal immense-granite blocks and the remnants of bygone-outbuildings. The re-appearance of the crumbling drystone walls indicates the track has reached the middle slope where there is a quick transition to the bottom due to a more direct route on this side of the mountain. Neatly terraced orchards roll downwards edged by thickets of oaks. A banked wood accommodates four gorgeous brown donkeys, three adults, and a foal. The donkeys escort us down the length of the wire fence that keeps them in the wood and of the track.

The breeze drops to leave humid air as the ride joins a long single vehicle dirt road through a sheltered valley where extensive orchards of mulberry and olive trees cover the lower gradients. The protecting hills and mountain pull down pale-grey clouds to hover above the ridges and peaks. The villas adjacent to the orchards are grandiose, modernized and expensive. Stone walls are of new designs and in good repair. Unusual for the Felanitx countryside the road is concrete and free of potholes. The level surface and length of the roadway make it perfect for a long-working trot.

After roughly 30 minutes of riding through this beautiful, tranquil and affluent valley, the horses are turned onto an offshoot track curving off a 45-degree bend that takes us back up and close to the foot of Sant Salvador. Rock formations on the crest of the mountain dominate the skyline. From this distance, below, the cross on the closest formation is a silhouette against the grey sky. Dipped down in the saddle of the mountain are the lines and sharp corners of the monastery complex. On the higher north end is another large silhouette. In spite of being indistinguishable and by the process of elimination I know this is the statue of Christ. The colossal size of the statue allows the eye to make out the outline of the great plinth it stands on.

Another demonstration of the wealth of the valley is a well-maintained orchard wall topped by a taut wire fence. Conversely, the bordering orchard doesn't bear boundaries, and our route moves onto a footpath crossing its meandering slope. The trees have ample interspace giving the orchard a natural field look and a view back down to the treetops lower down and back up the hill on the other side. The cloud starts to break and allows pockets of sunlight to beam down onto villa rooftops.

A wave of exhaustion hits me, and I have to make an extra effort to keep me and tired Maravillosso together. A change in terrain aides the final stage of the morning's ride. Leaving the openness of the orchard behind, the trail snakes up-and-down on tenuous-woodland footpaths in a terrain of steep banks and densely packed trees. In places, modest-clearings reveal secluded villas and outbuildings. The obstacle course of branches and abrupt-steep descents and ascents helps me stay alert and riding Maravillosso forward. Finally, the ride emerges from the trees into a spacious-clearing at the side of a road, where bushes and young trees form a patchy barrier at the roadside. Tucked away amid carob trees close to the back treeline is the Son Menut trailer. Lunch had already arrived. The horses are secured to trees and quickly dry off after their water down in the glorious rays of sun beneath a blue sky or if they choose in the shade of a tree.

Isabelle recognizes our picnic spot. This road was part of the route on the cycle safari she participated in yesterday. A short distance away from the east side of the town of Felanitx is the road up to the monastery. The picnic gets served up on a piece of land at the foot of the range. Overhead is the west side of the monastery complex. From here to the monastery, road users have to negotiate many hairpin bends on their way up the tree-covered mountainside. I have a hunch from Joe's reaction on hearing the route of the bike safari, Isabelle's cycle covered many more miles than mine. Joe is surprised when I mention, I too had been out for a cycle, albeit a more sedate one. Despite Isabelle's impressive-cycle, she doesn't take first prize. Anton, who is staying at Son Menut, had pretty much covered most of Mallorca since his arrival. While his wife has been improving her dressage skills, he's cycled great distances and visited Can Picafort and Cala Mesquida along the way.

Over lunch, Joe tells each of us a little bit about our horse. Maravillosso is a 10-year-old Spanish horse/Arab cross gelding. He's for sure inherited the refinement and prettiness of both breeds.

Joe reports it's been a great year for tourism in Mallorca. As a result of the current political or economic instability in the cheaper locations of Egypt and Greece many tourists had selected to holiday in the Balearic Islands – my holiday in Cairo last year is apparently against the trend. In my opinion, Mallorca is a beautiful island with a lot to offer: great scenery, relaxation, and good-Mediterranean food and wine.

In the process of packing up the trailer and preparing the horses, I acknowledge there are merely a couple more hours of riding Maravillosso. The return leg essentially uses the route taken before the earlier climb. Maravillosso is re-energized following his rest. Though, there is still the need to frequently trot to close up the gaps between us and the faster-long-stride walkers. There is also another spell of pony club manoeuvring through the strip of woodland coming up to re-cross the main road. Still, there is no problem with falling back in the canter.

Unfortunately, Noble's continual-employment at Son Menut is not looking secure. Every time the ride arrives at a long and straight byway, she wants to canter as fast as she can. She demonstrations her enthusiasm and dispute with Joe by jogging sideways on the spot. Joe responds by asking her to trot or canter only in the moments she is calm.

Our water break is in the shade at the side of a sleepy tree-lined lane. I stand holding Maravillosso's reins next to a tumble-down wall fringing a thicket of trees. Behind the wall is an unseen *finca* and garden. I can hear the cluck of chickens and children playing. Maravillosso doesn't take any notice he is busy picking shoots out from around the edges of the stones in the wall. Brown and dry the shoots don't look appetizing, but he seems to savour the taste. On the opposite side of the lane, the long-stride walkers stand underneath the overhanging branches of a pair of broad-silver-leaf trees, one of which contributes its trunk to serve as part of a modern version of the crumbling wall: in good repair and topped by identically cut stones. The ride has halted close to a paved and grand entrance belonging to a generous *finca*. Inside the neat and well-maintained property is a gravel drive winding through a garden of trees to end at a modern two-storey home with shutters framing sizable windows.

An hour later with the sun low in the sky, I find myself riding through familiar territory on straight dust tracks connected by 45-degree corners through a district of oak thickets and farmers' fields. We are back in Son Menut's neighbourhood, and the property is close. The air is still and hot enough for large pink sows to lay sprawled out basking in the rays penetrating their yard. Apart from us, tired and relaxed horses and riders, and the barking dogs there is no more activity for the remainder of the ride.

After walking around more bends, the ride reaches the start of the long track that joins the main road from Son Menut to the town of Felanitx. Joe angles Noble so he can look back at us, 'Here we will have our final canter.'

In humour and anticipation of Noble's enthusiasm, he adds, 'Hopefully we will stop at the end.'

With Noble leading and home over the hill, the horses take off. Within strides, a dog barks inside the gate of a solitary-dwelling at the side of the track. Chris is in front of me, and the dog startles his bay mare making her swerve to the left. A little surprised himself, Maravillosso swerves too. Chris and I hold secure and balanced soft seats and stay on our horses. Joe takes a quick glance back to check everyone is on board. It is the fastest canter yet, and I feel, Maravillosso extend into a gallop for a few strides to keep up with Chris's bay mare. Just as Joe brings the ride back to trot and walk, I recall his words of advice during the initial assessment: 'When we canter always keep the horses in single file behind one another then all you need to do is stay on and enjoy.'

This final canter is the most enjoyable.

Joe doesn't want to linger, so he instigates a brisk trot uphill to take a right, before the road bends, to join the rougher-surfaced lane. Maravillosso is running on homebound energy, so there is no longer any need for me to ride him forward. At a walk, I use a long-rein as the ride progresses through the hamlet, down the hill, and into Son Menut.

I untack Maravillosso, wash his bit, hose him down and take him to his stable. He contently tucks into his dinner as I say goodbye and pat him. He is a sweet horse, and I would be happy to take him home. Following a rest day tomorrow, another rider will have the privilege of riding him out and relish in the relaxation brought about by the Mallorca countryside and indulge in many fast canters.

With nothing but the minibus and airplanes to ride on tomorrow Son Menut red wine and complimentary bottles of Spanish Cava complement the evening meal in the restaurant. Though Brigot isn't here, her plan to stay at

Son Menut next year comes into the conversation. None of my fellow *Natural Parcs* programme guests have any plans to ride anywhere else yet. I, however, do have a plan. In contrast to the relaxation and tranquillity of a Mediterranean retreat my intentions shift to a different type of adventure. My goal is to meet the incredible surefooted hill-ponies of the Indian Himalayas. My next destination is the town of Leh situated on an elevation of 3,524 m (11,561 ft).

Further Information

If these stories have inspired you to pack your boots and travel off on a riding holiday of your own, you can find details of how I booked each mini-adventure at https://www.thehorseridingtourist.com/

On the destination pages of the website, there is a summary of when I travelled, the name of the travel provider, and any subsequent information relevant to the featured horse-riding holiday.
https://www.thehorseridingtourist.com/destinations/

There is also a helpful packing list to pick from and a page providing links to travel advice, health advice and money saving tips to use in the planning stage of overseas trips.
https://www.thehorseridingtourist.com/packing-list/

Go to my blog page to read about how to choose and prepare for a horse-riding holiday based on my own unique experiences.
https://www.thehorseridingtourist.com/blog-library/

Alternatively, if you have a specific question, please message me at:

Email: rachel@thehorseridingtourist.com
Twitter: https://twitter.com/THRTourist
Facebook: https://www.facebook.com/TheHorseRidingTourist/

Lightning Source UK Ltd.
Milton Keynes UK
UKHW010834140121
377036UK00002B/9